To

Geo T. Douis

with best wishes of

Geo M. Lawsa

april 8 — 35.

THE FOUR GOSPELS

ACCORDING TO THE
EASTERN VERSION

TRANSLATED FROM THE ARAMAIC
BY
GEORGE M. LAMSA
Author of *My Neighbor Jesus*

PHILADELPHIA
A. J. HOLMAN COMPANY
1933

Second Printing Jan., 1934

To

W. E. ROLLINS, D.D.

Dean of the

Protestant Episcopal Theological Seminary in Virginia

and

MRS. HELEN COLLINS ROLLINS

Jesus was born and reared in the East, under the influence of Eastern customs and practices, and he spoke in terms understood by the people of his time. It is, however, my conviction that his personality is far above everything that has been written and said about him. He is the portrait of God, and through him alone could we see God. The most significant fact to me, therefore, is this living personality who, by his miraculous powers, has transformed the life of mankind, and made sinners into saints, and given humanity a new hope.

G. M. L.

This symbol is the Aramaic character to designate Deity (Three Persons in One) and appears on most ancient Syriac manuscripts.

INTRODUCTION

When the King James Version was made, Europe was just emerging out of dark clouds. The political and religious situation was still chaotic. Nation after nation was eagerly striving for freedom. The ecclesiastical structure and its hierarchy were weakening under the impact of scientific and religious research. The time was ripe for a spiritual revival in all lands. There was also an eager demand for the Scriptures, and this was promptly met by devout scholars who offered translations.

These changes were largely stimulated by the industrial and commercial activities, which greatly incited hopes for a better understanding of the Orient and the world at large. Hitherto the East was practically unknown. Since the rise of Islam and the growth of the Turkish power, the East was isolated from Europe. It was this isolation which prompted Columbus to make his notable voyage in search of a way to the Orient and which resulted in the discovery of America. Indeed, there were but few adventurers who had crossed unknown seas and lands in search of fame and fortune. In those days travel was hazardous and expensive, and transportation was beset with severe difficulties. The world was unchartered and a few good roads were found only in some regions. The races of the Near East were, moreover, hostile to the peoples of Europe, due doubtless to the devastations caused by the Crusades in the name of Christ. Indeed, when a man undertook a long journey he was hardly expected to return alive. It took Marco Polo, an Italian adventurer, twenty years to visit the great Khan in the Far East and return home. The delay was no doubt caused by wars, revolutions, lack of caravans, severe winters in the several countries through which he passed. While he was learning the Asiatic languages he forgot his own mother tongue.

INTRODUCTION

It was only after the conquest of India by Great Britain and the rise of British power that any worthwhile contributions came from the Orient. In this particular period European nations were more interested in the search for gold and in acquiring new lands than in investigating the wisdom and religions of the East.

Under these circumstances, it is apparent how Eastern manners and customs continued to be as mysterious to the Occident, as those of the latter were to the Orient. Indeed, this strange misunderstanding still prevails. This is because Christianity is an Eastern religion and the Bible an Oriental book. This is why early and mediaeval artists portrayed Jesus and his disciples at the Last Supper, sitting on chairs at a luxurious table in the Western style; instead of sitting on the floor with their legs folded under them, their hats on their heads, their shoes removed, and a large tray containing two dishes, a few spoons and a jar of wine in front of them. These artists and authors of books were not aware that many things which were in good taste in the Occident were in bad form and even repulsive in the Orient. For instance, in the West men help and honor their wives; in the East wives are virtually the servants of their husbands, and never sit at a common meal with them. The Oriental retains his hat and removes his shoes when entering a house; this order is altogether reversed among Occidentals. In the East it would be scandalous to play music during the Church or Mosque services; the absence of music is almost inconceivable in Western services. If an Occidental observes an Oriental praying five times a day he would conclude that he is lazy or crazy; on the other hand, an Oriental is puzzled when the Occidental has to be urged to pray. Moreover, in some Eastern countries women are still purchased or acquired. Men often marry girls who are under age, but by an oral pledge the men do not take them as their wives until the age of maturity is reached. Wives are often driven out of their homes by their husbands with or without cause. All this is totally different in Western lands where women are respected and have more to say than their husbands.

Indeed customs constituted a great barrier between

the East and the West; to this was added the barrier of distance. This is one reason why so much misunderstanding exists between the Orient and the Occident. This is why some of the things in the Bible are magnified. For instance, the little lake in Galilee looks as if it was an enormous body of water, and the tiny boats appear as large ships. Tiny states of only a few square miles are regarded as kingdoms. Joshua conquered thirty-one kingdoms east of the Jordan, which had a territory of not more than a few hundred square miles, whose inhabitants were mostly shepherds and farmers (Joshua 12 : 24). Travellers are often disappointed when they see holy lands, which are so different to what they had pictured.

These and like differences illustrate the difficulties of Occidentals in understanding the languages and customs of Orientals. All the greater is our indebtedness to those translators of the Scriptures, who, in the face of unsurmountable difficulties, have given us versions which stand as monuments to their scholarship, zeal and devotion; and who challenge us to follow in their steps.

Prior to and since the Reformation many attempts have been made to translate the Holy Scriptures and to explain their message, which in the original language was simple and lucid; and to throw light on some obscure passages which have lost their original meaning when interpreted in terms of modern civilization and European customs. In spite of these numerous undertakings, the Bible still continues to perplex people. This fact explains why new translations of the Bible have continued to appear from time to time.

During all the centuries of scholarly endeavor and controversy the East has practically been silent. Hardly anything has been said for or against what the West has done with the Scriptures. This silence has been maintained from the days of Tatian, Ephraim Syrus, and Narsis, Assyrian writers who were noteworthy commentators. The reason for this was not lack of interest in what constitutes the basic principles of religion and thought. It was rather due to certain unavoidable circumstances.

INTRODUCTION

Eastern Christianity was prosecuting its work with vigorous enthusiasm, in the assured confidence that Christianity would soon become the universal religion in the East and the West. In those early days the Persian Empire alone had seven metropolitan provinces and eighty bishoprics, all the way from Armenia to India. Moreover, Christianity was winning favor in the eyes of the Persian Court. There was no thought that any reverses might interfere with the spread of the gospel message.

The horizon was then suddenly darkened by a cloud which appeared in South-west Arabia. The claims of Christianity and of the victorious Roman Empire were strenuously challenged. What at first appeared to the Christians as a despised heresy, espoused by a nomadic chief, assumed big proportions and vanquished the Christian forces in the East. Schools of Christian learning were closed, monasteries were deserted, churches were converted into mosques, books which did not agree with Moslem doctrines were burned, and writers of new books were punished. Christian scholars were conscripted to translate works of Greek and Syriac authors into Arabic, for propagating the new and militant faith of Islam, which was steadily ousting Christianity. Writers of commentaries, which even incidentally or unwittingly disagreed with the Koran, were promptly exiled or put to death. Christian authorship was under a severe ban. These unhappy events, accompanied with constant persecutions, put an end to any further attempts to throw light on the Holy Scriptures. In sheer destitution the Christians were ready to relinquish everything for the alternative of a restricted freedom to worship Jesus as their Lord and Saviour. Although deprived of schools and learning, the teachings of Jesus were largely preserved by customs and practices, which Islam could not displace, and by copies of the Scriptures, which escaped destruction.

The providence of God, however, wrought an extraordinary miracle. Other Christian literature suffered, but the Gospels of Jesus stood unchallenged. Even though the Koran became the revered book of the Moslems, Mohammed (570–632 A. D.) accepted the Gospels as the veritable word of God, as also did his successors, and all Moslems throughout the world. However, the version of the Gospels, honored by Mohammedans, is not the Vulgate of the Western world, which they repudiate as second-hand and as an unreliable translation. But it was the Eastern version of the Gospels, the Peshitta, which means clear, straight and popularly accepted. This name is justified by its clarity of style, directness of expression and simplicity of language. This was the version which the people of this region knew and used before they became Mohammedans. This is, moreover, the authentic and official version of what once constituted the original Eastern Church, the Mother Church of Christendom.

Years later when other peoples accepted Christianity, translations of the Peshitta were made into Greek, Armenian, Arabic, Persian, and other languages. Even the Christians of Malabar, India, who are known as the Christians of St. Thomas one of the apostles of our Lord, adopted the Peshitta from the earliest centuries. Indeed, it was the universally accepted version among all Christians in the East. And it has so continued down to the present day. Furthermore, the Eastern Christians never used the Vulgate Latin translation. It appeared in the East only after the coming of Western missionaries to the East a few decades ago, and it has been used by their converts.

The Eastern Version originally consisted of twenty-two books of the New Testament. The Revelation and the four Epistles of II Peter, II John, III John and Jude were not included. The Revelation was accepted after the Council of Nicaea, 325 A. D., but many of the Eastern bishops in Persia rejected it. The argument for priority on the basis of fewer books might be illustrated from the amendments to the Constitution of the United States. Suppose a thousand years hence two texts of this instrument were discovered, one containing the twelve early amendments and the other with twenty amendments, and these two texts were not dated. Surely the one with fewer amendments, even though a later copy of the original, would be accepted as the older, even though the other text with the twenty amendments was an earlier copy. Another argument for priority is that copies of the Eastern version, used for the training of the clergy, would suffer the loss of the first and last pages of the book by their careless handling and constant use of the book, and the date of their writing would become unknown. In the East when documents and books are worn out they are copied exactly and the originals are burned. This is due to the belief of the Eastern people that it is a sin to allow a book to fall to pieces. Then again, the dating of documents was unknown to earlier writers. Even if authors wished to date their writings, they would have hesitated because of the prejudice against dating them in the years of persecuting emperors, and because the teachings of Christianity were regarded as hostile to the Roman Empire. In such circumstances, even the authors of the Four Gospels omitted their names for fear of reprisals. Thus dates were not important. Furthermore, the originality of a document is not determined by the year but by the native context, the customs, the structure of the sentences, and the clarity of thought. That is to say, by internal and not external evidence.

It would seem that the appearance of other Aramaic versions, which differed from the Eastern Version, was due to the defeat of Rome and the treaty made by the Emperor Jovian with the Persian King Sapor (363 A. D.). By this pact Rome ceded five provinces in the Euphrates valley to Persia. The Christians of these provinces had hitherto been under Rome and subject to the ecclesiastical authority of Antioch. After the treaty they automatically came under the jurisdiction of the Eastern patriarch, whose See was at Seleucia, the imperial capital of the Persian Kings of the Sassanian dynasty. The patriarch of the East and his associates not only welcomed these Christian refugees, but also permitted them to use their own versions. These versions included portions of the New Testament not found in the Peshitta. This was doubtless due to the fact that such parts originated in the Eastern Roman Empire after the compilation of the Peshitta, and could not be sent to Persia because of the conflict which began soon after the death of Constantine and lasted for many years. It is unfortunate that these later versions, and the versions which the Jacobite Christians made in the fifth century, should be confused with the ancient Peshitta text, which was used in the native church of Persia, centuries before, and was quoted by Eastern writers of the second and third centuries.

Some illustrations of difficulties in translating the Aramaic text into Greek may interest the modern reader. These difficulties also prove the originality of the Eastern version.

(1) The Aramaic word for seed is *zara*, and the word for sower is *zarua*. The differences in the Aramaic formation of these words is so slight that the Greek translators overlooked and confused the word "seed" with the word sower (Matt. 13 : 18). It reads "the parable of the seed" according to the Eastern version, and not "the parable of the sower," according to the Western text. Such mistakes are unavoidable in a language like the Aramaic, where a word has many meanings and a dot misplaced altogether changes the meaning. This was especially true before vowel points were introduced, and when punctuation was not observed, and there was no uniformity in writing and copying.

(2) The Aramaic word *gamla* is the same word for "camel" and "a large rope." Matt. 19 : 24 should read, "It is easier for a rope to go through a needle's eye, etc."

(3) The Aramaic word for a certain large piece of money called *Kakra*, talent, is like the word used for province. The difference is distinguished by a single dot, according to the letter over which it is placed. Thus ܟܟܪܐ means coin, and ܟܟܪܐ means province. The confusion is seen in the parable of the nobleman, who rewarded his servants not with coins but with cities, which is improbable (Luke 19 : 13, 17, 24). This error was no doubt due to a copyist who placed the dot over the wrong letter. Such an error could not have occurred in the Greek version if it was the original, because the Greek has two

different words for coin and for city. Thus if the Peshitta was a translation from the Greek, the word would have been *medinata*, which means cities. In the case of the parable of the seed, likewise, it would have been "the parable of the sower." This further proves that the Peshitta is consistent in its report of the teachings of Jesus, which harmonized with contemporary customs.

It is also of interest to note the differences between versions. In the Greek version of St. John 12 : 40, we read:

> "He hath blinded their eyes, and hardened their heart; that they should not see with their eyes, nor understand with their heart; and be converted, and I should heal them."

The Eastern Version reads:

> "Their eyes have become blind and their heart darkened, so that they cannot see with their eyes nor understand with their heart, let them return and I will heal them."

The Aramaic word *avaro* means have become blind. The grammatical differences between "He made them blind" or "had become blind" is indicated by the final letter o which is the third person plural.

Furthermore, some Aramaic words were not translated into Greek because they were not clearly understood. Such words are *rakah*, to spit; *mammon*, wealth; *eth-patakh*, be opened. In other places Aramaic phrases are retained in their original form. Some Aramaic words, again, are translated to agree with the usage of the languages into which they were put. For instance, the Aramaic *tova*, means envied, expressing emulation, but it is translated "blessed" in the Beatitudes, for which the Aramaic is *brekha*. This word "blessed" and a few others are retained by me in this translation because there are no equivalents to express their meanings. On the other hand, some of the Aramaic colloquial and idiomatic expressions could hardly be translated into other languages without the loss of thought.

INTRODUCTION

It is a well known fact that languages undergo changes. Many words become obsolete and lose their meaning, especially when translated into other languages expressing different cultures. These original meanings could often be obtained by examining the phraseology and thought conveyed by the words. For instance, medical terms were unknown in the East, and even today they are little known. Indeed, the people still use ancient terms when describing various diseases. An insane man is called *dewana*, which literally means that he is possessed of a devil, or has become wild. Mark 1 : 34, according to the King James Version, reads that Jesus "suffered not the devils to speak because they knew him"; the Aramaic is that "he did not allow the insane to speak," after he had healed them, "because some of these were his acquaintances," and he did not want them to praise him. Mark 9 : 17 states that the boy had "a dumb spirit"; it means that this particular disease had caused dumbness in the boy and not that the spirit was dumb. Luke 11 : 14, in the King James Version, states that Jesus "was casting out a devil and it was dumb"; the Eastern version, which reflects the Aramaic style of speech, states that Jesus "was casting out a demon from a dumb man." In Luke 4 : 41, in the King James Version, "the devils came out of many, crying out and saying, Thou art Christ the Son of God"; the translation from the Aramaic is, "demons also came out of many, who cried out saying, You are the Christ the Son of God"; the sick did this after they were healed. It is hardly credible that the devils, who were cast out, would acknowledge Jesus as the Christ.

It is interesting to know that Eastern people still believe that every sickness is caused and controlled by demons. This crude belief is no doubt due to the fact that the actual causes of diseases were not known. Such beliefs in demonology are found not only among Semites but among all peoples living even today under primitive conditions, in Asia as well as in Europe and the United States. We are, however, grateful to science and truth for demonstrating that diseases are due to physical and nervous causes, delusions and fears, and have nothing to do with demons and evil spirits.

There are other instances which cause confusion when taken literally. The Aramaic *al* means "enter into," "attack," "chase"; but it has been exclusively translated "enter into," so as to imply, as in Matthew 8 : 31, that the demons entered into the swine. According to the context and the style of Aramaic speech, the word *al* here means that, not the demons but the lunatics attacked the swine. These lunatics were Syrians or Gadarenes, whose people kept swine, which were an abomination to the Jews. Jesus was a Jewish prophet. As a mark of appreciation of what Jesus was doing for them and as a proof of their conversion, these lunatics were willing to destroy the herd of swine which belonged to their people. This was doubtless one reason why the owners of the swine got into a panic and urged Jesus to leave their land, lest their business be completely destroyed by more conversions to the Jewish faith. On the other hand, the demons did not need the permission of Jesus to enter into the swine any more than they needed any permission to enter into the lunatics.

This word *al* is still used when it is said that "the oxen are entering into each other," or, "the men are entering into each other," where the reference is to their attacking one another in a fight. So also when a wolf attacks a fold, it is still said that "the wolf has entered into the sheep."

There are similar difficulties in the matter of colloquialisms. "He breathed on them," means that he stimulated their courage (John 20 : 22). "The zeal of thy house hath eaten me up" means the zeal for your house has made me courageous (John 2 : 17). Such difficulties are also evident in American colloquialisms, which could hardly be translated into Eastern languages. In English the word fire has several meanings, such as "to set fire to a house," "to fire a gun," "to fire a worker." In the last instance, an Eastern, unfamiliar with American customs, would understand that the worker was either burned or shot instead of being dismissed.

A comparison between the Aramaic and Greek texts, in the light of the above illustrations, cannot but lead to the conclusion in favor of the Aramaic origin of the Gospels.

The strongest argument, however, offering indisputable evidence, is that our Lord and his disciples spoke Aramaic. It was also the language of the Church in Jerusalem, Syria, and Mesopotamia. The "Hebrew tongue" means Aramaic, in which St. Paul spoke to the people of Jerusalem, and in which the ascended Jesus spoke to Saul on his way to Damascus (Acts 21 : 40; 22 : 2; 26 : 14). Indeed, this was the Apostle's mother tongue in which he prayed and expressed his deepest emotions. Compare Romans 8 : 15, Galatians 4 : 6; I Corinthians 16 : 22, where occur such Aramaic words as *abba*, father, and *marana tha*, O Lord come.

Even so far back as the seventh century B. C., Aramaic was the language of communication for commerce and diplomacy between the nations in Mesopotamia, Asia Minor and Palestine (cf. 2 Kings 18 : 26). The Greeks referred to this language as Syriac, because they confused Syria which is in the north of Palestine, with Assyria which is a totally different country between the Euphrates and Tigris rivers, east of Syria. This confusion exists even today in the United States. It is moreover a historical fact that Aramaic was the colloquial and literary language of Palestine, Syria, Asia Minor and Mesopotamia, from the fourth century B. C. to the ninth century A. D. After the Assyrian and Babylonian exile, Hebrew ceased to be spoken and gave way to Aramaic, which became the widely prevalent popular language. Jewish writers, from the days of Nehemiah and Ezra, wrote in Aramaic. This is further seen in the books of Daniel, the Psalter, and in the composition of other Old Testament books. Attempts were made to restore Hebrew by some Jewish scholars, who warned the people that the angels do not understand prayers offered in Aramaic and would therefore be handicapped in acting as their mediators with God. Other Jewish scholars defended Aramaic against such criticisms, adding that God himself spoke to Adam in Aramaic, and that Abraham was an Aramaean. Jacob's children were born and raised in Assyria, and later sojourned in Canaan, after which they migrated with him to Egypt.

During the reigns of the Achaemenian dynasty in Persia, beginning with Cyrus, 528 B. C., Aramaic was used as the official language for correspondence between the kings and their provincial governors as far as Egypt. As a matter of fact, Jewish literature after Christ was written mainly in Aramaic, and works in Hebrew were translated into Aramaic. Josephus, the Jewish historian, used Hebrew and Aramaic words indiscriminately. This is because Hebrew was an Aramaic dialect, and the differences between them were largely in matters of pronunciation rather than of meaning. After the destruction of the second Temple, the Jews became wholly an Aramaic-speaking people, and Hebrew became the language of the scholars.

Greek was seldom spoken except by the cultured few and by government officials. Indeed, the Jews obstinately resisted every attempt at Hellenization, as the Maccabaean struggle clearly indicates. The brief Greek rule over Syria and Mesopotamia might be compared with British rule in India, Mesopotamia and Palestine. British officers, governors and soldiers invariably acquire the native languages, but only a few natives know English. Some natives who do not speak English nevertheless adopt English names, such as George, Smith, Victoria, Henry. Their purpose in doing so is to win favor with their rulers. The same was true during the Greek conquest. Jews and Syrians adopted Greek names without necessarily implying that they used the Greek language in daily intercourse. The same course was followed by the Jews during the Babylonian exile. The Jews adopted Babylonian names. This custom is no doubt confusing to the Western mind, unfamiliar with the characteristic temperament of the Oriental. The Assyrians, for many centuries, have been ruled by Turkey, but they still speak and write their own language. A few Assyrians speak Turkish when dealing with officials of the government.

It is furthermore significant that the Aramaic text contains not a single reference to the Greek people. The Greek text of St. John's Gospel mentions that some "Greeks" desired to see Jesus (12 : 20). The word in the Eastern Version is *ammey* people, and the reference is to Gentile Idumaeans and Syrians. The woman of

Zarepath was a Syrian, according to the Eastern version, and not a Greek (Luke 4 : 26). These changes were probably made by the Greek translators, who wished to introduce some references to their own people in the Gospels. The Aramaic word for Greek is Yonaye (Cf. Ionian), but it never occurs in the Gospels, except in the single reference to the Greek language in the inscription on the Cross. Nor is there any mention of Greek culture, philosophy or customs, proving that they did not influence Jesus and his disciples, nor the early Christians.

The first Greek text of any importance was introduced by Erasmus to the Western world in 1516. In the preparation of this edition he had only ten manuscripts, the oldest of which belonged to the twelfth century. He did not know Aramaic nor had he access to any other than the above Greek manuscripts. Indeed, at this time the East was practically unknown. It thus happened that Greek became known in Europe as the original language in which the Gospels and the rest of the New Testament were written. As much is implied by the translators of the King James version in their little known Preface, which sets forth the circumstances that induced their undertaking. But facts hitherto unknown and now uncovered lead to a totally different conclusion.

It is important to know that the Eastern version, the first compilation of the New Testament scriptures, was made in Edessa. This was the capital of the buffer state of Ur-Hai, near Harran, where Aramaic was the spoken language. This state exchanged hands during the conflicts between the Roman and Persian Empires. From the fourth century, however, it had a type of Christianity, which was independent of Western influence. But Christianity was established here long before that time. The Church in Edessa was founded by Addai or Thaddeus, one of the Twelve who was sent to that city as a missionary; and St. Thomas, another of the apostles of our Lord, later went through that region. This city moreover was the center of Syriac learning and literature from earliest times, so that it justifiably won the title of the "Athens of Syria." In course of time it became the seat of Christian scholarship under the leadership of St.

Ephraim, who there founded a school or university. But even before his day the Gospels were well known in Mesopotamia and Persia, according to the testimony of Eusebius, who made quotations from the Aramaic writings of Hegesippus the defender of Christianity against Gnosticism. This is furthermore substantiated by the edition of the Gospels called the Diatessaron, prepared by Tatian an Assyrian, who lived in Mesopotamia about 172 A. D. But this compilation by Tatian was repudiated and copies burned.

Unfortunately those who associate the Aramaic text of the Peshitta with Rabbulas, bishop of Edessa in 435 A. D., overlook the fact that there were many bishops of this flourishing church at Edessa and Persia before he was born. How could these men have been elevated to the Episcopal See without written gospels, and how could Christianity have been propagated and survived throughout the East without the Scriptures? Rabbulas furthermore was an anti-Nestorian. If he had translated the gospels from the Greek, he would surely have included the Revelation, and the four omitted epistles of II Peter, II and III John, and Jude, and made the Eastern version to correspond with the Vulgate. But such was not the case. The version which existed before his day is known in some places as the Old Syriac. This is another name for the Peshitta because at this time Peshitta had already become old. Its origin is lost in obscurity, and references to this ancient version have doubtless been confused with another version called the *Damparshey*, derived from the Aramaic *parash* to select, and which was used as a lectionary. The existence of the Edessene Church from apostolic times and the venerable age of its Scriptures leads to the conclusion that the Aramaic version was a spontaneous growth, and that Edessa was the logical place for this growth. It might be said that this is merely tradition. But is not tradition another word for history? It is the living voice of the past conserving the values of its wisdom and experience, especially as during persecutions books were destroyed and burned. If we discount this voice then the past becomes a closed door, and we have no key to open it in the East or the West.

The original language of the Gospels therefore is the native Galilean Aramaic, the vernacular of northern Palestine, and not the Chaldean Aramaic which was spoken in southern Palestine. It was the same language that was spoken by the Assyrians, who were brought to the cities of Samaria and Galilee by the Assyrian kings after the ten tribes were carried into captivity (II Kings, 17 : 24 ff.). The manner of speech, the phraseology, the idioms, the orientation in the Gospels are vividly and distinctively northern Aramaic. Parables and allegories are all derived from Semitic customs, and there is no reference to incidents from alien sources. The constant repetitions are characteristic of Oriental usage. Such phrases as, "*Amen Amen amar na Lkhon,*" "Truly, truly, I say unto you," "In those days," "And it came to pass," "And he said to them," are peculiarly Aramaic. Then again the original has fewer words because the thought is conceived in the native tongue and easily expressed to the people of the same language. This is not the case with a translation which of necessity must use more words to convey the meaning. Consider the first clause of our Lord's Prayer. The Aramaic uses two words, *Avon dvashmaya*; the Greek uses six words, *Pater hemon ho en tois ouranois,* as also does the English, "Our Father who art in heaven." If the Eastern text was a translation from the Greek, more words would have been used in the Aramaic, and the translation would have had obscure and confusing phrases. This is not the case with the Peshitta, which consistently sustains its title as "clear." A translation frequently misses the real meaning of the original and often has to use synonyms to bring out shades of meaning. This is obvious to me because for years I have translated letters and documents for the United States Government and for several institutions. It is therefore easy from constant practice to say whether a writing is a translation or written in the original, especially in the case of my mother tongue the Aramaic.

It is also worth noting that the Eastern version retains all the Semitic names in their original form and pronunciation, which correspond with the Hebrew names. Compare the names in Matthew, Ch. 1 and Luke Ch. 3 in the original Aramaic text. Another interesting fact is that the Eastern version in referring to Peter always speaks of him as Simon and at times as Simon Kepa, (Stone). It was natural for the Greek translators to use only the Greek term, thus translating the Aramaic word *Kepa* into the Greek word *Petrus*. Contemporary issues moreover are not considered in detail as they were not raised at the time. Our Gospels are only an outline of the teaching of Jesus. If they were written outside the Semitic atmosphere and its related situations, the writers would doubtless have furnished explanations, and the gospel narratives would have been much longer. But such a course was superfluous. A Greek writer would have made comparisons between Semitic and Greek culture and customs, thus making them clearer to Greek readers.

The Gospels were written much earlier than they are supposed to have been. If they were of a late date the writers would not have been able to make direct and accurate quotations, as is done in the Sermon on the Mount and other sayings of Jesus. The nearest and shortest way to trace the authorship of the Gospels and the place they were written is to rely upon internal evidence.

The writers must have been Jews for they are familiar with the Old Testament Scriptures and with customs and manners, such as the passover and other festivals, as well as with the topography of Palestine. The authors wrote to their contemporaries. This is why they did not stress the general issues because the public knew them. Had the Gospels been written at a later date, the writers would have undoubtedly explained some of the issues, such as head-tax, Messianic expectations, etc., and the documents would have been much longer than they are. The opening sentences in St. Luke's gospel clearly implies that there were many other gospels written on scrolls and extensively circulated, and that they were the work of eye-witnesses who knew Jesus and who were associated with him. The place where these writings were produced must have been either Palestine or Edessa, the two great centers where Aramaic was spoken. On the other hand, there is no reason why these Aramaic-speaking countries should have their sacred scriptures written in a language which was alien to them. The evidence therefore is convincing and conclusive for an Aramaic original, and this is none other than the Peshitta.

My present translation is not intended to depreciate the noble work of European and American scholars, whom I hold in the highest esteem. My purpose is to present the thought and accuracy of the Eastern version while retaining its simplicity and directness, and reproducing as nearly as possible the shades of meaning in the original. Another purpose is to present the Eastern understanding of Jesus, as it is enshrined in the accepted version of the Four Gospels. It is moreover endorsed by the traditions and history of a people, distinguished by the sacrificial blood of martyrdoms, which date back to apostolic times and flows even to the present day. Though poor and reduced in numbers by incessant privations, these people once constituted what was recognized as the Mother Church. Today they are the only pure Semitic people in the Christian fold. They still speak the Aramaic language of our blessed Lord and Saviour with only a few inevitable changes, and they have retained the ancient and original version of the Holy Scriptures, without the change of revision. This has been endorsed by recent archaeological discoveries. With such a rich legacy they surely have the right to speak for themselves.

It is therefore a sacred privilege which has induced me, who belongs to this people, humbly to submit this translation to the fair judgment of Western people. I am happy to say that this is the first translation into English made from the Eastern version by a native, who was born and raised in a land where Aramaic continues to be spoken, as in the days of the first Christian century. The gratifying reception given my book, *My Neighbor Jesus*, encourages me to believe that this translation of the Four Gospels would make the fair figure of Jesus more attractive and his teachings more acceptable.

My thanks are due to the Rev. Oscar L. Joseph, Litt.D., an American scholar and author whose literary counsel is valued by leading publishers. He has helped in the choice of English so as to make it exact and lucid.

INTRODUCTION

It is with filial gratitude I hereby acknowledge my indebtedness to the Archbishop of Canterbury's Mission College in Urumiah, Persia, and to the Virginia Theological Seminary in Alexandria, from both of which I graduated. Words are inadequate to express my deep appreciation of many American friends who have encouraged me to make this translation, especially to Mrs. Ellen M. Wood for her deep interest. I am also grateful to Mr. J. Pierpont Morgan, for generous permission to use his Aramaic manuscripts in my researches; to Mr. Samuel G. Thomson for his help; and to Mrs. William B. Parsons, the late Mrs. Gardner Perry, Miss Anita G. Little, Mr. Harry I. Hunt, Mrs. Jas. C. Mackenzie, Mrs. Elizabeth White and others for their encouragement. It is truly the contribution of all these friends, whose purpose, in common with mine, has been to further the glory of Jesus Christ, our blessed Lord and Saviour.

George M. Lamsa.

WORDS WITH MANY MEANINGS

The following list of Aramaic words further illustrates the difficulties of the early translators from the Aramaic into Greek, at a time when questions of punctuation, accentuation and paragraphing were unknown. This is especially true of Aramaic, which is the richest and most expressive language of the Semitic group, but having a small vocabulary when compared with the Greek and Latin. This limitation of words made necessary the use of the same words with various shades of meanings. This is because Aramaic is one of the world's most ancient languages.

Translators are well aware of these grammatical difficulties, particularly in a language like Aramaic where a single dot above or under a letter radically changes the meaning of a word. These tiny dots are made by scribes, who are not authors but mere copyists, hired for this purpose by rich and by learned men. But owing to the humidity of the climate and the nature of the ink, blots appear on the pages when pressed against each other. Again because of exposure of a manuscript and its careless handling, flies alight on the pages and leave marks. Furthermore as the lines are crowded for lack of space, a dot placed above one letter may read as though it were placed under a letter in the previous line.

Some Aramaic words are written and pronounced alike, but their meaning differs according to the context. In other cases the differences are indicated by dots which alter the pronunciation. In yet other instances, if the translator does not speak the language from which he translates the meaning and usage of some words must be left to his knowledge and judgment.

WORDS WITH MANY MEANINGS

ܪܘܚܐ Rokha
- Spirit
- Wind
- Temper
- Pride
- Rheumatism

ܓܡܠܐ Gamla
- Large rope
- Camel
- Beam

ܐܬܪܐ Athra
- Country
- Place
- Chance
- Land
- Region

ܒܪܢܫܐ Barnasha
- Son of man
- Mankind
- Human being
- Man

ܫܥܐ Shaa
- Hour
- Time
- Turn

ܥܠܡܐ Alma
- World
- People

ܫܡܝܐ Shmaya
- Universe
- Heaven
- Sky

ܒܪܬܐ Barta
- Daughter
- Egg

ܥܠ Al
- Enter
- On
- By
- Attack
- Upon
- Because

ܡܠܐܟܐ Malakha
- Angel
- Messenger

ܫܠܡ Shlem
- Finished
- Fulfilled
- In peace
- Accomplished

ܛܥܐ Taa
- Forsake
- Mislead
- Lost
- Deceive

ܓܡܝܪܐ Gmira
- Complete
- Perfect
- Finished
- Comprehensive
- True

ܡܫܝܚܐ Mshikha
- Christ
- Anointed

ܡܫܚܐ Mishkha
- Oil
- Butter

WORDS WITH MANY MEANINGS

ܕܘܵܢܵܐ Dewana { Insane / Crazy / Lunatic

ܫܒ݂ܩ Shbak { Reserve / Keep / Spare / Leave / Forgive / Allow / Permit

ܫܹܕܵܢܵܐ Shedana { Insane / Crazy / Lunatic

ܕܹܘܵܐ Dewa { Wildman / Devil

ܡܵܢܹܐ Maney { Vessels / Utensils / Goods or Merchandise

Words spelled alike but pronounced differently, and with
different meanings.

ܓܲܪܒܹܐ Garbey { Leper
ܓܲܪܒ݂ܵܐ Garva { Muslin, Sheepskin

ܐܲܡܗܵܬ݂ܵܐ Amhatha { Maidservants
ܐܲܥܡܗܵܬ݂ܵܐ Aemhatha { Mothers

ܚܲܡܪܵܐ Khamra { Wine
ܚܡܵܪܵܐ Khmara { Donkey

ܟܲܟܪܵܐ Kakra { Talent
ܟܲܪܟ݂ܵܐ Karkha { Province

ܥܲܒ݂ܕܵܐ Avda { Servant
ܥܲܒ݂ܵܕܵܐ Avada { Work

ܡܲܠܟܵܐ Malka { King
ܡܲܠܟ݂ܵܐ Milka { Council

ܣܲܦܪܵܐ Sapra { Scribe
ܣܸܦܪܵܐ Sepra { Book, Reading

ܥܵܘܠܵܐ Awla { Iniquity
ܥܵܘܹܠܵܐ Awela { Baby

ܣܲܗܪܵܐ Sahra { Moon
ܣܵܗܕܵܐ Sahda { Witness

xxv

CONTENTS

The significant differences between this
translation and the Authorized King James
Version are indicated by Verse References
to that Version at the foot of each page.

THE GOSPEL ACCORDING TO
St. MATTHEW

CHAPTER 1

THE book of the genealogy of Jesus Christ, the son of David, the son of Abraham.

2 Abraham begot Isaac; Isaac begot Jacob; Jacob begot Judah and his brothers;

3 Judah begot Perez and Zerah of his wife Tamar; Perez begot Hezron; Hezron begot Aram;

4 Aram begot Aminadab; Aminadab begot Nahson; Nahson begot Salmon;

5 Salmon begot Boaz of his wife Rahab; Boaz begot Obed of his wife Ruth; Obed begot Jesse;

6 Jesse begot David the king; David the king begot Solomon of the wife of Uriah;

7 Solomon begot Rehoboam; Rehoboam begot Abijah; Abijah begot Asa;

8 Asa begot Jehoshaphat; Jehoshaphat begot Joram; Joram begot Uzziah;

9 Uzziah begot Jotham; Jotham begot Ahaz; Ahaz begot Hezekiah;

10 Hezekiah begot Manasseh; Manasseh begot Amon; Amon begot Josiah;

11 Josiah begot Jechoniah and his brothers, about the captivity of Babylon.

12 And after the captivity of Babylon, Jechoniah begot Shealtiel; Shealtiel begot Zerubbabel;

13 Zerubbabel begot Abiud; Abiud begot Eliakim; Eliakim begot Azor;

14 Azor begot Sadoc; Sadoc begot Achim; Achim begot Eliud;

15 Eliud begot Eleazar; Eleazar begot Matthan; Matthan begot Jacob;

16 Jacob begot Joseph the husband of Mary, of whom was born Jesus, who is called Christ.

17 ¶ Therefore all the generations, from Abraham down to David, are fourteen generations; and from David down to the Babylonian captivity, fourteen generations; and from the Babylonian captivity down to Christ, fourteen generations.

18 ¶ The birth of Jesus Christ was in this manner. While Mary his mother was acquired for a price for Joseph, before they came together, she was found with child of the Holy Spirit.

19 But Joseph her husband was a pious man, and did not wish to make it public; so he was thinking of divorcing her secretly.

20 While he was considering this, the angel of the Lord appeared to him in a dream, and said to him: O, Joseph, son of David, do not be afraid to take your wife Mary, because he that is to be born of her is of the Holy Spirit.

21 She will give birth to a son, and you will call his name Jesus; for he shall save his people from their sins.

22 ¶ All this happened, that what was spoken from the Lord by the prophet might be fulfilled,

23 Behold, a virgin will conceive and give birth to a son, and they shall call his name Immanuel, which is interpreted, Our God is with us.

24 When Joseph rose up from his sleep, he did just as the angel of the Lord commanded him, and he took his wife.

25 And he did not know her until she gave birth to her first born son; and she called his name Jesus.

CHAPTER 2

WHEN Jesus was born in Bethlehem of Judah, in the days of Herod the king, there came Magi from the East to Jerusalem.

2 And they were saying, Where is the King of the Jews, who has been born? For we have seen his star in the East, so we have come to worship him.

3 But when Herod the king heard it, he trembled, and all Jerusalem with him.

4 So he gathered together all the high priests and the scribes of the people, and he kept asking them, where the Christ will be born?

5 They said, In Bethlehem of Judah, for thus it is written in the book of the prophet,

6 Even you, Bethlehem of Judah, you are not insignificant in the eyes of the kings of Judah, for from you shall come out a king, who will shepherd my people Israel.

7 Then Herod called the Magi secretly, and he learned from them at what time the star appeared to them.

8 And he sent them to Bethlehem, and he said to them,

2

Go and enquire very carefully concerning the boy, and when you have found him, come back and let me know, so that I also may go and worship him.

9 When they had heard from the king, they went away; and behold, the same star that they had seen in the east was going before them, until it came and stood just above the place where the infant boy was.

10 When they saw the star, they rejoiced exceedingly.

11 And they entered the house, and they saw the infant boy with Mary, his mother; and they threw themselves down and worshipped him; and they opened their treasures and offered to him gifts —gold, and frankincense, and myrrh.

12 And they saw in a dream not to return to Herod, so they departed to their own country by another way.

13 When they had gone, the angel of the Lord appeared to Joseph in a dream, and said to him: Arise, take the infant boy and his mother, and escape to Egypt, and stay there until I tell you, for Herod is ready to demand the child so as to destroy him.

14 Then Joseph rose up, took the infant boy and his mother

in the night, and escaped to Egypt.

15 And he remained there until the death of Herod, so that what was said from the Lord by the prophet, might be fulfilled, I have called my son from Egypt.

16 ¶ When Herod saw that he was insulted by the Magi, he was greatly enraged, so he sent forth and had all the infant boys in Bethlehem and in its suburbs killed, from two years old and down, according to the time that he had enquired from the Magi.

17 Then was fulfilled what was said by the prophet Jeremiah who said,

18 A voice was heard in Ramah, weeping and wailing exceedingly, Rachel weeping for her sons, and she would not be comforted, because they could not be brought back.

19 ¶ When King Herod died, the angel of the Lord appeared in a dream to Joseph in Egypt.

20 And he said to him: Arise, take the boy and his mother, and go to the land of Israel, for those who were seeking the boy's life are dead.

21 So Joseph rose up, took the boy and his mother, and he came to the land of Israel.

22 But when he heard that Archelaus had become king

over Judaea, in the place of his father Herod, he was afraid to go there; and it was revealed to him in a dream to go to the land of Galilee.

23 And he came and dwelt in a city called Nazareth, so that what was said by the prophet, might be fulfilled, He shall be called a Nazarene.

CHAPTER 3

IN those days came John the Baptist; and he was preaching in the wilderness of Judaea,

2 Saying, Repent; for the kingdom of heaven is near.

3 For it was he of whom it was said by the prophet Isaiah, The voice which cries in the wilderness, Prepare the way of the Lord, and straighten his highways.

4 Now the same John's clothes were made of camel's hair, and he had leathern belts around his waist, and his food was locusts and wild honey.

5 Then there went out to him, Jerusalem and all of Judaea, and the whole country around Jordan.

6 And they were baptized by him in the river Jordan, as they confessed their sins.

7 But when he saw a great many of the Pharisees and Sadducees who were coming to be baptized, he said to them, O offspring of scorpions, who has warned you to escape from the anger which is to come?

8 Bring forth therefore fruits which are worthy of repentance;

9 And do not think and say within yourselves, We have Abraham as our father; for I say to you, that God can raise up children for Abraham from these stones.

10 Behold, the axe is already placed at the root of the trees; therefore, every tree which bears not good fruits shall be cut down and dropped in the fire.

11 I am just baptizing you with water for repentance; but he who is coming after me is greater than I, the one even whose shoes I am not worthy to remove; he will baptize you with the Holy Spirit and with fire.

12 Whose shovel is in his hand, and he purifies his threshings; the wheat he gathers into his barns, and the straw he burns up in the unquenchable fire.

13 ¶ Then Jesus came from Galilee to the Jordan to John, to be baptized by him.

14 But John tried to stop him and said, I need to be bap-

tized by you, and yet have you come to me?

15 But Jesus answered and said to him, Permit now, for this is necessary for us so that all righteousness may be fulfilled; and then he permitted him.

16 ¶ When Jesus was baptized, he immediately came out of the water; and the heavens were opened to him, and he saw the Spirit of God descending like a dove, and coming upon him;

17 And behold a voice from heaven which said, This is my beloved Son, with whom I am pleased.

CHAPTER 4

THEN Jesus was carried away by the Holy Spirit into the wilderness, to be tempted by the adversary.

2 So he fasted forty days and forty nights; but at last he was hungry.

3 And the tempter drew near and said to him, If you are the Son of God, tell these stones to become bread.

4 But he answered and said, It is written, that it is not by bread alone that man can live, but by every word which comes from the mouth of God.

5 Then the adversary took him to the holy city, and he made him to stand up on the pinnacle of the temple.

6 And he said to him, If you are the Son of God, throw yourself down; for it is written, that he will command his angels concerning you, and they will bear you up on their hands, so that even your foot may not strike a stone.

7 Jesus said to him, Again it is written, that you shall not try out the Lord your God.

8 Again the adversary took him to a very high mountain, and he showed him all the kingdoms of the world and their glory.

9 And he said to him, All of these I will give to you, if you will fall down and worship me.

10 Then Jesus said unto him, Go away, Satan, for it is written, you shall worship the Lord your God, and him only shall you serve.

11 Then the adversary left him alone; and behold the angels drew near and ministered unto him.

12 ¶ Now when Jesus heard that John was delivered up, he departed to Galilee.

13 And he left Nazareth, and came and settled in Capernaum, by the seaside, within the borders of Zabulon and of Napthali.

14 So that it might be ful-

filled, what was said by the prophet Isaiah, who said,

15 O land of Zabulon, O land of Napthali, the way to the sea, across the Jordan, Galilee of the Gentiles!

16 The people who dwelt in darkness saw a great light, and those who settled in the country and in the midst of the shadows of death, light shone on them.

17 ¶ From that time Jesus began to preach and to say, Repent, for the kingdom of heaven is coming near.

18 ¶ And while he was walking by the shore of the sea of Galilee, he saw two brothers, Simon who was called Peter and his brother Andrew, who were casting nets into the sea, for they were fishermen.

19 And Jesus said to them, Come after me, and I will make you to become fishers of men.

20 So they immediately left their nets and went after him.

21 And when he left that place he saw two other brothers, James the son of Zebedee and his brother John, in a ship with Zebedee their father, repairing their nets; and Jesus called them.

22 So they immediately left the ship and their father, and went after him.

23 ¶ And Jesus travelled throughout Galilee, teaching in their synagogues, and preaching the good news of the kingdom, and healing every kind of disease and sickness among the people.

24 And his fame was heard throughout Syria; so they brought to him all who were badly afflicted with divers sickness, and those who were tormented with pains, and the insane, and the epileptics, and the cripples; and he healed them.

25 So large crowds followed him from Galilee, and from the ten cities, and from Jerusalem and from Judaea, and from across the Jordan.

CHAPTER 5

WHEN Jesus saw the crowds, he went up to the mountain; and as he sat down, his disciples drew near to him.

2 And he opened his mouth and taught them, and he said,

3 Blessed are the poor in pride, for theirs is the kingdom of heaven.

4 Blessed are they who mourn, for they shall be comforted.

5 Blessed are the meek, for they shall inherit the earth.

6 Blessed are those who hunger and thirst for justice,

6

for they shall be well satisfied.

7 Blessed are the merciful, for to them shall be mercy.

8 Blessed are those who are pure in their hearts, for they shall see God.

9 Blessed are the peacemakers, for they shall be called sons of God.

10 Blessed are those who are persecuted for the sake of justice, for theirs is the kingdom of heaven.

11 ¶ Blessed are you, when they reproach you and persecute you, and speak against you every kind of bad word, falsely, for my sake,

12 Then be glad and rejoice, for your reward is increased in heaven; for in this very manner they persecuted the prophets who were before you.

13 ¶ You are indeed the salt of the earth; but if the salt should lose its savor, with what could it be salted? It would not be worth anything, but to be thrown outside and to be trodden down by men.

14 You are indeed the light of the world; a city that is built upon a mountain cannot be hidden.

15 Nor do they light a lamp and put it under a basket, but on a lamp holder, so it gives light to all who are in the house.

16 Let your light thus shine before men, so that they may see your good works and glorify your Father in heaven.

17 ¶ Do not expect that I have come to weaken the law or the prophets; I have not come to weaken, but to fulfil.

18 For truly I tell you, Until heaven and earth pass away, not even one yoth[1] or a dash shall pass away from the law until all of it is fulfilled.

19 Whoever therefore tries to weaken even one of these smallest commandments, and teaches men so, he shall be regarded as small in the kingdom of heaven; but anyone who observes and teaches them, he shall be regarded as great in the kingdom of heaven.

20 For I say to you, that unless your righteousness exceeds that of the scribes and Pharisees, you shall not enter the kingdom of heaven.

21 ¶ You have heard that it was said to those who were before you, You shall not kill, and whoever kills is guilty before the court.

22 But I say to you, that whoever becomes angry with his brother for no reason, is

---

[1] Yoth is the smallest letter in Aramaic and Hebrew.

Cf. dif. verses 10–12–17–19–22

guilty before the court: and whoever should say to his brother, Raca (which means, I spit on you) is guilty before the congregation; and whoever says to his brother, you are a nurse maid, is condemned to hell fire.

23 If it should happen therefore that while you are presenting your offering upon the altar, and right there you remember that your brother has any grievance against you;

24 Leave your offering there upon the altar, and first go and make peace with your brother, and then come back and present your offering.

25 Try to get reconciled with your accuser promptly, while you are going on the road with him; for your accuser might surrender you to the judge, and the judge will commit you to the jailer, and you will be cast into prison.

26 Truly I say to you, that you will never come out thence until you have paid the last cent.

27 ¶ You have heard that it is said, You shall not commit adultery.

28 But I say to you, that whoever looks at a woman with the desire to covet her, has already committed adultery with her in his heart.

29 If your right eye should cause you to stumble, pluck it out and throw it away from you; for it is better for you to lose one of your members, and not all of your body fall into hell.

30 And if your right hand should cause you to stumble, cut it off and throw it away from you; for it is better for you to lose one of your members, and not all of your body fall into hell.

31 It has been said that whoever divorces his wife, must give her the divorce papers.

32 But I say to you, that whoever divorces his wife, except for fornication, causes her to commit adultery; and whoever marries a woman who is separated but not divorced, commits adultery.

33 ¶ Again you have heard it was said to them who were before you, that you shall not lie in your oaths, but entrust your oaths to the Lord.

34 But I say to you, never swear; neither by heaven, because it is God's throne;

35 Nor by the earth, for it is a stool under his feet; nor by Jerusalem, for it is the city of a great king.

36 Neither shall you swear by your own head, because

8

you cannot create in it a single black or white hair.

37 But let your words be yes, yes, and no, no; for anything which adds to these is a deception.

38 ¶ You have heard that it is said, An eye for an eye, and a tooth for a tooth.

39 But I say to you, that you should not resist evil; but whoever strikes you on your right cheek, turn to him the other also.

40 And if anyone wishes to sue you at the court and take away your shirt, let him have your robe also.

41 Whoever compels you to carry a burden for a mile, go with him two.

42 Whoever asks from you, give him; and whoever wishes to borrow from you, do not refuse him.

43 ¶ You have heard that it is said, Be kind to your friend, and hate your enemy.

44 But I say to you, Love your enemies, and bless anyone who curses you, and do good to anyone who hates you, and pray for them who carry you away by force and persecute you.

45 So that you may become sons of your Father who is in heaven, who causes his sun to shine upon the good and upon the bad, and who pours down his rain upon the just and upon the unjust.

46 For if you love only those who love you, what reward will you have? do not even the publicans do the same thing?

47 And if you salute only your brothers, what is it more that you do? do not even the publicans do the same thing?

48 Therefore, you become perfect, just as your Father in heaven is perfect.

CHAPTER 6

BE careful concerning your alms, not to do them in the presence of men, merely that they may see them; otherwise you have no reward with your Father in heaven.

2 Therefore when you give alms, do not blow a trumpet before you, just as the hypocrites do in the synagogues and in the market places, so that they may be glorified by men. Truly I say to you, that they have already received their reward.

3 But when you give alms, let not your left hand know what your right hand is doing;

4 So that your alms may be done secretly, and your Father who sees in secret, shall himself reward you openly.

5 ¶ And when you pray, do

not be like the hypocrites, who like to pray, standing in the synagogues and at the street corners, so that they may be seen by men. Truly I say to you, that they have already received their reward.

6 But you, when you pray, enter into your inner chamber, and lock your door, and pray to your Father who is in secret, and your Father who sees in secret he himself shall reward you openly.

7 And when you pray, do not repeat your words like the pagans, for they think that because of much talking they will be heard.

8 Therefore, do not be like them, for your Father knows what you need, before you ask him.

9 Therefore pray in this manner: Our Father in heaven. Hallowed be thy name.

10 Thy kingdom come. Let thy will be done, as in heaven so on earth.

11 Give us bread for our needs from day to day.

12 And forgive us our offences, as we have forgiven our offenders;

13 And do not let us enter into temptation, but deliver us from error. Because thine is the kingdom and the power and the glory for ever and ever. Amen.

14 For if you forgive men their faults, your Father in heaven will also forgive you.

15 But if you do not forgive men, neither will your Father forgive even your faults.

16 ¶ When you fast, do not look sad like the hypocrites; for they disfigure their looks, so that they may appear to men that they are fasting. Truly I say to you, that they have already received their reward.

17 But you, when you fast, wash your face and anoint your head;

18 So that you may not appear to men that you are fasting, but to your Father who is in secret; and your Father who sees in secret, he will reward you.

19 ¶ Do not lay up for yourselves treasures buried in the ground, a place where rust and moth destroy, and where thieves break through and steal.

20 But lay up for yourselves a treasure in heaven, where neither rust nor moth destroy, and where thieves do not break through and steal.

21 For where your treasure is, there also is your heart.

22 The eye is the lamp of the body; if therefore your eye be clear, your whole body is also lighted.

Cf. dif. verses 11–12–13–15–19–22

23 But if your eye is diseased, your whole body will be dark. If therefore the light that is in you is darkness, how much more will be your darkness.

24 ¶ No man can serve two masters; for either he will hate the one, and like the other; or he will honor one, and despise the other. You cannot serve God and mammon (wealth).

25 For this reason, I say to you, Do not worry for your life, what you will eat, and what you will drink, nor for your body, what you will wear. Behold, is not life much more important than food, and the body than clothing?

26 Watch the birds of the sky, for they do not sow, neither do they harvest, nor gather into barns, and yet your Father in heaven feeds them. Are you not much more important than they?

27 Who is among you who by worrying can add one cubit to his stature?

28 Why do you worry about clothing? Observe the wild flowers, how they grow; they do not get tired out, nor do they spin.

29 But I say to you, that not even Solomon with all of his glory was covered like one of them.

30 Now if God clothes in such fashion the grass of the field, which today is and tomorrow falls into the fireplace, is he not much more to you, O you of little faith?

31 Therefore do not worry or say, What will we eat, or what will we drink, or with what will we be clothed?

32 For worldly people seek after all these things. Your Father in heaven knows that all of these things are also necessary for you.

33 But you seek first the kingdom of God and his righteousness, and all of these things shall be added to you.

34 Therefore do not worry for tomorrow; for tomorrow will look after its own. Sufficient for each day, is its own trouble.

CHAPTER 7

JUDGE not, that you may not be judged.

2 For with the same judgment that you judge, you will be judged, and with the same measure with which you measure, it will be measured to you.

3 Why do you see the splinter which is in your brother's eye, and do not feel the beam which is in your own eye?

4 Or how can you say to your brother, let me take out

the splinter from your eye, and behold there is a cross beam in your own eye?

5 O hypocrites, first take out the beam from your own eye, and then you will see clearly to get out the splinter from your brother's eye.

6 ¶ Do not give holy things to the dogs; and do not throw your pearls before the swine, for they might tread them with their feet, and then turn and rend you.

7 ¶ Ask, and it shall be given to you; seek, and you shall find; knock, and it shall be opened to you.

8 For whoever asks, receives; and he who seeks, finds; and to him who knocks, the door is opened.

9 Or who is the man among you, who when his son asks him for bread, why, will he hand him a stone?

10 Or if he should ask him for fish, why, will he hand him a snake?

11 If therefore you who err, know how to give good gifts to your sons, how much more will your Father in heaven give good things to those who ask him?

12 Whatsoever you wish men to do for you, do likewise also for them; for this is the law and the prophets.

13 ¶ Enter in through the narrow door, for wide is the door, and broad is the road which carries to destruction, and many are those who travel on it.

14 O how narrow is the door, and how difficult is the road which carries to life, and few are those who are found on it.

15 ¶ Be careful of false prophets who come to you in lamb's clothing, but within they are ravening wolves.

16 You will know them by their fruits. Why, do they gather grapes from thorns, or figs from thistles?

17 So every good tree bears good fruits; but a bad tree bears bad fruits.

18 A good tree cannot bear bad fruits, neither can a bad tree bear good fruits.

19 Any tree which does not bear good fruits will be cut down and cast into the fire.

20 Thus by their fruits you will know them.

21 ¶ It is not everyone who merely says to me, My Lord, my Lord, will enter into the kingdom of heaven, but he who does the will of my Father in heaven.

22 A great many will say to me in that day, My Lord, my Lord, did we not prophesy in your name, and in your name cast out devils, and in your name do many wonders?

23 Then I will declare to them, I have never known you; keep away from me, O you that work iniquity.

24 ¶ Therefore whoever hears these words of mine, and does them, he is like a wise man, who built his house upon a rock.

25 And the rain came down, and the rivers overflowed, and the winds blew, and they beat upon that house; but it did not fall down, because its foundations were laid upon a rock.

26 And whoever hears these words of mine, and does them not, he is like a foolish man, who built his house upon sand.

27 And the rain came down, and the rivers overflowed, and the winds blew, and they beat upon that house; and it fell down, and its fall was very great.

28 ¶ And it happened when Jesus finished these words, the crowds were stunned at his teaching.

29 For he taught them as one who had the power, and not like their own scribes and Pharisees.

CHAPTER 8

WHEN he came down from the mountain, large crowds followed him.

2 And behold a leper came and worshipped him, and said, My Lord, if you wish, you can cleanse me.

3 And Jesus stretched out his hand and touched him, and he said, I do wish, be cleansed. And in that hour his leprosy was cleansed.

4 Jesus then said to him, Look here, why are you telling it to men? go first and show yourself to the priests, and offer an offering as Moses has commanded, for a testimonial to them.

5 ¶ When Jesus entered Capernaum, a centurion approached him, and appealed to him,

6 Saying, My Lord, my boy is lying in the house, paralyzed, and suffering greatly.

7 Jesus said to him, I will come and heal him.

8 The centurion then answered and said, My Lord, I am not good enough that you should enter under the shadow of my roof; but just say a word, and my boy will be healed.

9 For I am also a man in government service, and there are soldiers under my command; and I say to this one, Go, and he goes; and to the other, Come, and he comes; and to my servant, Do this, and he does it.

10 When Jesus heard it, he was amazed, and he said to those who accompanied him, Truly I say to you, that not even in Israel have I found such faith as this.

11 And I say to you, that a great many will come from the east and from the west, and sit down with Abraham and Isaac and Jacob in the kingdom of heaven.

12 But the sons of the kingdom will be put out in the outer darkness; there shall be weeping and gnashing of teeth.

13 So Jesus said to the centurion, Go, let it be done to you according to your belief. And his boy was healed in that very hour.

14 ¶ And Jesus came to Simon's house, and he saw his mother-in-law laid up and sick with fever.

15 And he touched her hand, and the fever left her, and she got up and waited on them.

16 ¶ Now when evening came, they brought to him a great many lunatics, and he cured them just by a word; and he healed all who were badly afflicted.

17 So that what was spoken by the prophet Isaiah, might be fulfilled, who said, He will take our afflictions and bear our sickness.

18 ¶ When Jesus saw large crowds surrounding him, he gave orders to go to the crossing place.

19 And a scribe drew near and said to him, O my teacher, I will follow you wherever you go.

20 Jesus said to him, The foxes have holes, and the fowls of the sky a sheltering place, but the Son of man has no place even to lay his head.

21 Another of his disciples said to him, My Lord, permit me first to go and bury my father.

22 But Jesus said to him, Come after me, and let the dead bury their own dead.

23 ¶ And when Jesus went up into the boat, his disciples went up with him.

24 And behold the sea became very rough, so that the boat was almost covered by the waves; but Jesus was asleep.

25 And his disciples came near and woke him up, and said to him, Our Lord, save us, we are perishing.

26 Jesus said to them, Why are you fearful, O you of little faith? Then he got up and rebuked the wind and the sea, and there was a great calm.

27 But the men were sur-

prised, saying, Who is this man, that even the winds and the sea obey him?

28 ¶ And when Jesus came to the port on the other side, to the country of the Gadarenes, he was met by two lunatics,[1] who were just coming out of the cemetery. They were exceedingly vicious so that no man would dare to pass by that road.

29 And they cried aloud saying, What business have we together, Jesus, "son of God"? Have you come here to torment us before the time?

30 Now there was near by them a large herd of swine feeding.

31 And the lunatics kept asking him, saying, If you are going to heal us, permit us to attack[2] the herd of swine.

32 Jesus said to them, Go. And immediately they left and attacked the swine, and the whole herd went straight over the cliff, and fell into the sea, and were drowned in the water.

33 And they who fed them ran away and went to the city, and reported everything that happened, and about the lunatics.

34 So all the city went out to meet Jesus; and when they saw him, they urged him to depart from their borders.

CHAPTER 9

SO he went up into the boat, and crossed over and came to his own city.

2 And they brought to him a paralytic, lying on a quilt bed; and Jesus saw their faith, and he said to the paralytic, Have courage, my son, your sins have been forgiven.

3 Some of the scribes said among themselves, This man blasphemes.

4 But Jesus knew their thoughts, so he said to them, Why do you think evil in your hearts?

5 For which is easier to say, Your sins have been forgiven, or to say, Arise and walk?

6 But that you might know that the Son of man has authority on earth to forgive sins, then he said to the paralytic, Arise, take up your quilt-bed, and go to your home.

7 And he rose up and went to his home.

8 But when the crowds saw it, they were frightened, and they glorified God, because he had given such power as this to men.

[1] Aramaic *devana* means lunatic or insane; those suffering from mental diseases were supposed to be possessed of devils or evil spirits.
[2] Aramaic *al* means to attack, to chase, to enter.

Cf. dif. verses 28–29–31–33–2–8   15

9 ¶ And as Jesus passed from that place, he saw a man whose name was Matthew, sitting in the custom house, and he said to him, Follow me; and he got up and went after him.

10 ¶ And while they were guests in the house, a great many publicans and sinners came, and they sat as guests with Jesus and with his disciples.

11 And when the Pharisees saw it, they said to his disciples, Why does your master eat with publicans and sinners?

12 But when Jesus heard it, he said to them, Those who are well need no doctor, but those who are seriously sick.

13 Go and learn what this means, I want mercy and not sacrifice; for I came not to invite righteous men, but sinners.

14 ¶ Then the disciples of John came up to him, and said, Why do we and the Pharisees fast a great deal, and your disciples never fast?

15 Jesus said to them, Is it possible for those at the wedding feast to fast as long as the bridegroom is with them? But the days are coming, when the bridegroom will be taken from them, and then they will fast.

16 No man puts a new patch on an old garment, so as not to weaken that garment, and make the hole larger.

17 Neither do they pour new wine into worn out skins, so as not to rend the skins, and spill the wine, and the wine runs out, and the skins are ruined; but they pour new wine into new skins, and both of them are well preserved.

18 ¶ While he was speaking these things with them, a leader of the synagogue came near and worshipped him; and he said, My daughter has just died, but come and put your hand on her and she will live.

19 And Jesus and his disciples rose up and went with him.

20 ¶ And behold a woman who had the hemorrhage for twelve years, came up from behind him, and she touched the edge of his cloak.

21 For she was saying to herself, If I can only touch his garment, I will be healed.

22 And Jesus turned around and saw her and said to her, Have courage, my daughter, your faith has healed you; and the woman was healed in that very hour.

23 ¶ So Jesus arrived at the house of the synagogue leader, and saw the singers and the excited crowds.

Cf. dif. verses 12–14–16–17–20

24 And he said to them, That is enough; for the little girl is not dead, but she is asleep; and they laughed at him.

25 But when he had put the people out, he went in and held her by her hand, and the little girl got up.

26 And this news spread all over that country.

27 ¶ And as Jesus passed from there, he was delayed by two blind men, who were crying out and saying, Have mercy on us, O son of David.

28 And when he came into the house, the same blind men came up to him. Jesus said to them, Do you believe that I can do this? They said to him, Yes, our Lord.

29 Then he touched their eyes and said, Let it be to you according to your faith.

30 And immediately their eyes were opened; and Jesus charged them and said, See that no one know it.

31 But they went out and spread the news all over that country.

32 ¶ And when Jesus went out, they brought to him a dumb man who was demented.

33 And as soon as he was restored, the dumb man spoke, and the people were amazed and said, Such a thing has never been seen in Israel.

34 But the Pharisees said, He is casting out devils by the help of the prince of devils.

35 And Jesus travelled in all the cities and villages, teaching in their synagogues, and preaching the gospel of the kingdom, and healing every kind of sickness and disease.

36 ¶ When Jesus saw the multitudes, he had compassion on them, because they were tired out and scattered, like sheep which have no shepherd.

37 So he said to his disciples, The harvest is great, and the laborers are few;

38 Therefore urge the owner of the harvest to bring more laborers to his harvest.

CHAPTER 10

AND he called his twelve disciples, and gave them power over the unclean spirits, to cast them out, and to heal every kind of disease and sickness.

2 The names of the twelve apostles are these: The first of them Simon who is called Peter, and Andrew his brother; James the son of Zebedee, and John his brother;

3 Philip and Bartholomew,

Thomas and Matthew the publican, James the son of Alphaeus, and Lebbaeus surnamed Thaddaeus;

4 Simon the Zealot, and Judas of Iscariot, who betrayed him.

5 These twelve Jesus sent out, and charged them and said, Keep away from pagan practices, and do not enter a Samaritan city;

6 But above all, go to the sheep which are lost from the house of Israel.

7 And as you go, preach and say, that the kingdom of heaven is near.

8 Heal the sick, cleanse the lepers, cast out demons; freely you have received, freely give.

9 Do not accumulate gold, nor silver, nor brass in your purses;

10 Nor a bag for the journey, nor two shirts and shoes, nor a staff, for a laborer is at least worthy of his food.

11 Whatever city or town you enter, ask who is trustworthy in it, and remain there until you leave.

12 And when you enter into the house, salute the family.

13 And if the family is trustworthy, your salutation of peace shall come upon it; but if it is not trustworthy, your salutation shall return to you.

14 Whoever will not welcome you, and does not listen to your words, when you leave the house or the village, shake off the sand from your feet.

15 Truly I say to you, that it will be easier for the land of Sodom and Gomorrah on the day of judgment than for that city.

16 ¶ Behold, I am sending you like lambs among the wolves; therefore be wise as serpents, and pure as doves.

17 But be careful of men; for they will deliver you up to the courts, and they will scourge you in their synagogues;

18 And they will bring you before the presence of governors and kings for my sake, as a testimony to them and to the Gentiles.

19 But when they deliver you up, do not worry as to how or what you will speak; for it will be given to you in that very hour what you are to speak.

20 For it is not you who speak, but the Spirit of your Father, which speaks through you.

21 Brother will deliver up his own brother to death, and father his son; and children will rise up against their parents and put them to death.

22 And you will be hated by

everybody because of my name; but he who endures until the end shall live.

23 When they persecute you in this city, escape to the other; for truly I say to you, that you shall not finish converting all the cities of the house of Israel, until the Son of man returns.

24 No disciple is more important than his teacher, and no servant than his master.

25 It is enough for a disciple to be like his teacher, and for a servant to be like his master. If then, they have called the master of the house Beelzebub, how much more those of his household.

26 Therefore do not be afraid of them; for there is nothing covered that will not be uncovered, and hidden that will not be known.

27 What I tell you in the dark, tell it in the daylight; and what you hear with your ears, preach on the house tops.

28 Do not be afraid of those who kill the body, but who cannot kill the soul; but above all, be afraid of him who can destroy both the soul and the body in hell.

29 Are not two sparrows sold for a penny? and yet not one of them will fall on the ground without your Father's will.

30 But so far as you are concerned, even the hairs of your head are all numbered.

31 Therefore fear not; you are much more important than many sparrows.

32 Everyone therefore who will acknowledge me before men, I will also acknowledge him before my Father in heaven.

33 But whoever will deny me before men, I will also deny him before my Father in heaven.

34 ¶ Do not expect that I have come to bring peace on earth; I have not come to bring peace but a sword.

35 For I have come to set a man against his father, and a daughter against her mother, and a daughter-in-law against her mother-in-law.

36 And a man's enemies will be the members of his own household.

37 Whoever loves father or mother more than me is not worthy of me; and whoever loves son or daughter more than me is not worthy of me.

38 And whoever does not take up his cross and follow me is not worthy of me.

39 He who is concerned about his life shall lose it; and he who loses his life for my sake shall find it.

40 Whoever receives you,

receives me; and whoever receives me, receives him who sent me.

41 He who receives a prophet in the name of a prophet, shall receive a prophet's reward; and whoever receives a righteous man in the name of a righteous man, shall receive a righteous man's reward.

42 Anyone who gives a drink to one of these little ones, if only a cup of cold water, in the name of a disciple, truly I say to you, he shall never lose his reward.

CHAPTER 11

WHEN Jesus had finished commanding his twelve disciples, he departed from that place to teach and to preach in their cities.

2 But when John heard in prison of the works of Christ, he sent by his disciples,

3 And said to him, Are you the one who is to come, or are we to expect another one?

4 Jesus answered and said to them, Go and describe to John the things which you see and hear.

5 The blind see, and the lame walk, and the lepers are cleansed, and the deaf hear, and the dead rise up, and the poor are given hope.

6 And blessed is he who does not stumble on account of me.

7 ¶ When they went away, Jesus began to speak to the people concerning John, What did you go out to the wilderness to see? A reed which is shaken by the wind?

8 If not so, what did you go out to see? A man dressed in fine clothes? Behold those who wear fine clothes are in king's houses.

9 And if not so, What then did you go out to see? A prophet? Yes, I tell you, and much more than a prophet.

10 For this is he of whom it is written, Behold, I send my messenger before your face, to prepare the way before you.

11 ¶ Truly I say to you, that among those who are born of women, there has never risen one who is greater than John the Baptist; and yet even the least person in the kingdom of heaven is greater than he.

12 From the days of John the Baptist until now, the kingdom of heaven has been administered by force, and only those in power control it.

13 For all the prophets and the law] prophesied until John.

14 And if you wish, accept it, that he is Elijah who was to come.

20   *Cf. dif. verses 2–5–6–11–12*

15 He who has ears to hear, let him hear.

16 ¶ But to whom shall I liken this generation? It is like boys who sit in the street and call to their friends.

17 And say, We have sung to you, but you would not dance; and we have wailed to you but you did not mourn.

18 For John came, neither eating nor drinking, and they said he is crazy.

19 The Son of man came, eating and drinking, and they said, Behold, a glutton and a wine-bibber, and a friend of publicans and sinners. And yet wisdom is justified by its works.

20 ¶ Then Jesus began to reproach the cities in which his many works were done, and which did not repent. And he said,

21 Woe to you, Chorazin! woe to you, Bethsaida! for if in Tyre and Sidon had been done the works which were done in you, they might have repented in sackcloth and ashes.

22 But I say to you, It will be easier for Tyre and Sidon in the day of judgment, than for you.

23 And you, Capernaum, which have exalted yourself up to heaven, shall be brought down to Sheol; for if in Sodom had been done the works which were done in you, it would be standing to this day.

24 But I say to you, It will be easier for the land of Sodom in the judgment day, than for you.

25 ¶ At that time, Jesus answered and said, I thank you, O my Father, Lord of heaven and earth, because you have hidden these things from the wise and the men of understanding, and you have revealed them to children.

26 O yes, my Father, for such was your will.

27 Everything has been delivered to me by my Father, and no man knows the Son except the Father, nor does any man know the Father but the Son, and he to whomever the Son wishes to reveal.

28 ¶ Come unto me, all you who are tired out and carrying burdens, and I will give you rest.

29 Take my yoke upon you, and learn from me, for I am genial and meek in my heart, and you will find rest to your souls.

30 For my yoke is very pleasant, and my burden is lighter.

CHAPTER 12

AT that time, Jesus walked on the sabbath through the wheat fields; and his disciples became hungry, and they began to pluck ears of wheat and eat.

2 But when the Pharisees saw them, they said to him, Behold, your disciples are doing what is unlawful to do on the sabbath.

3 But he said to them, Have you not read what David did, when he and those who were with him were hungry?

4 How he entered into the house of God, and did eat bread that was on the table of the Lord, that which was not lawful for him to eat, nor for those who were with him, but only for the priests?

5 Or, have you not read in the book of law, that the priests in the temple disregard the sabbath, and yet are blameless?

6 But I say to you, that there is one here, who is greater than the temple.

7 But if you only knew what it means, I want mercy and not sacrifice, you would not condemn those who are blameless.

8 For the Son of man is Lord of the sabbath.

9 ¶ And Jesus departed from thence and came to their synagogue.

10 And there was a man there whose hand was withered. And they questioned him, saying, Is it lawful to heal on the sabbath? that they might accuse him.

11 He said to them, Who is the man among you who has only one sheep, and if it should fall into a pit on the sabbath, would he not take hold of it and lift it up?

12 How much more important is a man than a sheep? It is therefore lawful to do good on the sabbath.

13 Then he said to the man, Stretch out your hand. And he stretched out his hand, and it was restored like the other.

14 ¶ And the Pharisees went out, and they took counsel concerning him, so as to do away with him.

15 But Jesus knew of it, and he departed from thence; and a great many people followed him, and he healed them all.

16 And he charged them not to say where he was,

17 So that what was said by the prophet Isaiah might be fulfilled, who said,

18 Behold my servant with whom I am pleased, my beloved one, in whom my soul rejoices; I will put my Spirit upon him, and he will preach justice to the peoples.

19 He will not argue, nor will he cry aloud; and no man will hear his voice in the street.

20 He will not break even a

Cf. dif. verses 4–5–16–18–20

bruised reed, and he will not extinguish a flickering lamp, until he brings justice to victory;

21 And in his name will the peoples find hope.

22 ¶ Then they brought near to him a lunatic, who was also dumb and blind; and he healed him, so that the dumb and blind man could speak and see.

23 All the people were amazed and said, Perhaps this man is the son of David?

24 But when the Pharisees heard of it, they said, This man does not cast out demons, except by Beelzebub, the prince of demons.

25 But Jesus knew their thoughts, and said to them, Every kingdom which is divided against itself, will be destroyed; and every house or city that is divided against itself, will not stand.

26 And if Satan cast out Satan, he is divided against himself; how then will his kingdom stand?

27 So if I cast out demons by Beelzebub, by what do your sons cast them out? for this reason they will be your judges.

28 And if I cast out devils by the Spirit of God, then the kingdom of God has come near to you.

29 Or, how can a man enter into a strong man's house and plunder his goods, except he first bind the strong man, and then he plunders his house?

30 ¶ He who is not with me is against me; and he who does not gather with me, shall be dispersed.

31 Therefore I say to you, that all sins and blasphemies will be forgiven to men; but the blasphemy against the Spirit shall not be forgiven to men.

32 And whoever speaks a word against the Son of man, will be forgiven; but whoever speaks against the Holy Spirit shall not be forgiven, neither in this world nor in the world to come.

33 Either produce like a good tree with good fruits; or produce like a bad tree with bad fruits; for a tree is known by its fruits.

34 O generation of scorpions, how can you speak good things when you are bad? for the mouth speaks from the fullness of the heart.

35 A good man brings out good things from good treasures, and a bad man brings out bad things from bad treasures.

36 For I say to you, that for every foolish word which men

speak, they will have to answer for it on the day of judgement.

37 For by your words you shall be justified, and by your words you shall be found guilty.

38 ¶ Then some of the men of the scribes and Pharisees answered and said to him, Teacher, we would like to see a sign from you.

39 But he answered and said to them, An evil and adulterous generation wants a sign; and no sign will be given to it, except the sign of the prophet Jonah.

40 For as Jonah was in the whale's belly three days and three nights, so the Son of man will be in the heart of the earth, three days and three nights.

41 Even the men of Nineveh will rise up in judgement with this generation, and find it guilty; for they repented through the preaching of Jonah, and behold, a greater than Jonah is here.

42 The queen of the south will rise up in judgement with this generation, and find it guilty; for she came from the far ends of the earth that she might hear Solomon's wisdom, and behold a greater than Solomon is here.

43 When an unclean spirit goes out of a man, it travels in places where there is no water, and seeks rest, and does not find it.

44 Then it says, I will return to my own house from whence I came out; so it comes back and finds it empty, warm and well furnished.

45 Then it goes away and brings with it seven other spirits worse than itself, and they enter and live in it; and the end of that man becomes worse than at first. Such will happen to this evil generation.

46 ¶ While he was speaking to the people, his mother and his brothers came and stood outside, and they wanted to speak with him.

47 Then a man said to him, Behold your mother and your brothers are standing outside, and they want to speak with you.

48 But he answered and said to him who told him, Who is my mother and who are my brothers?

49 And he pointed his hand to his disciples and said, Behold my mother, and behold my brothers.

50 For whoever does the will of my Father in heaven, he is my brother and my sister and my mother.

CHAPTER 13

THAT same day Jesus went out of the house, and sat by the seaside.

2 And many people gathered around him, so that he had to go up and sit in a boat, and all the people stood on the seashore.

3 And he spoke many things to them in parables, and said, Behold the sower went out to sow;

4 And when he had sown, some seed fell on the roadside, and the fowls came and ate it.

5 Other fell upon the rock, where there was not sufficient soil; and it sprung up earlier because the ground was not deep enough;

6 But when the sun shone, it was scorched, and because it had no root, it dried up;

7 And other fell among thistles, and the thistles sprung up and choked it.

8 And other fell in good soil, and bore fruit, some one hundred, and some sixty, and some thirty.

9 He who has ears to hear, let him hear.

10 ¶ Then his disciples drew near to him and said, Why do you talk to them in parables?

11 He answered and said to them, Because to you it is granted to know the mystery of the kingdom of heaven, but it is not granted to them.

12 For to him who has, shall be given and it shall increase to him; but to him who has not, even that which he has shall be taken away from him.

13 This is the reason I speak to them in figures, because they see and yet cannot perceive; and they hear and yet do not listen, nor do they understand.

14 And in them is fulfilled the prophecy of Isaiah who said, Hearing you will hear, but you will not understand; and seeing you will see, but you will not know.

15 For the heart of this people has become hardened, and their ears hear heavily, and their eyes are dull; so that they cannot see with their eyes, and hear with their ears, and understand with their hearts; let them return, and I will heal them.

16 But as for you, blessed are your eyes for they see; and your ears for they hear.

17 For truly I say to you, a great many prophets and righteous men have longed to see what you see, and did not see it; and to hear what you hear, and did not hear it.

18 ¶ Now you listen to the parable of the seed.

19 Whoever hears the word of the kingdom and does not understand it, the evil one comes and snatches away the word which has been sown in his heart. This is that which was sown on the roadside.

20 That which was sown upon the rock, this is he who hears the word, and immediately accepts it with joy;

21 But it has no root in him, except for a while; and when trouble or persecution comes because of the word, he immediately stumbles.

22 That which was sown among thistles, this is he who hears the word, but worldly thoughts and the deception caused by riches choke the word, and it becomes fruitless.

23 That which was sown upon good soil, this is he who hears my word, and understands it, so he bears fruit and produces some one hundred, and some sixty, and some thirty.

24 ¶ He related another parable to them, and said, The kingdom of heaven is like a man who sowed good seed in his field.

25 And when the men slept, his enemy came and sowed tares among the wheat, and went away.

26 But when the blade sprang up and bore fruit, then the tares also appeared.

27 So the servants of the landowner came and said to him, Our lord, behold, did you not sow good seed in your field; whence did the tares come into it?

28 He said to them, An enemy did this; his servants then said to him, Do you want us to go and pick them out?

29 But he said to them, It might happen that while you are picking out the tares, you may uproot with them also the wheat.

30 Let them both grow together until the harvest; and at the harvest season, I will say to the reapers, Pick out first the tares, and bind them into bundles to be burned; but gather the wheat into my barns.

31 ¶ He related another parable to them, and said, The kingdom of heaven is like a grain of mustard seed, which a man took and sowed in his field.

32 It is the smallest of all seeds; but when it is grown, it is larger than all of the herbs; and it becomes a tree, so that the fowls of the sky come and nest in its branches.

33 ¶ He told them another parable. The kingdom of

Cf. dif. verses 19–21–22–23–29

heaven is like the leaven, which a woman took and buried in three measures of flour, until it was all leavened.

34 ¶ Jesus spoke all these things to the people in parables; and without parables he did not speak to them.

35 So that it might be fulfilled what was said by the prophet, who said, I will open my mouth in parables, and I will bring out secrets hidden before the foundation of the world.

36 Then Jesus left the multitudes and came to the house; and his disciples came up to him, and said, Explain to us the parable of the tares and the field.

37 He answered and said to them, He who sowed good seed is the Son of man.

38 The field is the world; the good seed are the sons of the kingdom; but the tares are the sons of evil.

39 The enemy who sowed them is Satan; the harvest is the end of the world; and the reapers are the angels.

40 Therefore, just as the tares are picked out and burned in the fire, so shall it be at the end of the world.

41 The Son of man will send his angels, and they will pick out from his kingdom all things which cause stumbling, and all workers of iniquity.

42 And they will throw them into the furnace of fire; there shall be weeping and gnashing of teeth.

43 Then the righteous ones shall shine as the sun in the kingdom of their Father. He who has ears to hear, let him hear.

44 ¶ Again, the kingdom of heaven is like a treasure which is hidden in the field, which a man discovered and hid, and because of his joy, he went and sold everything he had, and bought that field.

45 ¶ Again, the kingdom of heaven is like a merchant, who was seeking good pearls.

46 And when he had found one costly pearl, he went and sold everything he had, and bought it.

47 ¶ Again, the kingdom of heaven is like a net which was thrown into the sea, and it gathered fish of every kind.

48 When it was filled, they drew it to the shore, and sat down and sorted them; the good ones they put into bags, and the bad they threw away.

49 So will it be at the end of the world; the angels will go out and separate the bad from among the righteous,

50 And they will throw

them into the furnace of fire; there shall be weeping and gnashing of teeth.

51 ¶ Jesus said to them, Have you understood all of these things? They said to him, Yes, our Lord.

52 He said to them, Therefore every scribe who is converted to the kingdom of heaven, is like a man who is a householder, who brings out new and old things from his treasures.

53 ¶ When Jesus had finished these parables, he departed thence.

54 And he came to his own city; and he taught them in their synagogues, in such a way, that they were amazed and said, Where did he get this wisdom and these wonders?

55 Is he not the carpenter's son? is not his mother called Mary? and his brothers, James and Joses and Simon and Judah?

56 Are not all his sisters with us? Where did he get all these things?

57 And they were perplexed about him. But Jesus said to them, No prophet is insulted, except in his own city and in his own house.

58 And he did not perform many miracles there, because of their unbelief.

CHAPTER 14

AT that time Herod the tetrarch heard the news about Jesus.

2 And he said to his servants, This man is John the Baptist; he has risen from the dead; this is why great miracles are wrought by him.

3 ¶ For Herod had arrested John, and bound him, and put him in prison, because of Herodias, his brother Philip's wife.

4 For John had said to him, It is unlawful to have her as your wife.

5 So Herod wanted to kill him, but he was afraid of the people, because they accepted him as a prophet.

6 When Herod's birthday came, the daughter of Herodias danced before the guests, and it pleased Herod.

7 He therefore swore to her with oaths, that he would give her anything that she asked.

8 And she, because she was instructed by her mother, said, Give me right here on a tray the head of John the Baptist.

9 And the king was very sorry; but because of the oaths and the guests, he commanded that it be given to her.

10 So he sent and had John beheaded in the prison.

11 And his head was brought in on a tray, and given to the girl; and she took it to her mother.

12 Then his disciples came and took up his body and buried it, and they came and informed Jesus.

13 ¶ When Jesus heard it, he departed thence by boat, alone to a desert place; and when the people heard of it, they followed him by land from the cities.

14 And Jesus went out and saw large crowds, and he had pity for them, and he healed their sick.

15 ¶ When it was evening, his disciples came to him, and they said to him, This is a lonely place, and it is getting late; dismiss the people so that the men may go to the villages and buy food for themselves.

16 But he said to them, It is not necessary for them to go; you give them something to eat.

17 They said to him, We have nothing here, except five loaves of bread and two fish.

18 Jesus said to them, Bring them here to me.

19 And he ordered the people to sit down on the ground, and he took the five loaves of bread and the two fish, and he looked up to heaven and he blessed them, and he broke them, and gave them to his disciples, and the disciples placed them before the people.

20 So they all ate, and were satisfied; and they took up the fragments which were left over, twelve full baskets.

21 And the men who ate were five thousand, not counting the women and children.

22 ¶ And immediately he urged his disciples to go up into the boat, in advance of him to the crossing place, while he dismissed the people.

23 And when he had dismissed the people, he went up to the mountain alone to pray; and when darkness fell he was still there alone.

24 But the boat was many miles away from the land, tossed by the waves, for the wind was against it.

25 And in the fourth watch of the night, Jesus came to them, walking on[1] the water.

26 And his disciples saw him walking on the water, and they were scared, and they said, It is a false vision; and they cried out because of their fear.

[1] The Aramaic means *on* or *by*. There was no crossing at this time for the boat was at a distance from its starting point.

Cf. dif. verses 15–22–24–26, 29

27 But Jesus spoke to them at once and said, Have courage; it is I; do not be afraid.

28 And Peter answered and said to him, My Lord, if it is you, command me to come to you on the water.

29 Jesus said to him, Come. So Peter went down from the boat, and walked on the water, to come to Jesus.

30 But when he saw that the wind was severe, he was afraid, and began to sink, and he raised his voice and said, My Lord, save me.

31 And our Lord immediately stretched out his hand and grasped him; and he said to him, O you of little faith, why did you doubt?

32 And when they went up into the boat, the wind quieted down.

33 And they who were in the boat came and worshipped him; and they said, Truly you are the Son of God.

34 ¶ And they rowed and came to the land of Gennesaret.

35 And the men of that country recognized him, and they sent word to all the villages around them; so they brought to him all who were seriously sick.

36 And they besought him, that they might touch even the edge of his robe; and those who touched it were healed.

CHAPTER 15

THEN Pharisees and scribes from Jerusalem came up to Jesus, saying,

2 Why do your disciples disregard the tradition of the elders, and they do not wash their hands when they eat food?

3 Jesus answered and said to them, Why do you also disregard the commandment of God on account of your tradition.

4 For God said, Honor your father and your mother, and whoever curses his father and his mother, let him be put to death.

5 But you say, whoever says to a father or to a mother, whatever you may be benefited from me is Corban (my offering), he need not honor his father or his mother.

6 So you have rendered useless the word of God for the sake of your tradition.

7 O you hypocrites, the prophet Isaiah well prophesied concerning you and said,

8 This people honor me with their lips, but their heart is far away from me.

9 And they worship me in vain, when they teach the

doctrines of the commandments of men.

10 ¶ Then he called the people and said to them, Listen and understand.

11 It is not what enters into the mouth which defiles man; but what goes out of the mouth, that is what defiles man.

12 Then his disciples came up and said to him, Do you know that the Pharisees who heard this saying were offended?

13 But he answered and said to them, Every plant that my heavenly Father did not plant, shall be uprooted.

14 Leave them alone; they are blind guides of the blind. And if the blind lead around the blind, both will fall into a pit.

15 And Simon Peter answered and said to him, My Lord, explain this parable to us.

16 And he said to them, Even yet do you not understand?

17 Do you not know that what enters into the mouth goes into the stomach, and thence, through the intestines, is cast out?

18 But what comes out of the mouth comes out from the heart; and that is what defiles man.

19 For from the heart come out evil thoughts, such as fornication, murder, adultery, theft, false witness, blasphemy.

20 It is these that defile man; but if a man should eat when his hands are unwashed, he will not be defiled.

21 ¶ And Jesus went out from thence, and he came to the border of Tyre and Sidon.

22 And behold, a Canaanite woman from these borders, came out crying aloud, and saying, Have mercy on me, O my Lord, son of David; my daughter is seriously afflicted with insanity.

23 But he did not answer her. And his disciples came up to him and urged him, saying, Dismiss her, for she keeps crying aloud after us.

24 And he answered and said to them, I am not sent, except to the sheep which went astray from the house of Israel.

25 But she came and worshipped him, and said, My Lord, help me.

26 Jesus said to her, It is not right to take the children's bread and throw it to the dogs.

27 But she said Yes, my lord, even the dogs eat of the

crumbs which fall from the master's tray, and they live.

28 Then Jesus said to her, O woman, your faith is great; let it be to you as you wish; and her daughter was healed from that very hour.

29 ¶ And Jesus departed from thence, and he came toward the sea of Galilee; and he went up to a mountain and sat down there.

30 And a great many people came to him, who had with them the lame, blind, dumb, maimed, and many others; and they laid them down at the feet of Jesus, and he healed them.

31 So that the people wondered, to see the dumb speaking, and the maimed healed, and the lame walking, and the blind seeing; and they praised the God of Israel.

32 ¶ Jesus then called his disciples and said to them, I have compassion for this people, for they have remained with me three days, and they have nothing to eat; and if I dismiss them fasting, they might faint on the way; but this I do not wish to do.

33 His disciples said to him, Where can we get bread in this desolate place to feed all this people?

34 Jesus said to them, How many loaves of bread have you? They said to him, Seven, and a few small fish.

35 So he ordered the people to sit on the ground.

36 Then he took the seven loaves of bread and the fish, and gave thanks, and he broke them, and gave to his disciples, and the disciples gave them to the people.

37 And all of them did eat and were satisfied; and they took up of the fragments that were left over, seven full baskets.

38 And those who did eat were four thousand men, besides women and children.

39 And when he had dismissed the people, he went up to the boat and came to the border of Magadan.

CHAPTER 16

AND the Pharisees and Sadducees came up to him to tempt him; and they asked him to show them a sign from heaven.

2 But he answered and said to them, When it is evening, you say, It is clear, for the sky is red.

3 And in the morning you say, It is a winter day, for the sky is red and cloudy. O hypocrites, you know how to judge the face of the sky, but

the signs of the present time you are not able to distinguish.

4 A wicked and adulterous generation wants a sign; and no sign shall be given to it, except the sign of the prophet Jonah. And he left them and went away.

5 When his disciples came to the crossing place, they had forgotten to take bread with them.

6 ¶ He said to them, Look out and beware of the leaven of the Pharisees and of the Sadducees.

7 And they were reasoning among themselves and saying, It is because we have not brought bread.

8 But Jesus knew it and said to them, What are you thinking among yourselves, O you of little faith; is it because you have not brought bread?

9 Do you not yet understand? Do you not remember the five loaves of bread of the five thousand, and how many baskets you took up?

10 Neither the seven loaves of bread of the four thousand, and how many baskets you took up?

11 How is it that you did not understand that I was not talking to you about the bread, but to beware of the leaven of the Pharisees and of the Sadducees?

12 Then they understood, that he did not say that they should beware of the leaven of the bread, but of the teaching of the Pharisees and the Sadducees.

13 ¶ When Jesus came to the country of Caesarea of Philippi, he asked his disciples saying, What do the men say concerning me, that I am merely a son of man?

14 They said, There are some who say John the Baptist, others Elijah, and still others Jeremiah, or one of the prophets.

15 He said to them, Who do you say that I am?

16 Simon Peter answered and said, You are the Christ, the Son of the living God.

17 Jesus answered and said to him; Blessed are you, Simon son of Jonah, for flesh and blood did not reveal it to you, but my Father in heaven.

18 I tell you also that you are a stone, and upon this stone I will build my church; and the doors of Sheol shall not shut in on it.

19 I will give you the keys of the kingdom of heaven; and whatever you bind on earth shall be bound in heaven, and whatever you

release on earth shall be released in heaven.

20 Then he charged his disciples not to tell any man that he is the Christ.

21 ¶ From that time Jesus began to make known to his disciples, that he will shortly have to go to Jerusalem, and suffer a great deal from the elders, and the high priests and scribes, and be killed, and rise up on the third day.

22 So Peter took him aside and began to rebuke him, and he said, Far be it from you, my Lord, that this should happen to you.

23 But he turned and said to Peter, Get behind me, Satan, you are a stumbling-block to me; for you are not thinking of the things of God, but of men.

24 ¶ Then Jesus said to his disciples, He who wishes to come after me, let him deny himself, and take up his cross and follow me.

25 For whoever wishes to save his life shall lose it; and whoever loses his life for my sake shall find it.

26 For how will a man be benefited, if he should gain the whole world and lose his own soul? Or what shall a man give in exchange for his soul?

27 For the Son of man will come in the glory of his Father with his holy angels; and then he will reward each man according to his works.

28 Truly I say to you, There are men who stand here, who will not taste death, until they see the Son of man coming in his kingdom.

CHAPTER 17

AND after six days Jesus took Peter and James and his brother John, and brought them up to a high mountain alone.

2 And Jesus was transfigured before them, and his face shone like the sun, and his clothes turned white like light.

3 And there appeared to them Moses and Elijah, as they were talking with him.

4 Then Peter answered and said to Jesus, My Lord, it is better for us to remain here; and if you wish, we will make three shelters here, one for you, and one for Moses, and one for Elijah.

5 And while he was speaking, behold, a bright cloud overshadowed them, and a voice came out of the cloud saying, This is my beloved Son, I am pleased with him; hear him.

6 When the disciples heard it, they threw themselves on

34

their faces, and they were greatly frightened.

7 And Jesus came near them and touched them, and said, Arise, do not be afraid.

8 And they raised up their eyes, and they saw no man, except Jesus alone.

9 And as they were going down from the mountain, Jesus commanded them, and said to them, Do not speak of this vision in the presence of anyone, until the Son of man rises from the dead.

10 And his disciples asked him, and said, Why then do the scribes say that Elijah must come first?

11 Jesus answered and said to them, Elijah will come first, so that everything might be fulfilled.

12 But I say to you, Elijah has already come, and they did not know him, and they did to him whatever they pleased. Thus also the Son of man is bound to suffer from them.

13 Then the disciples understood that what he had told them was about John the Baptist.

14 ¶ And when they came to the people, a man approached him and knelt on his knees, and said to him,

15 My Lord, have mercy on me; my son is an epileptic and has become worse; he often falls into the fire, and often into the water.

16 And I brought him to your disciples, but they were not able to heal him.

17 Jesus answered and said, O faithless and crooked generation, how long shall I be with you? and how long shall I preach to you? bring him here to me.

18 And Jesus rebuked him, and the demon went out of him; and the boy was healed from that very hour.

19 Then the disciples came up to Jesus when he was alone, and said to him, Why could we not heal him?

20 Jesus said to them, Because of your unbelief; for truly I say to you, If there is faith in you even as a grain of mustard, you will say to this mountain, move away from here, and it will move away; and nothing would prevail over you.

21 Nevertheless this kind does not come out, except by fasting and prayer.

22 ¶ While they were returning through Galilee, Jesus said to them, The Son of man will shortly be delivered into the hands of men;

23 And they will kill him, and on the third day he will

rise up. And they were very much grieved.

24 ¶ And when they came to Capernaum, those who collect two coins of silver as head-tax came to Peter and said to him, Would not your master give his two coins?

25 He said to them, Yes. And when Peter entered the house, Jesus anticipated and said to him, What do you think, Simon? from whom do the kings of the earth collect custom duties and head-tax? from their sons, or from strangers?

26 Simon said to him, From strangers. Jesus said to him, Then the sons are free.

27 But so as not to offend them, go to the sea, and throw out a hook, and the first fish which comes up, open its mouth and you will find a coin; take it and give it for me and for you.

CHAPTER 18

AT that very hour the disciples came up to Jesus and said, Who is greatest in the kingdom of heaven?

2 So Jesus called a little boy, and made him to stand up in the midst of them,

3 And he said, Truly I say to you, Unless you change and become like little boys, you shall not enter into the kingdom of heaven.

4 Whoever therefore will humble himself like this little boy, shall be great in the kingdom of heaven.

5 And he who will welcome one like this little boy, in my name, welcomes me.

6 And whoever misleads one of these little ones who believe in me, it would be better for him that an ass' millstone were hanged on his neck and he were sunk in the depths of the sea.

7 ¶ Woe to the world because of offences! Offences are bound to come; but woe to the man by whose hand the offences come!

8 If your hand or your foot offends you, cut it off and throw it away from you; for it is much better for you to go through life lamed or maimed, rather than having two hands or two feet, and fall into the everlasting fire.

9 And if your eye offends you, remove it and throw it away from you; it is better for you to go through life with one eye, rather than having two eyes and fall into the gehenna[1] of fire.

10 See to it that you do not despise one of these little

[1] That is, hell.

ones; for I say to you, their angels always see the face of my Father in heaven.

11 For the Son of man has come to save what was lost.

12 What do you think? If a man should have a hundred sheep, and one of them is lost, would he not leave the ninety and nine on the mountain, and go in search of the one which is lost?

13 And if he should find it, truly I say to you, he rejoices over it more than over the ninety and nine which were not lost.

14 Even so, your Father in heaven does not want one of these little ones to be lost.

15 ¶ Now then, if your brother is at fault with you, go and rebuke him alone; if he listens to you, then you have won your brother.

16 But if he will not listen to you, take one or two with you, because at the mouth of two or three witnesses every word is sustained.

17 And if he will not listen to them, tell the congregation; and if he will not listen to the congregation, then regard him as a publican and a heathen.

18 Truly I say to you, Whatever you bind on earth will be bound in heaven, and whatever you release on earth will be released in heaven.

19 Again I say to you, that if two of you are worthy on earth, anything that they would ask, it will be done for them by my Father in heaven.

20 For wherever two or three are gathered in my name, I am there among them.

21 ¶ Then Peter came up and said to him, My Lord, if my brother is at fault with me, how many times should I forgive him? up to seven times?

22 Jesus said to him, I do not say to you up to seven times, but up to seventy times seven.

23 ¶ Therefore the kingdom of heaven is likened to a king who wanted to take an accounting from his servants.

24 And when he began to take the accounting, they brought to him one who owed ten thousand talents.

25 And as he could not pay, his lord commanded him to be sold, together with his wife and children, and all that he had, so he could pay.

26 The servant then fell down, worshipped him and said, My Lord, have patience with me, and I will pay you everything.

27 Then the master of that servant had pity, so he released him, and cancelled his debt.

28 But that servant went out, and found one of his fellow-servants, who owed him one hundred cents; and he seized him, and tried to choke him, saying to him, Give me what you owe me.

29 So his fellow-servant fell down at his feet, and begged him and said, Have patience with me, and I will pay you.

30 But he was not willing; and he went and had him put into prison, until he should pay him what he owed him.

31 When their fellow-servants saw what had happened, they were very sorry, and they came and informed their master of everything that had happened.

32 Then his master called him and said to him, O wicked servant, I cancelled all your debt because you begged me.

33 Was it not right for you to have mercy on your fellow-servant, just as I had mercy on you?

34 So his master was angry, and delivered him to the scourgers, until he should pay everything he owed him.

35 So will my Father in heaven do to you, if you do not forgive each man his brother's fault from your heart.

CHAPTER 19

WHEN Jesus had finished these sayings, he departed from Galilee, and came to the border of Judaea, at the crossing of the Jordan.

2 And a great many people followed him, and he healed them there.

3 ¶ And the Pharisees came up to him and were tempting him and saying, Is it lawful for a man to divorce his wife for any cause?

4 But he answered and said to them, Have you not read, that he who made from the beginning, made them male and female?

5 And he said, Because of this, a man shall leave his father and his mother, and shall be joined to his wife, and the two shall be one flesh.

6 Henceforth they are not two, but one body; therefore what God has joined together, man must not separate.

7 They said to him, Why then did Moses command to give a letter of separation and then divorce her?

8 He said to them, Moses,

considering the hardness of your heart, gave you permission to divorce your wives; but from the beginning it was not so.

9 But I say to you, Whoever leaves his wife without a charge of adultery and marries another commits adultery; and he who marries a woman thus separated commits adultery.

10 ¶ His disciples said to him, If there is so much scandal between man and woman, it is not worthwhile to marry.

11 He said to them, This saying does not apply to every man, but to whom it is needed.

12 For there are eunuchs who were born this way from their mother's womb; and there are eunuchs who were made eunuchs by men; and there are eunuchs who made themselves eunuchs for the sake of the kingdom of heaven. To him who can grasp, this is enough.

13 ¶ Then they brought little boys to him, that he may lay his hand on them and pray; and his disciples rebuked them.

14 But Jesus said to them, Allow the little boys to come to me, and do not stop them;

for the kingdom of heaven is for such as these.

15 And he laid his hand on them, and he went away from thence.

16 ¶ Then a man came up and said to him, O good[1] teacher, what is the best that I should do to have life eternal?

17 He said to him, Why do you call me good? There is no one who is good except the one God; but if you want to enter into life, obey the commandments.

18 He said to him, Which ones? And Jesus said to him, You shall not kill; You shall not commit adultery; You shall not steal; You shall not bear false witness;

19 Honor your father and your mother; and, Love your neighbor as yourself.

20 The young man said to him, I have obeyed all these from my boyhood, what do I lack?

21 Jesus said to him, If you wish to be perfect, go and sell your possessions and give them to the poor, and you will have a treasure in heaven; then follow me.

22 When the young man heard this word, he went away sad, for he had great possessions.

---

[1] Aramaic *tava* means wonderful.

Cf. dif. verses 9–10–11–12–21

39

5

23 ¶ Jesus then said to his disciples, Truly I say to you, It is difficult for a rich man to enter into the kingdom of heaven.

24 Again I say to you, It is easier for a rope[1] to go through the eye of a needle, than for a rich man to enter into the kingdom of God.

25 When the disciples heard it, they were exceedingly astonished, saying, Who then can be saved?

26 Jesus looked at them and said, For men this is impossible, but for God everything is possible.

27 ¶ Then Peter answered and said to him, Behold, we have left everything and followed you; what will we have?

28 Jesus said to them, Truly I say to you, that in the new world when the Son of man shall sit on the throne of his glory, you who have come after me shall also sit on twelve chairs, and you shall judge the twelve tribes of Israel.

29 And every man who leaves houses, or brothers, or sisters, or father, or mother, or wife, or children, or fields, for my name's sake, shall receive a hundredfold, and shall inherit everlasting life.

30 But many who are first shall be last, and the last first.

CHAPTER 20

FOR the kingdom of heaven is like a man, who is a householder, who went out early in the morning to hire laborers for his vineyard.

2 He bargained with the laborers for a penny a day, and sent them to his vineyard.

3 And he went out at the third hour, and saw others standing idle in the market place.

4 And he said to them, You also go to the vineyard, and I will give you what is right. And they went.

5 And he went out again at the sixth and at the ninth hour, and did the same.

6 And towards the eleventh hour he went out and found others standing idle, and he said to them, Why do you stand all day idle?

7 They said to him, Because no man has hired us. He said to them, You also go to the vineyard, and you will receive what is right.

8 When evening came, the owner of the vineyard said to his steward, Call the laborers and pay them their wages; and begin from the last ones to the first.

[1] The Aramaic word *gamla* means rope and camel.

Cf. dif. verses 24–28–2

9 When those of the eleventh hour came, they each received a penny.

10 But when the first ones came, they expected to receive more; but they also got each one a penny.

11 And when they received it, they murmured against the householder,

12 Saying, These last ones have worked only one hour, and you have made them equal with us, who have borne the weight of the day and its heat.

13 He answered and said to one of them, My friend, I am not doing you an injustice; did you not bargain with me for a penny?

14 Take what is yours and go away; I wish to give to this last one the same as to you.

15 Have I no right to do what I wish with mine own? Or are you jealous because I am generous?

16 Even so the last shall be first, and the first last; for many are called, but few are chosen.

17 ¶ Now Jesus was ready to go up to Jerusalem; and he took his twelve disciples apart on the road, and he said to them,

18 Behold, we are going up to Jerusalem, and the Son of man will be delivered to the high priests and the scribes, and they will condemn him to death.

19 And they will deliver him to the Gentiles and they will mock him, and scourge him, and crucify him; and on the third day he will rise up.

20 ¶ Then the mother of the sons of Zebedee came up to him, together with her sons; and she worshipped him, and requested something of him.

21 He said to her, What do you wish? She said to him, Command that these two sons of mine sit, one at your right and one at your left, in your kingdom.

22 Jesus answered and said, You do not know what you are asking. Can you drink the cup that I am ready to drink, or be baptized with the baptism with which I am to be baptized? They said to him, We can.

23 He said to them, Indeed my cup you shall drink, and the baptism with which I am to be baptized, you too shall be baptized with; but to sit at my right and at my left, that is not mine to give, but it is for those for whom it is prepared by my Father.

24 When the ten heard it, they were angry at the two brothers.

25 And Jesus called them and said, You know that the princes of the people are also their owners; and their officials rule over them.

26 Let not this be so among you; but whoever wishes to be great among you, let him be a minister to you;

27 And whoever wishes to be first among you, let him be a servant to you:

28 Just as the Son of man did not come to be ministered to, but to minister, and to give his life as a salvation for the sake of many.

29 ¶ And when Jesus went out of Jericho a large crowd followed him.

30 And behold, two blind men were sitting by the roadside, and when they heard that Jesus was passing by, they cried aloud, saying, Have mercy upon us, O Lord, son of David.

31 But the people rebuked them to keep quiet; but they cried louder, saying, Our Lord, have mercy upon us, son of David.

32 And Jesus stopped and called them, and he said, What do you wish me to do for you?

33 They said to him, Our Lord, that our eyes may be opened.

34 And Jesus had mercy upon them, so he touched their eyes; and immediately their eyes were opened, and they followed him.

CHAPTER 21

WHEN he came near to Jerusalem, he came to Bethphage on the side of the Mount of Olives. Jesus then sent two of his disciples,

2 And he said to them, Go to that village which is in front of you, and straightway you will find an ass which is tied up, and a colt with her; untie and bring them to me.

3 And if any man should say anything to you, tell him that our Lord needs them; and he will immediately send them here.

4 All this happened, so that what was said by the prophet, might be fulfilled, who said,

5 Tell the daughter of Zion, Behold your king is coming to you, meek, and riding upon an ass, and upon a colt, the foal of an ass.

6 And the disciples went and did as Jesus had commanded them.

7 And they brought the ass and the colt, and they put their garments on the colt, and Jesus rode on it.

8 And a great many people spread their garments on the road; and others cut down

42

branches from the trees and spread them on the road.

9 And the people who were going before him and coming after him, were shouting and saying, Hosanna to the son of David; Blessed is he who comes in the name of the Lord; Hosanna in the highest.

10 When he entered Jerusalem, the whole city was stirred up, and they were saying, Who is this man?

11 And the people were saying, This is the prophet, Jesus, from Nazareth in Galilee.

12 ¶ And Jesus entered into the temple of God, and put out all who were buying and selling in the temple, and he overturned the trays of the money-changers and the stands of those who sold doves.

13 And he said to them, It is written, My house shall be called the house of prayer; but you have made it a bandits' cave.

14 And in the temple they brought to him the blind and the lame, and he healed them.

15 But when the high priests and the Pharisees saw the wonders that he did, and the boys who were crying aloud in the temple, and saying, Hosanna to the son of David, they were displeased.

16 And they said to him, Do you hear what they are saying? Jesus said to them, Yes; have you never read, From the mouth of little children and of boys you made praise?

17 ¶ And he left them, and went outside of the city to Bethany, and he lodged there.

18 In the morning, as he returned to the city, he became hungry.

19 And he saw a fig tree on the roadside, and he came to it and found nothing on it except leaves; and he said to it, Let there be no fruit on you again for ever. And shortly the fig tree withered.

20 When the disciples saw it, they were amazed and said, How is it that the fig tree has withered so soon?

21 Jesus answered and said to them, Truly I say to you, If you have faith, and do not doubt, you will perform a deed not only like this of the fig tree, but should you say even to this mountain, Remove and fall into the sea, it shall be done.

22 And everything that you will ask in prayer and believe, you shall receive.

23 ¶ When Jesus came to the temple, the high priests

and the elders of the people came up to him, while he was teaching, and said to him, By what authority do you do these things? and who gave you this authority?

24 Jesus answered and said to them, I will also ask you a word, and if you tell me, I will then tell you by what authority I do these things.

25 Whence is the baptism of John? Is it from heaven, or from men? And they reasoned with themselves, saying, If we should say from heaven, he will say to us, Why then did you not believe him?

26 And if we should say, from men, we are afraid of the people, for all of them regard John as a prophet.

27 So they answered and said to him, We do not know. Jesus said to them, Neither will I tell you by what authority I do these things.

28 ¶ What do you think? A man had two sons, and he came to the first one and said to him, My son, go and work today in the vineyard.

29 He answered and said, I do not want to, but later he regretted and went.

30 And he came to the other one and said to him likewise.

And he answered and said, Here am I, my Lord, and yet he did not go.

31 Which of these two did the will of his father? They said to him, The first one. Jesus said to them, Truly I say to you, that even the publicans and the harlots will precede you into the kingdom of God.

32 For John came to you in a righteous way, and you did not believe him; but the publicans and the harlots believed him; but you, even though you saw, did not repent, so that later you may believe him.

33 ¶ Hear another parable. There was a man who was a householder, and he planted a vineyard, and fenced it, and he dug in it a winepress, and built a tower, and then he leased it to laborers, and went away on a journey.

34 And when the fruit season was at hand, he sent his servants to the laborers, that they might send him of the fruits of his vineyard.

35 And the laborers seized his servants, and some were beaten, and some were stoned, and some were killed.

36 Again he sent other servants, many more than the first; and they did likewise to them.

37 At last he sent his son to them, saying, They might feel ashamed before my son.

38 But when the laborers saw the son, they said among themselves, This is the heir; come, let us kill him and retain his inheritance.

39 So they seized him, and took him out of the vineyard, and killed him.

40 When therefore the owner of the vineyard comes, what will he do to those laborers?

41 They said to him, He will destroy them severely, and lease his vineyard to other laborers, who will give him fruits in their seasons.

42 Jesus said to them, Have you never read in the scripture, The stone which the builders rejected, the same became the corner-stone; this was from the Lord, and it is a marvel in our eyes?

43 Therefore I say to you, that the kingdom of God will be taken away from you, and will be given to a people who bear fruits.

44 And whoever falls on this stone will be broken, and on whomever it falls it will scatter him.

45 ¶ When the high priests and Pharisees heard his parables, they understood that he was speaking against them.

46 So they wanted to arrest him, but they were afraid of the people, because they regarded him as a prophet.

CHAPTER 22

AND Jesus answered again by parables, and said,

2 The kingdom of heaven is like a king who gave a marriage-feast for his son.

3 And he sent his servants to call those who were invited to the marriage-feast, but they would not come.

4 Again he sent other servants and said, Tell those who are invited, Behold my supper is ready, and my oxen and fatlings are killed, and everything is prepared; come to the marriage-feast.

5 But they sneered at it, and went away, one to his field, another to his business;

6 And the rest seized his servants and insulted them, and killed them.

7 When the king heard it he was angry; and he sent out his armies and destroyed those murderers, and burned their city.

8 Then he said to his servants, Now the marriage-feast is ready, and those who were invited were unworthy.

9 Go, therefore, to the main roads, and whomever you

may find, invite them to the marriage-feast.

10 So the servants went out to the roads and gathered together every one they could find, bad and good; and the wedding-house was filled with guests.

11 When the king entered to see the guests, he saw there a man who was not wearing wedding garments.

12 And he said to him, My friend, how did you enter here, when you do not have wedding garments? And he was speechless.

13 Then the king said to the servants, Bind his hands and his feet and take him out into the darkness; there shall be weeping and gnashing of teeth.

14 For many are invited, and few are chosen.

15 ¶ Then the Pharisees went away and took counsel how to trap him by a word.

16 So they sent to him their disciples together with the Herodians, and they said to him, Teacher, we know that you are true, and you teach the way of God justly; and you do not favor any man, for you do not discriminate between men.

17 Tell us, therefore, what do you think? Is it lawful to pay head-tax to Caesar, or not?

18 But Jesus knew their evil, and said, Why do you tempt me, O hypocrites?

19 Show me the head-tax penny. And they brought to him a penny.

20 And Jesus said to them, Whose is this image and inscription?

21 They said, Caesar's. He said to them, Give therefore to Caesar what is Caesar's, and to God what is God's.

22 And when they heard it, they were amazed; and they left him and went away.

23 ¶ That same day the Sadducees came and said to him, There is no resurrection of the dead; and they asked him,

24 And said to him, Teacher, Moses has told us, If a man die without sons, let his brother take his wife, and raise up offspring for his brother.

25 Now there were with us seven brothers; the first married and died, and because he had no sons, he left his wife to his brother.

26 Likewise the second, also the third, up to the seventh.

27 And after them all the woman also died.

28 Therefore at the resurrection, to which of these seven will she be a wife? for they all married her.

Cf. dif. verses 10–15–16–17–19–23

29 Jesus answered and said to them, You err, because you do not understand the scriptures nor the power of God.

30 For at the resurrection of the dead, they neither marry women, nor are women given to men in marriage, but they are like the angels of God in heaven.

31 But concerning the resurrection of the dead, have you not read what was said to you by God, saying,

32 I am the God of Abraham, the God of Isaac, the God of Jacob? And yet God is not the God of the dead, but of the living.

33 And when the people heard it, they were amazed at his teaching.

34 ¶ But when the Pharisees heard that he had silenced the Sadducees, they gathered together.

35 And one of them who knew the law, asked him, testing him,

36 Teacher, which is the greatest commandment in the law?

37 Jesus said to him, Love the Lord your God with all your heart, and with all your soul, and with all your power, and with all your mind.

38 This is the greatest and the first commandment.

39 And the second is like to it, Love your neighbor as yourself.

40 On these two commandments hang the law and the prophets.

41 ¶ While the Pharisees were gathered together, Jesus asked them,

42 And he said, What do you say concerning the Christ? whose son is he? They said to him, son of David.

43 He said to them, How is it then that David through the Spirit calls him Lord? For he said,

44 The Lord said to my Lord, Sit at my right hand, until I put your enemies under your feet.

45 If David then calls him Lord, how can he be his son?

46 And no man was able to answer him, and from that day no man dared to question him.

CHAPTER 23

THEN Jesus spoke with the people and with his disciples.

2 And he said to them, The scribes and the Pharisees sit on the chair of Moses.

3 Therefore whatever they tell you to obey, obey and do it, but do not do according to their works; for they say and do not.

4 And they bind heavy burdens, and put them on men's shoulders, but they themselves are not willing to touch them, even with their finger.

5 And all their works they do, just to be seen by men; for they widen the fringes of their garments, and they lengthen the ends of their robes,

6 And they like the chief places at feasts, and the front seats in the synagogues,

7 And the greetings in the streets, and to be called by men, Rabbi.

8 But you do not be called, Rabbi; for one is your Master, and all you are brethren.

9 And call no one on earth, father, for one is your Father in heaven.

10 Nor be called leaders, for one is your leader, the Christ.

11 But he who is greatest among you, let him be your minister.

12 For whoever exalts himself shall be humbled; and whoever humbles himself shall be exalted.

13 ¶ Woe to you, scribes and Pharisees, hypocrites! for you embezzle the property of widows, with the pretense that you make long prayers; because of this you shall receive a greater judgment.[1]

14 Woe to you, scribes and Pharisees, hypocrites! for you have shut off the kingdom of heaven against men; for you do not enter into it yourselves, and do not permit those who would enter.

15 Woe to you, scribes and Pharisees, hypocrites! for you traverse sea and land to make one proselyte; and when he becomes one, you make him the son of hell twice more than yourselves.

16 Woe to you, blind guides, for you say, Whoever swears by the temple, it is nothing; but whoever swears by the gold which is in the temple, he is guilty!

17 O you fools and blind! for which is greater, the gold or the temple that sanctifies the gold?

18 And whoever swears by the altar, it is nothing; but whoever swears by the offering that is on it, he is guilty.

19 O you fools and blind! for which is greater, the offering, or the altar that sanctifies the offering?

20 Therefore he who swears by the altar, he swears by it and by everything that is on it.

21 And whoever swears by the temple, swears by it and by him who dwells in it.

[1] The order of verses 13 and 14 is reversed in the Eastern Version.

Cf. dif. verses 4–5–10–13

22 And he who swears by heaven, swears by the throne of God, and by him who sits on it.

23 Woe to you, scribes and Pharisees, hypocrites! for you take tithes on mint, dill and cummin, and you have overlooked the more important matters of the law, such as justice, mercy and trustworthiness. These were necessary for you to have done, and the same by no means to have left undone.

24 O blind guides, who strain out gnats and swallow camels!

25 ¶ Woe to you, scribes and Pharisees, hypocrites! you clean the outside of the cup and of the dish, but inside they are full of extortion and iniquity.

26 Blind Pharisees! clean first the inside of the cup and of the dish, so that their outside may also be clean.

27 Woe to you, scribes and Pharisees, hypocrites! for you are like tombs painted white, which look beautiful from the outside, but inside are full of dead bones and all kinds of corruption.

28 Even so, from the outside you appear to men to be righteous, but from within you are full of iniquity and hypocrisy.

29 Woe to you, scribes and Pharisees, hypocrites! for you build the tombs of the prophets, and you decorate the graves of the righteous;

30 And you say, If we had been in the days of our forefathers, we would not have been partakers with them in the blood of the prophets.

31 Now you testify concerning yourselves, that you are the children of those who killed the prophets.

32 You also fill up the measure of your fathers.

33 O you serpents, and seed of scorpions! how can you flee from the judgment of hell?

34 ¶ Because of this, I am sending to you prophets and wise men and scribes; some of them you will kill and crucify; and some you will scourge in your synagogues, and pursue them from city to city;

35 So that all the blood of the righteous shed on the ground may come on you, from the blood of Abel the righteous down to the blood of Zachariah, son of Barachiah, whom you killed between the temple and the altar.

36 Truly I say to you, All of these things shall come upon this generation.

37 O Jerusalem, Jerusalem, murderess of the prophets, and stoner of those who are sent to her! how often I wanted to gather together your children, just like a hen which gathers her chickens under her wings, and yet you would not!

38 Behold, your house will be left to you desolate.

39 For I say to you, from now you will not see me until you say, Blessed is he who comes in the name of the Lord.

CHAPTER 24

AND Jesus went out of the temple to go away; and his disciples came up to him, and were showing him the building of the temple.

2 But he said to them, Behold, do you not see all of these? truly I say to you, Not a stone shall be left here upon a stone, which will not be torn down.

3 ¶ While Jesus sat on the Mount of Olives, his disciples came up talking among themselves, and they said to him, Tell us when these things will happen, and what is the sign of your coming, and of the end of the world?

4 Jesus answered and said to them, Be careful that no man deceives you.

5 For many will come in my name, and say, I am the Christ, and they will deceive many.

6 You are bound to hear of revolutions and rumors of wars; look out and do not be disturbed; for all of these things must come to pass, but the end is not yet.

7 For nation will rise against nation, and kingdom against kingdom; and there will be famines and plagues and earthquakes, in different places.

8 But all these things are just the beginning of travail.

9 Then they will deliver you over to be oppressed, and they will kill you; and you will be hated by all nations for my name's sake.

10 Then many will stumble, and they will hate one another, and betray one another.

11 And many false prophets will rise, and will mislead a great many.

12 And because of the growth of iniquity, the love of many will become cold.

13 But he who has patience to the end, he will be saved.

14 And this gospel of the kingdom shall be preached throughout the world as a testimony to all the nations; then the end will come.

A NEW COMMENTARY
ON THE GOSPELS

by

GEORGE M. LAMSA

Based on the Aramaic, the language which Jesus spoke, and the unfamiliar ancient customs of the East which have remained unchanged during all the centuries since the time of Jesus, this Commentary meets a long-felt need. It is the first explanatory work ever written by an Oriental scholar born, reared and educated in the Aramaic of his tribe with the further advantage of a higher education in English institutions. Mr. Lamsa has the ability and the power to interpret these ancient customs and writings due to the heritage of his birth and his personal knowledge from living with his tribe.

The Gospels are only an outline of the life and preaching of Jesus. They were written by the disciples for the contemporary general public who knew Jesus and were familiar with the general issues of the times. The Commentary clears briefly the difficult passages in the Gospels and explains Oriental manners and customs by interpreting all into modern thought. Ambiguous and obscure sayings of Jesus are thus made logical and clear.

Mr. Lamsa not only explains why Jesus gave certain utterances in the language of His day but the issues which gave rise to such expressions. For example, Jesus was asked about taxation, "Is it lawful to give tribute unto Caesar, or not?" The Gospels do not explain the issues that caused this inquiry. The Eastern Version states that this was a head tax. All citizens of the Roman Empire were compelled to pay many taxes on property. These property taxes were not resented as were the head taxes, or the grouping of human beings with animals. Such a head tax by a temporal power was religiously unlawful to the Jew whose only allegiance was pledged to God and who paid two shekels per man into the Temple treasury. Even today the peoples of the East resent head tax and some governments in order to avoid trouble include this under disguise.

To Be Published By

A. J. HOLMAN COMPANY
1224 ARCH STREET, PHILADELPHIA

Inquiries Invited to Be Filed for Complete Information
When Published

15 When you see the sign of the refuse of desolation, as spoken by the prophet Daniel, accumulating in the holy place, whoever reads will understand it.

16 Then let those who are in Judaea, flee to the mountain.

17 And he who is on the roof, let him not come down to take things out of his house.

18 And he who is in the field, let him not return back to take his clothes.

19 But woe to those who are with child, and to those who give suck in those days!

20 Pray that your flight may not be in winter, nor on the sabbath.

21 For then will be great suffering, such as has never happened from the beginning of the world until now, and never will be again.

22 And if those days were not shortened, no flesh would live; but for the sake of the chosen ones those days will be shortened.

23 Then if any man should say to you, Behold, here is the Christ, or there, do not believe it.

24 For there will rise false Christs and lying prophets, and they will show signs and great wonders, so as to mis-lead, if possible, even the chosen ones.

25 Behold, I have told you in advance.

26 Therefore, if they should say to you, Behold, he is in the desert, do not go out; or, behold, he is in the room, do not believe it.

27 For just as the lightning comes out from the east, and is seen even in the west, such will be the coming of the Son of man.

28 For wherever the corpse is, there will the eagles gather.

29 ¶ Immediately after the suffering of those days, the sun will be darkened, and the moon will not give her light, and the stars will fall from the sky, and the powers of the universe will be shaken.

30 Then the sign of the Son of man will appear in the sky; and then all the generations of the earth will mourn, and they will see the Son of man coming on the clouds of the sky, with an army and great glory.

31 And he will send his angels with a large trumpet, and they will gather his chosen ones from the four winds, from one end of universe[1] to the other.

[1] The Aramaic *shmaya* means heaven, universe and sky. Cf. vv. 30, 31, 35, 36.

Cf. dif. verses 15–21–26–27–30–31

32 From the fig tree learn a parable. As soon as its branches become tender and bring forth leaves, you know that summer is coming.

33 So even you, when you see all these things, know that it has arrived at the door.

34 Truly I say to you, that this generation will not pass away, until all these things happen.

35 Even heaven and earth will pass away, by my words shall not pass away.

36 ¶ But concerning that day and that hour, no man knows, not even the angels of heaven, but the Father alone.

37 Just as in the days of Noah, so will be the coming of the Son of man.

38 For as the people before the flood were eating and drinking, marrying and giving in marriage, until the day Noah entered into the ark,

39 And they knew nothing until the flood came and carried them all away; such will be the coming of the Son of man.

40 Then two men will be in the field, one will be taken away and the other left.

41 Two women will be grinding at the hand-mill, one will be taken and the other left.

42 ¶ Be alert, therefore, for you do not know at what hour your Lord will come.

43 But know this much, that if the master of the house knew at what watch of the night the thief comes, he would keep awake and would not let his house be plundered.

44 For this reason, you also be ready, for the Son of man will come at an hour when you do not expect him.

45 Who then is the faithful and wise servant, whom his Lord has appointed over his household, to give them food in due time?

46 Blessed is that servant, when his Lord comes and finds him so doing.

47 Truly I say to you, he will appoint him over all that he has.

48 But if a bad servant should say in his heart, My Lord will delay his coming,

49 And he begins to beat his fellow-servants, and to eat and drink with the drunkards,

50 The Lord of that servant will come on a day when he does not expect, and at an hour that he does not know.

51 And he will severely scourge him, and give him a

portion like that of the hypocrites; there will be weeping and gnashing of teeth.

CHAPTER 25

THEN the kingdom of heaven will be like ten virgins, who took their lamps, and went out to greet the bridegroom and the bride.

2 Five of them were wise, and five were foolish.

3 And the foolish ones took their lamps, but took no oil with them.

4 But the wise ones took oil in the vessels with their lamps.

5 As the bridegroom was delayed, they all slumbered and slept.

6 And at midnight there was a cry, Behold, the bridegroom is coming; go out to greet him.

7 Then all the virgins got up and fixed their lamps.

8 And the foolish ones said to the wise ones, Give us some of your oil, for our lamps are going out.

9 Then the wise ones answered and said, Why, there would not be enough for us and for you; go to those who sell and buy for yourselves.

10 And while they went to buy, the bridegroom came; and those who were ready entered with him into the wedding house, and the door was locked.

11 Afterward the other virgins also came and said, Our Lord, our Lord, open to us.

12 But he answered and said to them, Truly I say to you, I do not know you.

13 Be alert, therefore, for you do not know, that day nor the hour.

14 ¶ It is just like a man who went on a journey, who called his servants and put his wealth in their charge.

15 To one he gave five talents, to one two, to another one; to each one according to his ability; and immediately he went on a journey.

16 The one who received five talents then went and traded with them, and he earned five others.

17 Likewise the second one, he gained by trading two others.

18 But he who received one, went and dug in the ground, and hid his lord's money.

19 After a long time, the lord of those servants returned, and took an accounting from them.

20 Then the one who received five talents came up, and offered five others, and he said, My lord, you gave me five talents, behold, I have gained five others to them.

21 His lord said to him, Well done, good and reliable servant; you have been faithful over a little, I will appoint you over much; enter into your master's joy.

22 Then the one with the two talents came and he said, My lord, you gave me two talents, behold I have gained two others to them.

23 His lord said to him, Well done, good and reliable servant, you have been faithful over a little, I will appoint you over much; enter into your master's joy.

24 Then the one who received one talent also came up, and he said, My lord, I knew you that you are a hard man, and you reap where you did not sow, and gather where you did not scatter.

25 So I was afraid, and I went and hid your talent in the ground; here it is, it is your own one.

26 His lord answered and said to him, O wicked and lazy servant, you knew me that I reap where I did not sow, and I gather where I did not scatter.

27 You should then have put my money in the exchange, and when I returned I would have demanded my own with interest.

28 Therefore take away the talent from him, and give it to the one who has ten talents.

29 For to him who has, it shall be given, and it shall increase to him; but he who has not, even that which he has shall be taken away from him.

30 And the idle servant they threw out into the outer darkness; there will be weeping and gnashing of teeth.

31 ¶ When the Son of man comes in his glory, and all his holy angels with him, then he will sit upon the throne of his glory.

32 And all nations will gather before him; and he will separate them one from another, just as a shepherd separates the sheep from the goats;

33 And he will set the sheep at his right, and the goats at his left.

34 Then the king will say to those at his right, Come, you blessed of my Father, inherit the kingdom which has been prepared for you from the foundation of the world.

35 For I was hungry, and you gave me to eat; I was thirsty, and you gave me to drink; I was a stranger and you took me in;

36 I was naked, and you

Cf. dif. verses 21–25–27–29–30

covered me; I was sick, and you visited me; I was in prison, and you came to me.

37 Then the righteous will say to him, Our Lord, when did we see you hungry, and feed you? or thirsty and gave you drink?

38 And when did we see you a stranger, and took you in? Or that you were naked, and covered you?

39 And when did we see you sick, or in the prison, and come to you?

40 The king then will answer and say to them, Truly I say to you, Inasmuch as you have done to one of these least brethren, you did it to me.

41 Then he will also say to those at his left, Go away from me, you cursed, to the everlasting fire, that which is prepared for the adversary and his angels.

42 For I was hungry, and you did not give me to eat; I was thirsty, and you did not give me to drink;

43 I was a stranger, and you did not take me in; I was naked, and you did not cover me; I was sick and in prison, and you did not visit me.

44 Then they also will answer and say, Our Lord, when did we see you hungry, or thirsty, or a stranger, or naked, or sick, or in the prison, and did not minister to you?

45 Then he will answer and say to them, Truly I say to you, Inasmuch as you did not do to one of these least ones, you also did not do it to me.

46 And these shall go into everlasting torment, and the righteous into eternal life.

CHAPTER 26

WHEN Jesus had finished all these sayings, he said to his disciples,

2 You know that after two days will be the passover, and the Son of man will be betrayed to be crucified.

3 Then the high priests and the scribes and the elders of the people assembled at the court yard of the high priest, who is called Caiaphas.

4 And they took counsel concerning Jesus, to arrest him by a snare and kill him.

5 And they said, Not on the feast day, so as not to cause a riot among the people.

6 ¶ And when Jesus was at Bethany, in the house of Simon the leper,

7 A woman came up to him with an alabaster vessel of precious perfume, and she poured it upon the head of Jesus, while he was reclining.

8 When his disciples saw it,

they were displeased, and said, Why is this loss?

9 For it could have been sold for a great deal, and given to the poor.

10 But Jesus understood it and said to them, Why are you troubling the woman? she has done a good work to me.

11 For you always have the poor with you, but you will not have me always.

12 But this one who poured the perfume on my body, did it as for my burial.

13 And truly I say to you, Wherever this my gospel is preached throughout the world, what she has done will also be told as a memorial to her.

14 ¶ Then one of the twelve, called Judas of Iscariot, went to the high priests;

15 And he said to them, What are you willing to give me, and I will deliver him to you? And they promised him thirty pieces of silver.

16 And from that time he sought an opportunity to betray him.

17 ¶ On the first day of unleavened bread, the disciples came up to Jesus and said to him, Where do you wish that we may prepare the passover for you to eat?

18 And he said to them, Go into the city to a certain man, and say to him, Our master says, My time has come, I will observe the passover with my disciples at your place.

19 And his disciples did as Jesus had commanded them; and they prepared the passover.

20 And when it was evening, he was reclining with his twelve disciples.

21 And while they were eating, he said, Truly I say to you, that one of you will betray me.

22 And they felt very sad, and began to say to him one by one, Why, is it I, my Lord?

23 And he answered and said, He who dips his hand with me in the dish, he will betray me.

24 The Son of man is going through, just as it is written concerning him; but woe to the man by whose hand the Son of man is betrayed! it would have been far better for that man never to have been born.

25 Then Judas the traitor answered and said, Master, perhaps it is I? Jesus said to him, You say that.

26 ¶ While they were eating, Jesus took bread and blessed it, and he broke it, and gave it to his disciples,

and he said, Take, eat; this is my body.

27 Then he took the cup and gave thanks, and gave it to them and said, Take, drink of it, all of you.

28 This is my blood of the new covenant which is shed for many for the remission of sins.

29 But I say to you, from now on I shall not drink from this fruit of the vine, until the day when I drink it anew with you in the kingdom of God.

30 And they offered praise, and went out to the Mount of Olives.

31 ¶ Then Jesus said to them, All of you will deny me this night; for it is written, I will smite the shepherd, and the sheep of his flock will be scattered.

32 But after I am risen, I will be in Galilee before you.

33 Peter answered and said to him, Even if every man should deny you, I will never deny you.

34 Jesus said to him, Truly I say to you, that in this very night, before the cock crows, you will deny me three times.

35 Peter said to him, Even if I must die with you, I will never deny you. All the disciples said likewise.

36 ¶ Then Jesus came with them to a place which is called Gethsemane, and he said to his disciples, Sit down here, while I go to pray.

37 And he took Peter and the two sons of Zebedee, and he began to be sorrowful and oppressed.

38 He said to them, My soul is sorrowful even to death; wait for me here, and watch with me.

39 And he went a little further and fell on his face, and he prayed saying, O my Father, if it be possible, let this cup pass from me; but let it be, not as I will but as you.

40 Then he came to his disciples and found them sleeping, and he said to Peter, So, you were not able to watch with me even for one hour?

41 Awake and pray, that you may not enter into temptation; the spirit indeed is ready, but the body is weak.

42 He went away again the second time and prayed and said, O my Father, if this cup cannot pass, and if I have to drink it, let it be according to your will.

43 He came again and found them sleeping, for their eyes were heavy.

44 And he left them and went away again and prayed the third time, and he said the same word.

45 Then he came to his disciples and said to them, Sleep from now on and get your rest; behold, the hour has come, and the Son of man will be delivered into the hands of sinners.

46 Arise, let us go; behold, he who is to deliver me has arrived.

47 ¶ While he was speaking, behold, Judas the traitor, one of the twelve, came and with him a large crowd with swords and staves, from the high priests and the elders of the people.

48 Now Judas the traitor had given them a sign, saying, He whom I kiss, it is he, arrest him.

49 And immediately he came up to Jesus and said, Peace, Master; and he kissed him.

50 Jesus said to him, Is it for this that you have come, my friend? Then they came near and laid hands on Jesus, and arrested him.

51 And behold, one of those who were with Jesus stretched out his hand and drew a sword, and struck it at the servant of the high priest, and cut off his ear.

52 Then Jesus said to him,

Return the sword to its place; for all who take swords will die by swords.

53 Or do you think that I cannot ask of my Father, and he will now raise up for me more than twelve legions of angels?

54 How then could the scriptures be fulfilled, that it must be so?

55 At that very hour Jesus said to the people, Have you come out with swords and staves to arrest me like a bandit? I sat with you every day, teaching in the temple, and you did not arrest me.

56 But this has happened so that the scriptures of the prophets might be fulfilled. Then all the disciples left him, and fled.

57 ¶ And those who had arrested Jesus took him to Caiaphas the high priest, where the scribes and the elders had assembled.

58 But Simon Peter followed him afar off, up to the courtyard of the high priest, and he went inside and sat with the soldiers, to see the end.

59 Now the high priests and the elders and the whole council were seeking witnesses against Jesus, so that they might put him to death.

60 But they could not find any; then there came a great

Cf. dif. verses 49–50–53–55–59–60

many false witnesses; but at the end two came forward,

61 And said, This man said, I can tear down the temple of God, and build it in three days.

62 And the high priest stood up and said to him, You are not answering anything. What is it that these men testify against you?

63 But Jesus was silent. Then the high priest answered and said to him, I adjure you by the living God, to tell us if you are the Christ, the Son of God?

64 Jesus said to him, You say that. But I say to you that from henceforth you will see the Son of man sitting at the right hand of the power, and coming upon the clouds of the sky.

65 The high priest then rent his clothes and said, Behold, he is blaspheming; why therefore do we need witnesses? behold, you have now heard his blasphemy.

66 What else do you want? They answered and said, He is guilty of death.

67 Then they spat on his face, and struck him on his head, and others beat him,

68 Saying, O Christ, prophesy to us, who smote you?

69 ¶ Now Peter sat outside in the courtyard; and a maid servant came up to him, and said to him, You also were with Jesus the Nazarene.

70 But he denied it before all of them, and said, I do not understand what you are saying.

71 And as he was going to the porch, another one saw him, and she said to them, This man was also there with Jesus the Nazarene.

72 Again he denied it with oaths, I do not know the man.

73 After a while, those who were standing came up, and said to Peter, Truly you also are one of them, for even your speech proves it.

74 Then he began to curse and to swear, I do not know the man. At that very hour the cock crowed.

75 And Peter remembered the word of Jesus, which he had said to him, Before the cock crows, you will deny me three times. And he went outside and wept bitterly.

CHAPTER 27

WHEN it was morning, the high priests and the elders of the people took counsel concerning Jesus, how to put him to death.

2 So they bound him, and took him and delivered him to Pilate the governor.

3 ¶ Then Judas the traitor, when he saw that Jesus was convicted, repented, and went away and brought back the same thirty pieces of silver to the high priests and the elders.

4 And he said, I have sinned, because I have betrayed innocent blood. But they said to him, What is that to us? You know better.

5 Then he threw the silver in the temple, and departed; and he went and hanged himself.

6 The high priests took the silver and said, It is not lawful to put it in the house of offerings, because it is the price of blood.

7 And they took counsel, and bought with it the potter's field, for a cemetery for strangers.

8 On this account that field was called The field of blood, to this day.

9 ¶ Then what was spoken by the prophet was fulfilled, who said, I took the thirty pieces of silver, the costly price which was bargained with the children of Israel.

10 And I gave them for the potter's field, as the Lord commanded me.

11 And Jesus stood before the governor; and the governor asked him and said to him, Are you the king of the Jews? Jesus said to him, You say that.

12 And while the chief priests and elders were accusing him, he gave no answer.

13 Then Pilate said to him, Do you not hear how much they testify against you?

14 But he did not answer him, not even a word; and because of this he marvelled greatly.

15 Now on every feast day it was the custom of the governor to release one prisoner to the people, anyone whom they wanted.

16 They had a well known prisoner, called Bar-Abbas, who was bound.

17 When they were gathered together, Pilate said to them, Whom do you want me to release to you? Bar-Abbas, or Jesus who is called the Christ?

18 For Pilate knew that because of envy they had delivered him.

19 ¶ When the governor was sitting on his judgement seat, his wife sent to him and said to him, Have nothing to do with that righteous man; for today I have suffered a great deal in my dream because of him.

20 But the high priests and

the elders urged the people to ask for Bar-Abbas, and to destroy Jesus.

21 And the governor answered and said to them, Which of these two do you want me to release to you? They said, Bar-Abbas.

22 Pilate said to them, What shall I then do with Jesus who is called the Christ? They all said, Let him be crucified.

23 Pilate said to them, What evil has he done? But they cried out the more and said, Let him be crucified.

24 ¶ Now when Pilate saw that he was gaining nothing, but that instead confusion was increasing, he took water and washed his hands before the people, and said, I am innocent of the blood of this righteous man; do as you please.

25 All the people then answered and said, Let his blood be on us and on our children.

26 ¶ Then he released to them Bar-Abbas, and had Jesus scourged with whips, and delivered to be crucified.

27 Then the soldiers of the governor took Jesus into the Praetorium, and the whole company gathered around him.

28 And they removed his clothes and put on him a scarlet robe.

29 And they wove a crown of thorns and put it on his head, and a reed in his right hand; and they knelt on their knees before him, and they were mocking him and saying, Hail, King of the Jews!

30 And they spat on his face, and took the reed and struck him on his head.

31 And when they had mocked him, they took off the robe from him and put on him his own clothes, and took him away to be crucified.

32 And as they were going out, they found a man of Cyrene, whose name was Simon, whom they compelled to carry his cross.

33 ¶ And they came to a place which is called Golgotha, which is interpreted The Skull.

34 And they gave him to drink vinegar mixed with gall; and he tasted it, but he would not drink.

35 ¶ And when they had crucified him, they divided his clothes by casting lots.

36 And they were sitting there and watching him.

37 And they placed above his head in writing the reason for his death: THIS IS JESUS THE KING OF THE JEWS.

38 ¶ And there were crucified with him two bandits, one on his right and one on his left.

39 And those who passed by blasphemed against him, nodding their heads,

40 And saying, O you who can tear down the temple and build it in three days, deliver yourself, if you are the Son of God, and come down from the cross.

41 The high priests likewise were mocking, together with the scribes, the elders and the Pharisees.

42 And they were saying, He saved others, but he cannot save himself. If he is the King of Israel, let him now come down from the cross, so that we may see and believe in him.

43 He trusted in God; let him save him now, if he is pleased with him; for he said, I am God's Son.

44 The bandits also, who were crucified with him were reproaching him.

45 ¶ Now from the sixth hour, there was darkness over all the land, until the ninth hour.

46 And about the ninth hour, Jesus cried out with a loud voice and said, Eli, Eli, lmana shabachthani! which means,

My God, My God, for this I was kept![1]

47 Some of the men who were standing by, when they heard it, said, This man has called for Elijah.

48 And immediately one of them ran and took a sponge, and he filled it with vinegar, and put it on a reed, and gave him to drink.

49 But the rest said, Hush, let us see if Elijah will come to save him.

50 ¶ But Jesus again cried out with a loud voice, and gave up his breath.

51 And immediately the door curtains of the temple were rent in two, from the top to the bottom; and the earth quaked, and the rocks split;

52 And the tombs were opened; and the bodies of a great many saints who were sleeping in death rose up,

53 And they went out; and after his resurrection, they entered into the holy city, and appeared to a great many.

54 ¶ When the centurion and those who were with him watching Jesus, saw the earthquake and all that happened, they were very much frightened, and they said, Truly this man was the Son of God.

55 There were also many

[1] This was my destiny for which I was born.

Cf. dif. verses 39-44-46-49-50-51-53

women there, who were looking from afar, those who had followed Jesus from Galilee, and who used to minister to him.

56 One of them was Mary of Magdala; and Mary the mother of James and Joses, and the mother of the sons of Zebedee.

57 ¶ When evening came, there came a rich man of Arimathaea, whose name was Joseph, who was also a disciple of Jesus.

58 He went to Pilate and asked for the body of Jesus. And Pilate commanded that the body should be given to him.

59 So Joseph took the body, and wrapped it in a shroud of fine linen,

60 And laid it in his own new tomb which was hewn in a rock; and they rolled a large stone, and placed it against the door of the tomb, and went away.

61 And there were there Mary of Magdala and the other Mary, who were sitting opposite the tomb.

62 ¶ The next day, which is after Friday, the high priests and the Pharisees came together to Pilate,

63 And they said to him, Our lord, we have just remembered that that deceiver used to say when he was alive, After three days I will rise again.

64 Now, therefore, command that precautions be taken at the tomb for three days. It is probable that his disciples may come and steal him at night, and then say to the people, He has risen from the dead; and the last deception will be worse than the first.

65 Pilate said to them, You have guards; go and take precautions as best you know.

66 So they went and kept a watch at the tomb, and together with the guards they sealed the stone.

CHAPTER 28

IN the evening of the sabbath day, when the first day of the week began, there came Mary of Magdala and the other Mary, to see the tomb.

2 And behold, a great earthquake took place; for the angel of the Lord came down from heaven, and went up and rolled away the stone from the door, and sat on it.

3 His appearance was like lightning, and his garments white as snow.

4 And for fear of him the guards who were watching

trembled, and became as if they were dead.

5 But the angel answered and said to the women, You need not be afraid; for I know that you are seeking Jesus who was crucified.

6 He is not here, for he has risen, just as he had said. Come in, see the place where our Lord was laid.

7 And go quickly, and tell his disciples that he has risen from the dead; and behold, he will be before you in Galilee; there you will see him; behold, I have told you.

8 And they went away hurriedly from the tomb with fear and with great joy, running to tell his disciples.

9 And behold, Jesus met them, and said to them, Peace be to you. And they came up and laid hold of his feet, and worshipped him.

10 Then Jesus said to them, Do not be afraid; but go and tell my brethren to go to Galilee, and there they shall see me.

11 ¶ When they were going, some of the guards came into the city, and told the high priests everything that had happened.

12 So they gathered with the elders and took counsel; and they gave money, not a small sum, to the guards.

13 Telling them, Say that his disciples came by night, and stole him while we were sleeping.

14 And if this should be heard by the governor, we will appeal to him, and declare that you are blameless.

15 So they took the money, and did as they were instructed; and this word went out among the Jews, until this day.

16 ¶ The eleven disciples then went to Galilee to a mountain, where Jesus had promised to meet them.

17 And when they saw him, they worshipped him; but some of them were doubtful.

18 And Jesus came up and spoke with them, and said to them, All power in heaven and on earth has been given to me. Just as my Father has sent me I am also sending you.

19 Go, therefore, and convert all nations; and baptize them in the name of the Father and of the Son and of the Holy Spirit;

20 And teach them to obey everything that I have commanded you; and, behold, I am with you all the days, to the end of the world. Amen.

Cf. dif. verses 14–18

THE GOSPEL ACCORDING TO
St. MARK

CHAPTER 1

THE beginning of the gospel of Jesus Christ, the Son of God.

2 As it is written in Isaiah the prophet, Behold I send my messenger before your face, that he may prepare your way.

3 The voice that cries in the wilderness, Make ready the way of the Lord, and straighten his high ways.

4 John was in the wilderness, baptizing and preaching the baptism of repentance for the forgiveness of sins.

5 And the whole province of Judaea went out to him, and all the people of Jerusalem; and he baptized them in the river Jordan, when they confessed their sins.

6 ¶ John wore a dress of camel's hair, with a girdle of leather fastened around his loins; and his food was locusts and wild honey.

7 And he preached saying, Behold, there is coming after me one who is mightier than myself, even the strings of whose shoes I am not good enough to bend down and untie.

8 I have baptized you with water; but he will baptize you with the Holy Spirit.

9 ¶ And it came to pass in those days, Jesus came from Nazareth of Galilee, and was baptized in the Jordan by John.

10 And immediately, as he went up out of the water, he saw the sky was clear open, and the Spirit as a dove came down upon him.

11 And a voice came from heaven, You are my beloved Son, I am pleased with you.

12 And immediately the Spirit drove him out into the wilderness.

13 And he was there in the wilderness forty days, being tried out by Satan; and he was with the wild beasts; and the angels ministered to him.

14 ¶ But after John was delivered up, Jesus came to

Galilee, preaching the gospel of the kingdom of God,

15 And saying, The time has come to an end, and the kingdom of God is at hand; repent and believe in the gospel.

16 While he walked along the sea of Galilee, he saw Simon and Andrew his brother throwing their nets into the sea; for they were fishermen.

17 And Jesus said to them, Come after me, and I will make you fishers of men.

18 And straightway they left their nets, and went after him.

19 And when he went a little further, he saw James the son of Zebedee and his brother John; they also were in a boat mending their nets.

20 And he called them; and immediately they left their father Zebedee with the hired men, and went after him.

21 When they entered into Capernaum, straightway he taught on the sabbaths in their synagogues.

22 And they were amazed at his teaching; for he taught them as one with an authority, and not like their scribes.

23 ¶ And there was in their synagogue a man who had in him an unclean spirit; and he cried out,

24 And said, Jesus of Naza-reth, what have we in common? Have you come to destroy us? I know you, who you are, "Holy One of God."

25 And Jesus rebuked him and said, Be silent, and come out of him.

26 And the unclean spirit threw him down, and cried out in a loud voice, and left him.

27 And they were all astonished, and kept asking one another saying, What does this mean? and what is this new teaching, that with such a power he commands even unclean spirits and they obey him?

28 ¶ And his fame immediately spread throughout the country of Galilee.

29 Then they went out of the synagogue, and came to the house of Simon and Andrew, together with James and John.

30 And Simon's mother-in-law was laid up with fever; and they spoke to him about her.

31 And he went and held her hand, and lifted her up; and immediately the fever left her, and she ministered to them.

32 In the evening towards sunset, they brought to him all who were seriously sick, and the insane.

Cf. dif. verses 24–32

33 And the whole city was gathered at the door.

34 And he healed many who were seriously sick with divers diseases, and he restored many who were insane; and he did not allow the insane to speak because some of them were his acquaintances.

35 And in the morning he rose up very early and went away to a lonely place, and there prayed.

36 And Simon and those who were with him were looking for him.

37 And when they found him, they said to him, Everyone wants you.

38 He said to them, Let us walk to the neighboring towns and cities, so that I may preach there also; because I came for this.

39 And he preached in all their synagogues throughout Galilee, and cast out demons.

40 And there came to him a leper, and fell down at his feet, and begged him, saying, If you will, you can make me clean.

41 And Jesus had mercy on him, and stretched out his hand and touched him, and said, I am willing; be clean.

42 And in that hour his leprosy disappeared from him, and he became clean.

43 And he rebuked him and put him out,

44 And said to him, Look here, why are you telling it to the people? but go away, show yourself to the priests, and offer an offering for the sake of your cleansing, according to what Moses commanded, as their testimonial.

45 But when he went out, he began to publish it still more, and to spread the word, so that Jesus was no longer able to enter the city openly, but he remained outside in a lonely place; and yet they came to him from every place.

CHAPTER 2

AND Jesus entered again into Capernaum for a few days; and when they heard that he was in a house,

2 A great many gathered together so that it was impossible to hold them, not even in front of the entrance; so he spoke a few words to them.

3 And they came to him, and brought to him a paralyzed man, carried between four men.

4 But as they were unable to come near him because of the crowd, they went up to the roof and uncovered it over the place where Jesus was; and they lowered the

quilt-bed in which the paralyzed man lay.

5 When Jesus saw their faith, he said to the paralytic, My son, your sins are forgiven.

6 Now some of the scribes and Pharisees were sitting there, and they reasoned in their hearts,

7 Why does this man speak blasphemy? who can forgive sins except God only?

8 But Jesus perceived in his spirit that they were reasoning among themselves, and he said to them, Why do you reason these things in your heart?

9 Which is the easier, to say to the paralytic, Your sins are forgiven; or to say, Rise, take up your quilt-bed and walk?

10 But that you may know that the Son of man has power on earth to forgive sins, he said to the paralytic,

11 I tell you, Rise, take up your quilt-bed, and go to your house.

12 And immediately he rose, and took up his quilt-bed and went out before the eyes of them all; and they were all amazed, and gave glory to God, saying, We have never seen anything like it.

13 ¶ And he went out again by the seaside, and all the people kept coming to him, and he taught them.

14 And as he passed by, he saw Levi the son of Alphaeus, sitting at the custom house, and he said to him, Follow me; and he got up and followed him.

15 And it happened that while he was a guest at his house, a great many publicans and sinners were also guests with Jesus and his disciples; for there were many, and they followed him.

16 And when the scribes and the Pharisees saw him eating with the publicans and the sinners, they said to his disciples, Why does he eat and drink with publicans and sinners?

17 When Jesus heard it, he said to them, Those who are healthy need no doctor, but those who are seriously sick; I came not to call the righteous, but the sinners.

18 The disciples of John and of the Pharisees were fasting; and they came and said to him, Why do the disciples of John and of the Pharisees fast, and your own disciples do not fast?

19 Jesus said to them, Why, can the sons of the wedding feast fast as long as the bridegroom is with them? No!

20 But the days will come when the bridegroom is taken away from them, then in that day they will fast.

21 No man puts a new patch and sews it on a worn out garment, so that the new patch may not weaken the old, and the hole become larger.

22 And no man pours new wine into old wine-skins, so that the wine may not rend the skins, and the skins be ruined, and the wine run out; but they pour new wine into new wine-skins.

23 ¶ And it happened that while Jesus was going through the wheat fields on the sabbath, his disciples walked and pulled up the ears of wheat.

24 And the Pharisees said to him, Look what they are doing on the sabbath! that which is unlawful.

25 Jesus said to them, Have you not read what David did, when he was in need and hungry, he and those who were with him?

26 How he entered into the house of God when Abiathar was the chief priest, and ate the bread which was on the table of the Lord, which was not lawful to be eaten except by the priests, and he gave it also to those who were with him?

27 And he said to them, The sabbath was created for the sake of man, and not man for the sake of the sabbath.

28 The Son of man therefore is the Lord also of the sabbath.

CHAPTER 3

JESUS entered again into the synagogue, and there was there a man whose hand was withered.

2 And they watched him if he would heal him on the sabbath, that they might accuse him.

3 And he said to the man whose hand was withered, Stand up in the midst.

4 Then he said to them also, Is it lawful to do good or evil on the sabbath, to save a life or to destroy it? But they were silent.

5 And he looked at them with anger, sad because of the hardness of their hearts; and he said to the man, Stretch out your hand, and he stretched it out; and his hand was restored.

6 ¶ And the Pharisees immediately went out with the Herodians, and they took counsel concerning him how to do away with him.

7 So Jesus went to the sea with his disciples; and a great many people from Gali-

lee followed him, and from Judaea,

8 And from Jerusalem, and from Idumaea, and from around the Jordan, and from Tyre, and from Sidon; large crowds, who had heard all that he was doing, came to him.

9 And he said to his disciples to bring the boat near to him, because of the crowds, so that they might not press on him.

10 For he was healing so many, that others pushed toward him so as to touch him.

11 And those who were afflicted with unclean spirits, when they saw him, fell down before him, and cried saying, You are indeed the Son of God.

12 And he cautioned them a great deal, not to make him known.

13 ¶ And he went up to the mountain, and called those he wanted; and they came to him.

14 And he chose twelve to be with him, that he might send them to preach,

15 And to have power to heal the sick, and cast out devils.

16 And Simon he surnamed Peter.

17 And James the son of Zebedee, and John the brother of James, he surnamed B'nai Rakhshi, which means sons of thunder,

18 And Andrew, and Philip, and Bartholomew, and Matthew, and Thomas, and James the son of Alphaeus, and Thaddaeus, and Simon the Zealot,

19 And Judas of Iscariot, who betrayed him. And they came into the house.

20 And the people gathered again, so that they could not find bread to eat.

21 And his relatives heard it, and went out to arrest him, for they said, He has lost his mind.

22 ¶ And the scribes who had come down from Jerusalem said, Beelzebub is with him, and, By the prince of demons he is casting out demons.

23 And Jesus called them, and said to them in parables, How can Satan cast out Satan?

24 If a kingdom is divided against itself, that kingdom cannot stand.

25 And if a household is divided against itself, that household cannot stand.

26 And if Satan rises up against himself and is divided, he cannot stand, but that is his end.

27 No man can enter into a

Cf. dif. verses 17–21

strong man's house and plunder his goods, unless he first bind the strong man; and then he plunders his house.

28 Truly I say to you, that all sins and blasphemies which men blaspheme, shall be forgiven to them.

29 But he who blasphemes against the Holy Spirit, shall never be forgiven, but is guilty before the everlasting judgment.

30 Because they said, He has an unclean spirit.

31 ¶ Then there came his mother and his brothers, and stood outside, and they sent in to call him.

32 But the people were sitting around him; and they said to him, Behold, your mother and your brothers are outside, asking for you.

33 And he answered and said to them, Who is my mother, and who are my brothers?

34 And he looked at those who sat near him and said, Behold my mother, and behold my brothers.

35 For whoever does the will of God, is my brother and my sister and my mother.

CHAPTER 4

AGAIN he began to teach by the seaside; and many people gathered unto him, so that he went up and sat in a boat in the sea; and all the people stood on the land by the sea.

2 And he taught them much by parables, and in his teaching he said,

3 Listen; Behold, a sower went out to sow.

4 And when he had sown, some fell on the roadside, and the fowls came and ate it.

5 Other fell upon the rock, where there was not sufficient soil; and it sprung up earlier because the ground was not deep enough;

6 But when the sun shone, it was scorched, and because it had no root, it dried up.

7 And other fell among thistles, and the thistles sprung up and choked it, and it bore no fruit.

8 But other fell in good soil, and it sprung up and grew and bore fruit, some thirty, and some sixty, and some one hundred.

9 And he said, He who has ears to hear, let him hear.

10 When they were alone by themselves, those who were with him together with the twelve asked him about that parable.

11 And Jesus said to them, To you is given to know the mystery of the kingdom of God, but to the outsiders

everything has to be explained by parables.

12 For seeing they see, and yet do not perceive; and hearing they hear, and yet do not understand; if they return, their sins would be forgiven.

13 And he said to them, Do you not know this parable? how then will you know all the parables?

14 ¶ The sower who sowed, sowed the word.

15 Those on the roadside are those in whom the word is sown; and when they have heard it, Satan comes immediately and takes away the word which is sown in their hearts.

16 And those which were sown upon the rock, are those who when they have heard the word, immediately receive it with joy;

17 And they have no root in themselves, but last for a while; and when trouble or persecution comes because of the word, they soon stumble.

18 And those which were sown among thistles, are those who have heard the word,

19 And the thoughts of this world, and the deception of wealth, and the lusts of other things, enter in and choke the word, and bear no fruit.

20 And those which were sown in good soil, are those who hear the word, and receive it and bear fruit, one thirty, and one sixty, and one a hundred.

21 ¶ And he said to them, Is a lamp brought and put under a basket or under a bed? Is it not put on a lampholder?

22 For there is nothing hidden which will not be uncovered; and nothing in secret which will not be revealed.

23 If any man has ears to hear, let him hear.

24 ¶ And he said to them, Take heed what you hear; with what measure you measure it will be measured to you; and increase especially to them who hear.

25 For he who has, to him will be given; and he who has not, even that which he has will be taken away from him.

26 ¶ And he said, Such is the kingdom of God, like a man who casts seed in the ground.

27 And he sleeps and rises up night and day, and the seed springs up and grows, while he is not aware of it.

28 For the earth causes it to yield fruit; and yet first it becomes a blade of grass, then an ear, and at last a full grain in the ear.

Cf. dif. verses 12–21–24–27

29 But when the fruit is ripe, then immediately comes the sickle, because the harvest is ready.

30 ¶ And he said, To what shall we compare the kingdom of God? and with what parable shall we picture it?

31 It is just like a grain of mustard seed, which, when it is sown in the earth, is the smallest of all the seeds on earth.

32 And when it is sown, it springs up and becomes greater than all the herbs, and puts forth large branches, so that the birds can settle under their shadow.

33 ¶ Jesus talked to them with parables as these, such parables as they were able to hear.

34 And without parables he did not speak to them; but to his disciples, among themselves, he explained everything.

35 On that day, at evening, he said to them, Let us cross over to the landing place.

36 And they left the people, and took him away while he was in the boat. And there were other boats with them.

37 And there arose a heavy storm and wind, and the waves kept falling into the boat, so that the boat was nearly filled up.

38 But Jesus was sleeping on a blanket in the stern of the boat; and they came and roused him and said to him, Teacher, do you not care that we are perishing?

39 So he got up, and rebuked the wind, and said to the sea, Peace, be still. And the wind quieted down, and there was a great calm.

40 And he said to them, Why are you so fearful? and why do you have no faith? And they were exceedingly afraid, and said to each other, Oh, who is this, that even the winds and the sea obey him?

CHAPTER 5

AND they reached the port on the other side of the sea, in the country of the Gadarenes.

2 And as he went out of the boat, he was met by a man from the cemetery, who had an unclean spirit.

3 He lived in the cemetery, and no man could bind him in chains;

4 Because whenever he was bound with fetters and chains, he broke the chains and cut the fetters, and no man could control him.

5 And always, night and day, he was in the cemetery and in the mountains, crying

aloud and cutting himself with stones.

6 When he saw Jesus from afar, he ran and worshipped him,

7 And he cried with a loud voice and said, What have we got together, Jesus, Son of the most high God? I adjure you by God, not to torment me.

8 For he said to him, Get out of the man, O you unclean spirit.

9 And he asked him, What is your name? And he said to him, Our name is Legion, because we are many.

10 And he begged him much that he would not send him out of the country.

11 Now there was there, near the mountain a large herd of swine feeding.

12 And the lunatics begged him saying, Send us to the swine, that we may attack[1] them.

13 And he permitted them. And the lunatics went out, and attacked the swine; and the herd ran to the steep rocks, and fell into the sea; they were about two thousand, and they were drowned in the water.

14 And those who fed them, fled, and told it in the city and also in the villages. So they went out to see what had happened.

15 And they came to Jesus, and saw the lunatic,[2] clothed and well behaved, and sitting down; even the one who once had the legion in him; and they were afraid.

16 And those who saw it told them just how it happened to the lunatic and also to the swine.

17 So they began to urge him to leave their border.

18 As he went up to the boat, the lunatic begged him to remain with him.

19 And he would not permit him, but said to him, Go to your home, to your own people, and tell them what the Lord has done for you, and had mercy on you.

20 And he went away, and began to preach in the ten cities about what Jesus had done for him; and they were all surprised.

21 ¶ When Jesus crossed in the boat to the other side, large crowds again gathered around him, while he was by the sea.

22 And there came one of the leaders of the synagogue,

[1] The same Aramaic word *al* means to attack and to enter. If it meant "enter into" it would have read *al bekhaw*.

[2] Mark here refers to one lunatic who conversed with Jesus and then he mentions lunatics in ver. 12. There were doubtless many. Cf. Matt. 8: 28.

whose name was Jairus; and when he saw him, he fell at his feet,

23 And he beseeched him much and said to him, My daughter is very seriously ill; come and lay your hand on her, and she will be healed, and live.

24 So Jesus went with him; and a large multitude followed him, and they pressed on him.

25 And there was a woman who had the hemorrhage for twelve years,

26 Who had suffered much at the hands of many doctors, and had spent everything she had, and was not helped at all, but rather became worse.

27 When she heard concerning Jesus, she came through the dense crowd from behind him, and touched his cloak.

28 For she said, If I can only touch his cloak, I will live.

29 And immediately the hemorrhage was dried up; and she felt in her body that she was healed of her disease.

30 Jesus instantly knew that some power had gone out of him; so he turned around to the people and said, Who touched my garments?

31 His disciples said to him, You see the people pressing on you, and yet you say, Who touched me?

32 And he was looking round to see who had done this.

33 But the woman, frightened and trembling, because she knew what had happened to her, came and fell before him, and told him the whole truth.

34 He said to her, My daughter, your faith has healed you; go in peace, and be healed of your disease.

35 While he was still talking, some men came from the house of the leader of the synagogue, saying, Your daughter is dead; why do you trouble the teacher?

36 Jesus heard the word which they spoke, and he said to the leader of the synagogue, Fear not, only believe.

37 And he did not permit any man to go with him, except Simon Peter, and James, and John the brother of James.

38 And they came to the house of the leader of the synagogue, and he saw them in a tumult, weeping and wailing.

39 So he entered and said to them, Why are you excited

and crying? The little girl is not dead, but she is asleep.

40 And they laughed at him. But Jesus put them all out, and took the little girl's father and mother and those who were with him, and he entered where the little girl was laid.

41 And he took the little girl by her hand, and said to her, Talitha, koomi, which means, Little girl, rise up.

42 And immediately the little girl got up and walked; for she was twelve years old. And they were astonished with a great astonishment.

43 And he commanded them that no man should know this; and he told them to give her something to eat.

CHAPTER 6

AND Jesus went out from thence, and came to his own city; and his disciples followed him.

2 When the sabbath came, he began to teach in the synagogue, and many who heard him were surprised, and said, Whence did he receive all this? and what wisdom is this which is given to him, that wonders like these are wrought by his hands?

3 Is he not the carpenter, the son of Mary, and the brother of James and Joses and Judas and Simon? and behold, are not his sisters here with us? And they denounced him.

4 And Jesus said to them, There is no prophet who is insulted, except in his own city, and among his own brothers, and in his own house.

5 And he could not perform even a single miracle there, except that he laid his hand on a few sick people and healed them.

6 And he wondered at their lack of faith. And he travelled in the villages teaching.

7 ¶ Then he called his twelve, and began to send them two by two; and he gave them power over the unclean spirits, to cast them out.

8 And he commanded them not to take anything for the journey, except a staff only; no bag, no bread, no copper money in their purses;

9 But to wear sandals, and not to wear two shirts.

10 And he said to them, Whatever house you enter, stay there until you leave that place.

11 And whoever will not receive you, nor hear you, when you leave that place, shake off the sand under your feet as a testimony to them. Truly I say to you, It will be easier for Sodom and Gomorrah in

the day of judgement than for that city.

12 ¶ And they went out and preached that they should repent.

13 And they cast out many demons, and anointed with oil many who were sick, and they were healed.

14 ¶ And Herod the king heard about Jesus, for his name was known to him; and he said, John the Baptist has risen from the dead; this is why miracles are worked by him.

15 Others said, He is Elijah. And yet others, He is a prophet, just like one of the prophets.

16 But when Herod heard it, he said, John, whom I beheaded; it is he who has risen from the dead.

17 ¶ For this same Herod had sent out and arrested John, and cast him in prison, because of Herodias, wife of his brother Philip, whom he had married.

18 For John had said to Herod, It is not lawful for you to marry your brother's wife.

19 But Herodias was bitter towards him, and wanted to kill him; but she could not.

20 For Herod was afraid of John, because he knew that he was a righteous and holy man, and he guarded him; and he heard that he was doing a great many things, and he heard him gladly.

21 Then came a state day, when Herod on his birthday gave a banquet to his officials, and captains, and the leading men of Galilee.

22 And the daughter of Herodias entered in and danced, and she pleased Herod and the guests who were with him; and the king said to the little girl, Ask me whatever you wish, and I will give it to you.

23 And he swore to her, Whatever you ask me, I will give you, as much as half of my kingdom.

24 She went out and said to her mother, What shall I ask him? She said to her, The head of John the Baptist.

25 And immediately she entered cautiously to the king, and said to him, I do wish in this very hour that you may give me on a tray the head of John the Baptist.

26 And the king was exceedingly sorry; but because of the oaths, and because of the guests, he did not wish to refuse her.

27 But the king immediately sent the executioner, and commanded to bring the

head of John. And he went and beheaded John in the prison,

28 And brought it on a tray and gave it to the girl; and the girl gave it to her mother.

29 And when his disciples heard of it, they came and took up his body and buried it in a grave.

30 ¶ And the apostles gathered together unto Jesus, and told him everything they had done, and what they had taught.

31 And he said to them, Come, let us go to the wilderness all alone, and rest awhile; for there were many coming and going, and they had no chance even to eat.

32 So they went away in a boat to a desert place by themselves.

33 And many people saw them when they were leaving, and they knew them, and from all the cities they hurried by land and reached the place before him.

34 And when Jesus went out he saw large crowds, and he had compassion on them, because they were like sheep without a shepherd; and he began to teach them a great many things.

35 ¶ And when it was getting late, his disciples came up to him and said to him,

This is a desert place, and it is getting late.

36 Dismiss them, so that they may go away to the farms and villages around us, and buy bread for themselves; for they have nothing to eat.

37 He said to them, You give them to eat. They said to him, Shall we go and buy two hundred penny's worth of bread, and give it to them to eat?

38 He said to them, Go and see how many loaves of bread you have got here. And when they found out, they said to him, Five loaves of bread and two fishes.

39 And he commanded them to make everyone sit down in groups on the grass.

40 So they sat down in groups, by hundreds and by fifties.

41 Then he took the five loaves of bread and the two fish, and he looked up to heaven, and he blessed and broke the loaves of bread, and gave them to his disciples to place before them; and they divided the two fish among them all.

42 And they all ate and were satisfied.

43 And they took up the fragments of bread, twelve full baskets, and also of the fish.

Cf. dif. verses 33–36

44 And those who ate the bread were five thousand men.

45 ¶ And immediately he urged his disciples to go up into the boat, and go in advance of him to the port at Bethsaida, while he dismissed the people.

46 And when he had dismissed them, he went up to the mountain to pray.

47 When evening came, the boat was in the midst of the sea, and he was alone on the land.

48 And he saw them struggling as they were rowing, for the wind was against them; and in the fourth watch of the night, Jesus came to them, walking on the water, and he wanted to pass by them.

49 But when they saw him walking on the water, they thought it was a false vision, and they cried out;

50 For they all saw him and were frightened. And immediately he spoke to them and said, Have courage, it is I, do not be afraid.

51 And he went up to them into the boat, and the wind quieted down; and they marvelled exceedingly, and were astonished in themselves.

52 For they did not understand the miracle of the loaves of bread, because their hearts were confused.

53 ¶ And when they had crossed to the port, they came to the land of Gennesaret.

54 And when they went out of the boat, the people of that place immediately knew him.

55 And they came running throughout that land; and began to bring those who were seriously sick, carrying them in quilt-beds, where they heard he was.

56 And wherever he entered into villages and cities, they laid the sick in the streets, and begged him even to touch the edge of his robe; and all who touched him were healed.

CHAPTER 7

THEN there gathered unto him Pharisees and scribes, who had come from Jerusalem.

2 And they saw some of the men of his disciples eating bread with their hands unwashed; and they reproached them.

3 For all the Jews, even the Pharisees, unless their hands are washed carefully would not eat, because they strictly observe the tradition of the elders.

4 Even the things from the market, if they are not

washed, they would not eat them. And there are a great many other things, which they have accepted to obey, such as the washing of cups and pots, and copper utensils, and the bedding of dead men.

5 And the scribes and Pharisees asked him, Why do your disciples not walk according to the tradition of the elders, but eat bread with their hands unwashed?

6 He said to them, The prophet Isaiah well prophesied about you, O hypocrites, as it is written, This people honor me with their lips, but their heart is far away from me.

7 And they worship me in vain, when they teach the doctrines of the commandments of men.

8 For you have ignored the commandment of God, and you observe the tradition of men, such as the washing of cups and pots, and a great many other things like these.

9 He said to them, Well you do injustice to the commandment of God so as to sustain your own tradition.

10 For Moses said, Honor your father and your mother; and he who curses father or mother, let him be put to death.

11 But you say, If a man say to his father or his mother, What is left over is Corban (my offering);

12 And yet you do not let him do anything for his father or mother.

13 So you dishonor the word of God for the sake of the tradition, which you have established; and you do a great many like these.

14 ¶ Then Jesus called all the people and said to them, Hear me, all of you, and understand.

15 There is nothing outside of a man, if it should enter into him, which can defile him; but what goes out of him, that defiles the man.

16 Who has ears to hear, let him hear.

17 When Jesus entered into the house because of the people, his disciples asked him concerning that parable.

18 And he said to them, So even you are puzzled. Do you not know that whatever enters into a man from outside cannot defile him?

19 Because it does not enter into his heart, but into his stomach, and then is thrown out through the intestines, thereby purifying the food.

20 It is what goes out of man, which defiles the man.

21 For from within, from the

heart of men go out evil thoughts, such as fornication, adultery, theft, murder,

22 Extortion, wickedness, deceit, lust, an evil eye, blasphemy, pride, foolishness;

23 All these evils go out from within, and they defile the man.

24 ¶ Jesus moved away from thence, and came to the borders of Tyre and Sidon, and he entered into a house, and did not want any one to know about him. And yet he could not hide himself.

25 For immediately a woman heard about him, whose daughter had an unclean spirit; and she came and fell at his feet.

26 But the woman was a heathen, from Phoenicia in Syria; and she besought him to cast out the demon from her daughter.

27 And Jesus said to her, Let the children be first filled; for it is not right to take the children's bread and throw it to the dogs.

28 But she answered and said to him, Yes, my lord; even the dogs eat the children's crumbs under the trays.

29 Jesus said to her, Go your way; just because of this word, the demon has gone out of your daughter.

30 So she went to her house, and she found her daughter lying in bed, and the demon gone out of her.

31 ¶ Again Jesus went out from the border of Tyre and Sidon, and came to the sea of Galilee, to the border of the ten cities.

32 And they brought to him a deaf and dumb man; and they asked him to lay his hand on him.

33 So he drew him aside from the people, and put his fingers into his ears, then he spat, and touched his tongue;

34 And he looked up to heaven and sighed, and he said to him, Ethpatakh, which means, Be opened.

35 And in that very hour his ears were opened, and the knot of his tongue was loosened, and he spoke plainly.

36 And he warned them not to tell this to any man; but the more he warned them, so much the more they published it.

37 And they were greatly astonished, saying, He does everything so well. He makes the deaf hear, and the dumb to speak.

CHAPTER 8

IN those days, when there was a large multitude, and they had nothing to eat, he called his disciples and said to them,

2 I have pity for this people, for they have remained with me three days, and they have nothing to eat;

3 And if I dismiss them to their homes, while they are fasting, they will faint on the way, for some of them have come from a distance.

4 His disciples said to him, How can any man here in this lonely place, feed all of these with bread?

5 And he asked them, How many loaves have you? They said to him, Seven.

6 So he commanded the people to sit on the ground; and he took the seven loaves of bread, and he blessed them, and broke them, and gave them to his disciples to set them; and they set them before the people.

7 And there were a few fishes; he blessed them also, and commanded to set them before them.

8 So they ate and were satisfied, and they took up seven baskets of fragments which were left over.

9 The men who ate were about four thousand; and he dismissed them.

10 ¶ And immediately he went up into the boat with his disciples, and he came to the country of Dalmanutha.

11 And the Pharisees came out and began to question him, and they asked him for a sign from heaven, so as to test him.

12 And he sighed in his spirit and said, Why does this generation want a sign? truly I say to you, No sign will be given to this generation.

13 And he left them, and went up into the boat, and departed from that port.

14 ¶ And they had forgotten to take bread; except one loaf they had none with them in the boat.

15 And he commanded them and said to them, Look out, and beware of the leaven of the Pharisees and of the leaven of Herod.

16 They were reasoning among themselves and saying, It is because we have no bread.

17 But Jesus knew it and said to them, What are you thinking, because you have no bread? Do you not even yet know, and do you not understand? Is your heart still hard?

18 You have eyes, and yet do you not see? you have ears, and yet do you not hear? And do you not remember?

Cf. dif. verses 10–13

19 When I broke the five loaves of bread for the five thousand, how many full baskets of fragments did you take up? They said to him, Twelve.

20 He said to them, And when the seven for the four thousand, how many baskets full of fragments did you take up? They said, Seven.

21 He said to them, How is it then that even yet you cannot understand?

22 ¶ And he came to Bethsaida; and they brought to him a blind man, and they besought him to touch him.

23 And he took the blind man by the hand and brought him outside the town; and he spat on his eyes, and put his hands on him, and asked him what he saw.

24 And he looked and said, I see men like trees, walking.

25 Again he put his hands over his eyes, and he was restored, and saw everything clearly.

26 And he sent him to his house, saying, Do not enter even into the town, nor tell it to anyone in the town.

27 ¶ And Jesus went out, and his disciples, to the towns of Caesarea of Philippi; and on the road he asked his disciples and said to them,

What do men say about me, that I am?

28 They said, John the Baptist; and others, Elijah; and yet others, One of the prophets.

29 Jesus said to them, But you, whom do you say I am? Simon Peter answered and said to him, You are the Christ, the Son of the living God.

30 And he warned them not to tell any man about him.

31 ¶ Then he began to teach them, that the Son of man will have to suffer a great deal, and be rejected by the elders, and the high priests, and the scribes, and be killed, and rise again on the third day.

32 And he spoke that word openly. So Peter took him aside and began to rebuke him.

33 But he turned around and looked on his disciples, and he rebuked Simon, and said, Get behind me, Satan; for you are not thinking the things of God, but of men.

34 And Jesus called the people together with his disciples, and said to them, He who wishes to come after me, let him deny himself, and take up his cross, and follow me.

35 For whoever wishes to save his life will lose it; and whoever loses his life for my sake and the sake of my Gospel, he will save it.

36 For how could a man be benefited, if he should gain the whole world and lose his life?

37 Or what could a man give in exchange for his life?

38 Whoever, therefore, is ashamed of me and of my words in this sinful and adulterous generation, the Son of man will also be ashamed of him, when he comes in the glory of his Father with his holy angels.

CHAPTER 9

AND he said to them, Truly I say to you, that there are men standing here, who shall not taste death, till they see that the kingdom of God has come with power.

2 ¶ And six days after, Jesus took Peter, and James, and John, and brought them up to a high mountain alone; and he was transfigured before their eyes.

3 His clothes shone, and became white like snow, in such a manner that men on earth cannot make white.

4 And there appeared to them Moses and Elijah, talking with Jesus.

5 And Peter said to him, Teacher, it is better for us to remain here; and let us make three shelters, one for you, and one for Moses, and one for Elijah.

6 For he did not know what he was saying, for they were in fear.

7 And there was a cloud overshadowing them, and a voice out of the cloud said, This is my beloved Son; hear him.

8 And suddenly, when the disciples looked around, they saw no man, except Jesus alone with them.

9 And as they came down from the mountain, he commanded them not to tell any man what they had seen, until the Son of man has risen from the dead.

10 So they kept that saying to themselves, and they wanted to know what "risen from the dead" means.

11 ¶ And they asked him, saying, Why then do the scribes say that Elijah must first come?

12 He said to them, Elijah does come first, to prepare everything; and as it is written concerning the Son of man, that he will suffer much and be rejected.

13 But I say to you, that Elijah has also come, and

Cf. dif. verses 3–6–12

they did with him whatever they pleased, as it is written of him.

14 ¶ And when he came to his disciples, he saw a large crowd with them, and the scribes debating with them.

15 And immediately all the people saw him, and were greatly surprised, and they ran to greet him.

16 And he asked the scribes, What do you debate with them?

17 One of the multitude answered and said, Teacher, I brought my son to you, for he has a spirit of dumbness.

18 And whenever it seizes him, it troubles him; and he foams, and gnashes his teeth, and gets worn out. And I asked your disciples to cast it out, but they could not.

19 Jesus answered and said to him, O faithless generation, how long shall I be with you? and how long shall I preach to you? bring him to me.

20 And they brought the boy to Jesus; and when the spirit seized him, it immediately troubled him; and he fell on the ground, gasping and foaming.

21 So Jesus asked his father, How long has he been like this? He said to him, From his childhood.

22 And many times it has thrown him into the fire and into the water to destroy him; but whatever you can do, help me, and have mercy on me.

23 Jesus said to him, If you can believe, everything is possible to him who believes.

24 And immediately the father of the boy cried out weeping, and said, I do believe, help my little belief.

25 When Jesus saw that people were running and gathering to him, he rebuked the unclean spirit and said to it, O deaf and dumb spirit, I command you, come out of him, and do not enter him again.

26 And the epileptic cried out much, and was tortured, and the spirit went out; then the boy became as if dead, so that many could say, He is dead.

27 Then Jesus took him by the hand, and lifted him up.

28 When Jesus entered the house, his disciples asked him privately, Why could we not cast it out?

29 He said to them, This kind cannot be cast out by anything, except by fasting and prayer.

30 And when they went out from thence, they passed through Galilee; and he did not want any man to know about him.

31 For he taught his disciples, and said to them, The Son of man will be delivered into the hands of men, and they will kill him; and after he is killed, he will rise on the third day.

32 But they did not understand the saying, and they were afraid to ask him.

33 ¶ And they came to Capernaum; and when they entered the house, he asked them, What were you reasoning among yourselves on the road?

34 But they kept silent, for on the road they had argued with one another, which was the greatest of them.

35 And Jesus sat down, and he called the twelve and said to them, He who wishes to be first, let him be the last of every man, and the minister of every man.

36 And he took a little boy, and made him to stand in the midst; then he took him in his arms, and said to them,

37 Whoever receives a boy like this in my name, he receives me; and he who receives me, does not receive me, but him who has sent me.

38 ¶ John said to him, Teacher, we saw a man casting out demons in your name; and we forbade him, because he did not follow us.

39 Jesus said to them, Do not forbid him; for there is no man who performs miracles in my name, who will hastily speak evil of me.

40 Therefore, he who is not against you is for you.

41 For whoever gives you to drink even a cup of water only, because you represent the name of Christ, truly I say to you that his reward shall not be lost.

42 And whoever shall cause one of these little ones who believe in me to stumble, it were better for him that an ass' mill stone were hanged on his neck and then he were thrown into the sea.

43 If your hand offends you, cut it off; it is much better for you to go through life maimed, than to have two hands and go to Gehenna,[1]

44 Where their worm does not die, and their fire does not quench.

45 And if your foot offends you, cut it off; it is much better for you to go through life lame, than to have two feet, and fall into Gehenna,

46 Where their worm does not die, and their fire does not quench.

[1] That is, hell.

47 And if your eye offends you, remove it; it is better for you to enter the kingdom of God with one eye, than to have two eyes, and fall into the Gehenna of fire,

48 Where their worm does not die, and their fire does not quench.

49 For everything will be salted on fire, and every sacrifice will be salted with salt.

50 O how good is salt; but if the salt should lose its savor, with what could it be salted? Let there be salt in you, and be in peace with one another.

CHAPTER 10

AND he departed from thence, and came to the border of Judaea, at the crossing of the Jordan; and a great many people went to him there, and he taught them again, as he was accustomed to do.

2 ¶ And the Pharisees came up to him, tempting him and asking, Is it lawful for a man to desert his wife?

3 He said to them, What did Moses command you?

4 They said, Moses gave us permission to write a letter of separation, and then to divorce.

5 Jesus answered and said to them, It was because of the hardness of your heart, he wrote for you this particular law.

6 But from the very beginning God made them male and female.

7 For this reason a man shall leave his father and his mother and follow his wife.

8 And both shall be one flesh; henceforth they are not two, but one flesh.

9 What therefore God has joined, let no man separate.

10 ¶ And his disciples again asked him about this in the house.

11 And he said to them, Whoever divorces his wife and marries another, commits adultery.

12 And if a woman divorces her husband, and marries another, she commits adultery.

13 ¶ And they brought little boys to him, that he might touch them; but his disciples rebuked those who brought them.

14 But when Jesus saw it, he was displeased, and he said to them, Allow the little boys to come to me, and do not forbid them; for the kingdom of God is for such as these.

15 Truly I say to you, Whoever does not receive the

kingdom of God like a little boy shall not enter it.

16 Then he took them in his arms, and put his hand on them, and blessed them.

17 ¶ While he was on the way, a man ran up and fell on his knees, and he asked him, saying, O good Teacher, what shall I do to inherit life eternal?

18 Jesus said to him, Why do you call me good? there is no one who is good, except the one God.

19 You know the commandments, Do not commit adultery, Do not steal, Do not murder, Do not bear false witness, Do not oppress, Honor your father and mother.

20 But he answered and said to him, Teacher, all of these I have obeyed from my boyhood.

21 Then Jesus looked at him and loved him, and he said to him, You lack one thing; go, sell everything you have, and give it to the poor, and you shall have a treasure in heaven; and take up your cross and follow me.

22 But he felt sad because of this saying, and he went away depressed; for he had great wealth.

23 Then Jesus looked at his disciples and said to them, How hard it is for those who have wealth, to enter into the kingdom of God!

24 But the disciples were surprised at his words. And Jesus answered again and said to them, My sons, how hard it is for those who trust in their wealth, to enter into the kingdom of God!

25 It is easier for a rope to enter through the eye of a needle, than for a rich man to enter into the kingdom of God.

26 But they were the more surprised, saying among themselves, Who then can be saved?

27 Jesus looked at them, and said to them, With men this is impossible, but not with God; for everything is possible with God.

28 Then Peter began to say, Behold, we have left everything and followed you.

29 Jesus answered and said, Truly I say to you, There is no man who leaves houses, or brothers, or sisters, or father, or mother, or wife, or children, or fields, for my sake and for the sake of my gospel,

30 Who shall not receive now, in this time, an hundredfold, houses, and brothers and sisters, and maidservants, and children, and fields, and other worldly

pursuits, and in the world to come life everlasting.

31 Many who are first shall be last, and the last first.

32 ¶ While they were going up on their way to Jerusalem, Jesus was ahead of them; and they were amazed; and they followed him with fear. And he took his twelve aside, and began to tell them what was surely to happen to him.

33 Behold, we are going up to Jerusalem, and the Son of man will be delivered to the high priests and the scribes, and they will condemn him to death, and deliver him to the Gentiles.

34 And they will mock him, and scourge him, and spit in his face, and kill him; and on the third day he will rise up.

35 ¶ And James and John, the sons of Zebedee, came up to him and said to him, Teacher, we wish you would do for us whatever we ask.

36 He said to them, What do you wish me to do for you?

37 They said to him, Grant us to sit, one at your right and one at your left, in your glory.

38 He said to them, You do not know what you are asking; can you drink the cup which I drink? and be baptized with the baptism with which I am to be baptized?

39 They said to him, We can. Jesus said to them, The cup which I shall drink you will drink too; and with the baptism with which I am baptized, you will be baptized too;

40 But to sit at my right and at my left, that is not mine to give; except to those for whom it is prepared.

41 When the ten heard it, they began to murmur at James and John.

42 Jesus called them and said to them, You know that those who consider themselves princes of the people, are their owners too; and their officials rule over them.

43 Let not this be so among you; but he who wishes to be great among you, let him be a minister to you.

44 And anyone of you who wishes to be first, let him be a servant of every man.

45 For also the Son of man did not come to be ministered to, but to minister, and to give his life as a salvation for the sake of many.

46 ¶ And they came to Jericho; and when Jesus went out of Jericho with his disciples and a large crowd, a blind man, Timaeus, the son of Timaeus, sat by the roadside begging.

47 When he heard that it

was Jesus of Nazareth, he began to cry aloud and say, O son of David, have mercy on me.

48 And many rebuked him to keep quiet, but he cried out the more, saying, O son of David, have mercy on me.

49 Then Jesus stopped and commanded to call him. So they called the blind man, and said to him, Have courage, rise; he is calling you.

50 And the blind man threw off his robe, and he got up, and went to Jesus.

51 Jesus said to him, What do you wish me to do for you? The blind man said to him, Master, that I may see.

52 And Jesus said to him, See; your faith has healed you. And immediately he saw, and went on the way.

CHAPTER 11

WHEN he came near to Jerusalem, towards Bethphage and Bethany at the Mount of Olives, he sent two of his disciples,

2 And he said to them, Go to the village in front of us; and as soon as you enter it, you will find a colt which is tied up, on which no man of the sons of men has ever ridden; untie it and bring it.

3 And if any man should say to you, Why are you doing this? say to him that our Lord needs it; and immediately he will send it here.

4 So they went and found the colt tied by the door, outside, in the street. And as they were untying it,

5 Some of the men who stood there said to them, What are you doing, are you untying the colt?

6 And they said to them as Jesus had instructed them; and they permitted them.

7 And they brought the colt to Jesus, and they put their garments on it, and Jesus rode on it.

8 And many spread their garments on the road; and others cut down branches from the trees, and spread them on the road.

9 And those who were in front of him, and those who were behind him, were crying and saying, Hosanna; Blessed is he who comes in the name of the Lord;

10 And blessed is the kingdom of our father David, which comes; Hosanna in the highest.

11 ¶ And Jesus entered Jerusalem, into the temple; and he saw everything, and when evening came, he went out to Bethany with the twelve.

Cf. dif. verses 52–2–4–5–6–10–11

12 ¶ And the next day, when they went out of Bethany, he became hungry.

13 And he saw a fig tree in the distance, which had leaves on it. So he came to it to see if he could find anything on it; and when he came he found nothing on it except leaves; for it was not yet time for the figs.

14 And he said to it, From now and forever, let no man eat of your fruit. And his disciples heard it.

15 ¶ And they came to Jerusalem; and Jesus entered into the temple of God, and began to cast out those who were buying and selling in the temple; and he overturned the trays of the money-changers, and the stands of those who sold doves;

16 And he would not allow any man to bring goods into the temple.

17 And he taught them and said to them, Is it not written, My house shall be called the house of prayer for all the peoples? But you have made it a bandits' cave.

18 And the high priests and the scribes heard it, and they sought how to do away with him; for they were afraid of him, because all the people were amazed at his teaching.

19 And when evening came, they went outside of the city.

20 ¶ And in the morning, as they were passing, they saw the fig tree withered from its roots.

21 And Simon remembered, and said to him, Master, behold, the fig tree which you cursed has withered.

22 Jesus answered and said to them, If you have faith in God,

23 Truly I say to you, Whoever should say to this mountain, Remove and fall into the sea, and does not doubt in his heart, but believes that what he says will be done, whatever he says will be done to him.

24 Therefore I say to you, Anything you pray for and ask, believe that you will receive it, and it will be done for you.

25 And when you stand up to pray, forgive whatever you have against any man, so that your Father in heaven will forgive you your trespasses.

26 But if you will not forgive, even your Father in heaven will not forgive you your trespasses.

27 ¶ And they came again to Jerusalem; and while he was walking in the temple,

the high priests, and the scribes, and the elders came to him.

28 And they said to him, By what authority do you do these things? and who gave you this authority to do these things?

29 Jesus said to them, I will also ask you a word to tell me, and then I will tell you by what authority I do these things.

30 Whence is the baptism of John, from heaven, or from men? Tell me.

31 And they reasoned among themselves and said, If we should say to him, from heaven, he will say to us, Why then did you not believe him?

32 And if we should say, from men, there is the fear of the people, for all of them regard John as a true prophet.

33 So they answered and said to Jesus, We do not know. He said to them, I will also not tell you by what authority I do these things.

CHAPTER 12

AND he began to speak to them in parables. A man planted a vineyard, and fenced it all around, and he dug in it a wine-press, and built a tower in it, and then he leased it to laborers, and went on a journey.

2 And in due season he sent his servant to the laborers, to receive some of the fruits of the vineyard.

3 But they beat him, and sent him away empty.

4 And again he sent to them another servant; they stoned him also, and wounded him, and sent him away in disgrace.

5 And again he sent another, but they killed him; and he sent many other servants, some of them they beat, and some they killed.

6 But finally, he had a very beloved son, and he sent him to them last of all, for he said, They might feel ashamed before my son.

7 But the laborers said among themselves, This is the heir; come, let us kill him, and the inheritance will be ours.

8 And they took and killed him, and threw him outside of the vineyard.

9 What then will the owner of the vineyard do? he will come and destroy those laborers, and give the vineyard to others.

10 Have you not read this scripture, The stone which the builders rejected, the same became the corner-stone?

11 This was from the Lord, and it is a wonder in our eyes.

12 ¶ They wanted to seize him, but they were afraid of the people; for they knew that he spoke this parable against them; and they left him and went away.

13 ¶ And they sent to him some men of the scribes and of the Herodians, that they might trap him by a word.

14 They came and asked him, Master, we know that you are true, and you do not favor any man; for you are impartial, and you teach the way of God in truth. Is it lawful to give head-tax to Caesar or not?

15 Shall we give or shall we not give? But he knew their scheme, and said to them, Why do you tempt me? Bring me a penny, that I may see it.

16 And they brought it to him. He said to them, Whose is this image and inscription? They said, Caesar's.

17 Jesus said to them, Give to Caesar what is Caesar's, and to God what is God's. And they were amazed at him.

18 ¶ Then the Sadducees came to him, those who say there is no resurrection; and they asked him, saying,

19 Teacher, Moses wrote to us, that if a man's brother die, and leave a wife, and leave no children, his brother should take his wife, and raise up offspring for his brother.

20 Now there were seven brothers; the first one took a wife and died, and left no offspring.

21 Then the second one married her, and he died; he also left no offspring; and likewise the third one.

22 So all seven of them married her, and left no offspring. And after them all the woman also died.

23 Therefore at the resurrection, whose wife will she be? for all seven had married her.

24 Jesus said to them, Do you not err, because you do not understand the scriptures, nor the power of God?

25 For when they rise from the dead, they neither marry women, nor are women given in marriage to men; but they are like the angels in heaven.

26 Now concerning the rising of the dead, have you not read in the book of Moses, how God said to him from the bush, I am the God of Abraham and the God of Isaac and the God of Jacob?

27 And yet he was not the

God of the dead, but of the living. You therefore greatly err.

28 ¶ And one of the scribes came near and heard them debating, and he saw that he gave them a good answer. So he asked him, Which is the first commandment of all?

29 Jesus said to him, The first of all commandments is, Hear, O Israel, the Lord our God is one Lord;

30 And you must love the Lord your God with all your heart, and with all your soul, and with all your mind, and with all your power; this is the first commandment.

31 And the second is like to it, You must love your neighbor as yourself. There is no other commandment greater than these.

32 The scribe said to him, Well, teacher, you have said the truth, that he is one, and there is no other beside him;

33 And that a man should love him with all the heart, and with all the mind, and with all the soul, and with all the power, and love his neighbor as himself; this is far more important than all burnt offerings and sacrifices.

34 When Jesus saw that he replied wisely, he answered and said to him, You are not far from the kingdom of God.

And no man dared again to question him.

35 ¶ And Jesus answered and said, as he taught in the temple; How do the scribes say, that Christ is the son of David?

36 For David himself said through the Holy Spirit, The Lord said to my Lord, Sit on my right hand, until I put your enemies a stool under your feet.

37 Now therefore David himself calls him my Lord, and how can he be his son? And all the people heard him with pleasure.

38 ¶ And in his teaching he said to them, Beware of the scribes, who like to walk in long robes, and love to be saluted in the streets,

39 And the front seats in the synagogues, and the head places at banquets;

40 Those who embezzle the property of widows, with the pretense of making long prayers. They shall receive greater judgment.

41 ¶ And when Jesus sat towards the treasury, he watched how the people cast their alms into the treasury; and many rich men were casting a great deal.

42 And there came a poor widow, and she cast in two coins, which are farthings.

43 And Jesus called his disciples, and said to them, Truly I say to you, that this poor widow has cast in the treasury more than all the men who are casting;

44 For all of them cast of their abundance; but she of her poverty cast everything she had, even all of her possessions.

CHAPTER 13

WHEN Jesus went out of the temple, one of his disciples said to him, Teacher, behold, look at those stones and those buildings.

2 Jesus said to him, Do you see these great buildings? Not a stone shall be left here upon another stone, which shall not be torn down.

3 ¶ While Jesus sat on the Mount of Olives, towards the temple, Peter and James and John and Andrew asked him alone,

4 Tell us when these things will happen, and what is the sign when all these things are about to be fulfilled?

5 Then Jesus began to tell them; Be careful that no man deceive you.

6 For many will come in my name, and say, I am he; and they will deceive many.

7 And when you hear of wars and rumors of revolutions, do not be afraid; for this is bound to happen, but the end is not yet.

8 For nation will rise against nation, and kingdom against kingdom; and there will be earthquakes in different places, and there will be famines and uprisings. These things are just the beginning of travail.

9 Look out for yourselves; for they will deliver you to the judges, and they will scourge you in their synagogues; and you will stand before kings and governors for my sake, and as a testimony to them.

10 But my gospel must first be preached among all nations.

11 When they bring you up to deliver you, do not worry beforehand what you will speak; and do not think of anything except what is given you in that very hour; speak that; for it is not you that speak, but the Holy Spirit.

12 A brother will deliver his brother to death, and a father his son; and the children will rise up against their parents, and put them to death.

13 And you will be hated by all men because of my name; but he who has pa-

tience to the end, will be saved.

14 But when you see the sign of the refuse of desolation, as spoken by the prophet Daniel, accumulating where it should not be, whoever reads can understand it. Then let those who are in Judaea flee to the mountain;

15 And he who is on the roof, let him not come down, and not enter to take anything out of his house;

16 And he who is in the field, let him not return back to take his clothes.

17 But woe to those who are with child, and to those who give suck in those days!

18 Pray that your flight may not be in winter.

19 For in those days there will be suffering, such as has never been from the beginning of the creation, which God created until now, and never will be again.

20 And if the Lord had not shortened those days, no flesh would live; but for the sake of the chosen ones, which he chose, he shortened those days.

21 Then if any man should say to you, Behold, here is the Christ; or, behold, there; do not believe it.

22 For there will rise false Christs, and lying prophets, and they will show signs and wonders, and mislead, if possible, even the chosen ones.

23 But you be careful; behold, I have told you everything in advance.

24 ¶ But in those days, after that suffering, the sun will be darkened, and the moon will not give her light,

25 And the stars will fall down from the sky, and the powers of the universe will be shaken.

26 Then they will see the Son of man coming in the clouds, with a great army and with glory.

27 Then he will send his angels, and gather his chosen ones from the four winds, from the utmost part of the earth to the utmost part of heaven.

28 From the fig tree learn a parable. When its branches become tender and bring forth leaves, you know that summer is coming.

29 So even you, when you see all these things happen, understand that it is near the door.

30 Truly I say to you that this generation will not pass away, until all these things happen.

31 Heaven and earth will pass away, but my words shall not pass away.

32 But concerning that day and that hour, no man knows, not even the angels of heaven, neither the Son, except the Father.

33 Look out, be alert and pray; for you do not know when the time is.

34 It is just like a man who went on a journey, and left his house, and gave authority to his servants, and to each man his work, and he commanded the porter to keep awake.

35 Be alert therefore, for you do not know when the owner of the house will come, in the evening, or at midnight, or at the cock-crow, or in the morning.

36 He might come suddenly, and find you asleep.

37 What I say to you I say to all of you, Be alert.

CHAPTER 14

AFTER two days, the passover of unleavened bread was to come; and the high priests and the scribes were seeking how to seize him by craft and kill him.

2 And they said, Not during the feast, for it may cause a riot among the people.

3 ¶ When he was in Bethany, in the house of Simon the leper, while he reclined, there came a woman who had with her an alabaster vessel of perfume of pure nard, of good quality and very expensive; and she opened it, and poured it upon the head of Jesus.

4 But there were some men of the disciples who were displeased within themselves, and said, Why was this perfume wasted?

5 For it could have been sold for more than three hundred pennies and given to the poor. So they annoyed her.

6 Jesus said, Leave her alone; why do you trouble her? she has done a good work to me.

7 For you always have the poor with you, and when you wish, you can do good to them; but I am not always with you.

8 But this one has done it with what she had; she anointed my body in advance as for the burial.

9 And truly I say to you, Wherever this my gospel is preached throughout the world, what she has done will also be told as a memorial to her.

10 ¶ Then Judas of Iscariot, one of the twelve, went to the high priests, to deliver Jesus to them.

11 When they heard it, they were glad, and promised to

give him money. So he sought an opportunity to deliver him.

12 ¶ On the first day of unleavened bread, on which the Jews sacrifice the passover, his disciples said to him, Where do you wish that we go and prepare the passover for you to eat?

13 And he sent two of his disciples, and said to them, Go to the city, and behold you will meet a man carrying a vessel of water; follow him.

14 And wherever he enters, say to the owner of the house, Our master says, Where is the guestchamber, where I may eat the passover with my disciples?

15 And he will show you a large upper room furnished and prepared; there make ready for us.

16 And his disciples went out and came to the city, and they found just as he had told them; and they prepared the passover.

17 ¶ And when it was evening, he came with his twelve.

18 And when they were reclining and eating, Jesus said, Truly I say to you, One of you who eats with me, he will betray me.

19 They began to feel troubled, and said to him one by one, Why, is it I?

20 But he said to them, One of the twelve who dips with me in the dish.

21 The Son of man will go, as it is written of him; but woe to the man by whose hand the Son of man is betrayed! it would have been far better for that man never to have been born.

22 ¶ While they were eating, Jesus took bread, and blessed it, and he broke it, and gave it to them, and he said to them, Take it; this is my body.

23 And he took the cup, and gave thanks, and he blessed it, and gave it to them, and they all drank of it.

24 And he said to them, This is my blood of the new covenant, which is shed for the sake of many.

25 Truly I say to you, I shall not drink again of the fruit of the vine, until that day in which I drink it new in the kingdom of God.

26 ¶ And they offered praise, and went out to the Mount of Olives.

27 Then Jesus said to them, All of you will deny me this night; for it is written, I will smite the shepherd, and his sheep will scatter.

28 But when I am risen, I will be in Galilee before you.

29 Peter said to him, Even if all of them should deny you, but not I.

30 Jesus said to him, Truly I say to you, that you, today, in this night, before the cock crows twice, will deny me three times.

31 But he kept telling him still more, Even if I must die with you, I will never deny you, O my Lord. All the disciples said also, like him.

32 ¶ And they came to a place, which is called Gethsemane; and he said to his disciples, Sit down here, while I pray.

33 And he took with him Peter and James and John, and he began to be sorrowful and oppressed.

34 And he said to them, My soul is sorrowful even to death; wait for me and keep awake.

35 And he went a little aside, and fell on the ground, and prayed, that if it were possible, the hour might pass away from him.

36 And he said, *Abba, Ave,* O Father, my Father, you can do everything; make this cup pass away from me; but not according to my will, but yours.

37 And he came and found them sleeping, and he said to Peter, Simon, are you sleeping? could you not keep awake even for one hour?

38 Awake and pray, that you may not enter into temptation; the spirit indeed is willing and ready, but the body is weak.

39 He went away again and prayed, and he said the same word.

40 And he returned again, and came and found them sleeping, because their eyes were heavy; and they did not know what to say to him.

41 Then he came the third time, and said to them, From now on sleep and get rest; the end has arrived and the hour has come; and behold, the Son of man will be delivered into the hands of sinners.

42 Arise, let us go; behold, he who is to deliver me is near.

43 ¶ While he was speaking, Judas of Iscariot, one of the twelve, came and many people, with swords and staves, from the high priests and the scribes and the elders.

44 And the traitor who was to do the delivering gave them a sign, and he said, He whom I kiss, it is he; seize him carefully, and take him away.

45 And immediately he

drew near and said to him, My teacher, my teacher, and he kissed him.

46 And they laid hands on him and arrested him.

47 But one of those who stood by drew a sword, and struck it at the servant of the high priest, and cut off his ear.

48 And Jesus answered and said to them, Have you come out against me as against a bandit, with swords and staves to arrest me?

49 I was with you every day teaching in the temple, and you did not arrest me; but this has happened so that the scriptures might be fulfilled.

50 Then his disciples left him and fled.

51 And a young man was following him, naked, with a loin cloth around him; and they seized him.

52 But he left the loin cloth, and fled naked.

53 ¶ And they took Jesus to Caiaphas the high priest; and there gathered to him all the high priests and the scribes and the elders.

54 But Simon followed him afar off, up to the courtyard of the high priest; and he sat with the servants, warming himself before the fire.

55 The high priests and the whole council were seeking testimony against Jesus so that they might put him to death; but they could not find it.

56 For even though many testified against him, their testimonies were not worthy.

57 Then some men, who were false witnesses, stood up against him, and said,

58 We heard him say, I will tear down this temple which is made with hands, and in three days I will build another which is not made with hands.

59 But even this testimony was not worthy.

60 Then the high priest stood up in the midst, and asked Jesus, and said, Do you not answer? what do these testify against you?

61 But Jesus was silent, and made no answer. Again the high priest asked him, and said, Are you the Christ, the Son of the Blessed One?

62 Jesus said to him, I am; and you will see the Son of man sitting at the right hand of power, and coming upon the clouds of the sky.

63 Then the high priest tore his robe, and said, Why therefore do we need witnesses?

64 Behold, you have heard blasphemy from his own mouth; what do you think?

Cf. dif. verses 51–56–57–59–63–64

And they all decided that he is guilty of death.

65 Then some of the men began to spit on his face, and to cover his face, and to strike him on his head, saying, Prophesy; and the soldiers smote him on his cheeks.

66 ¶ And when Simon was below in the courtyard, there came a young maidservant of the high priest;

67 And she saw him warming himself, and looked at him, and said to him, You also were with Jesus the Nazarene.

68 But he denied it and said, I do not understand what you are saying. Then he went out to the porch, and the cock crowed.

69 And the same young maid saw him, and began to say to those who stood by, This one also is one of them.

70 But he denied it again. And a little later, those who stood by said to Peter, Truly you are one of them, for you also are a Galilean, and even your speech is like theirs.

71 And he began to curse and to swear, I do not know this man of whom you speak.

72 At that very hour the cock crowed the second time. And Simon remembered the word that Jesus said to him, Before the cock crows twice you will deny me thrice. And then he began to weep.

CHAPTER 15

AND immediately in the morning the high priests took counsel together with the elders and the scribes and with the whole council; and they bound Jesus and took him away, and delivered him to Pilate the governor.

2 And Pilate asked him, Are you the King of the Jews? He answered and said to him, You say that.

3 And the high priests accused him of many things.

4 Then Pilate asked again and said to him, Do you not answer? see, how many are testifying against you.

5 But Jesus gave no answer, so that Pilate marvelled.

6 ¶ Now it was the custom on every feast to release to them one prisoner, whom they asked for.

7 There was one called Bar-Abbas, who was bound with those who made insurrection, and who had committed murder during the insurrection.

8 And the people cried out, and began to ask, to do for them according to the custom.

9 Pilate answered and said, Are you willing that I release to you the King of the Jews?

10 For Pilate knew that the high priests had delivered him because of envy.

11 But the high priests incited the people the more, that he should release Bar-Abbas to them.

12 Pilate said to them, What then do you wish me to do to this man whom you call "the King of the Jews"?

13 And they cried out again, Crucify him!

14 Then Pilate said to them, What evil has he done? but they cried aloud the more, Crucify him!

15 Now Pilate wanted to do the will of the people; so he released Bar-Abbas to them, and he delivered to them Jesus, scourged, to be crucified.

16 Then the soldiers took him to the inner courtyard, which is the Praetorium; and they called together the whole company.

17 And they dressed him in purple, and wove a crown of thorns and put it on him.

18 And they began to salute him, Hail, O King of the Jews.

19 And they struck him on his head with a reed, and spat on his face, and knelt on their knees and worshipped him.

20 And when they had mocked him, they took off the purple, and put on him his own clothes, and took him out to crucify him.

21 ¶ And they compelled one who was passing by, Simon the Cyrenian, who was coming from the field, the father of Alexander and Rufus, to carry his cross.

22 And they brought him to Golgotha, a place which is interpreted The Skull.

23 And they gave him to drink wine mixed with myrrh; but he would not take it.

24 And when they had crucified him, they divided his clothes, and cast lots on them, what each man should take.

25 It was the third hour when they crucified him.

26 And the reason for his death was inscribed in writing, THIS IS THE KING OF THE JEWS.

27 And they crucified with him two bandits, one on his right and one on his left.

28 And the scripture was fulfilled which said, He was reckoned with the wicked.

29 ¶ Even those who passed by blasphemed against him, nodding their heads and saying, O destroyer of the tem-

ple and builder of it in three days,

30 Deliver yourself and come down from the cross.

31 The high priests likewise were laughing among themselves, with the scribes, and saying, He saved others; but he cannot save himself.

32 "O Christ, the King of Israel!" let him now come down from the cross, so that we may see and believe in him. Even those who were crucified with him reproached him.

33 And when the sixth hour was come, there was darkness over all the land, until the ninth hour.

34 And at the ninth hour, Jesus cried out with a loud voice, and said, Eli, Eli, Lmana, shabachthani! which means, My God, my God, for this I was kept!

35 Some of the men who were standing by, when they heard it, said, He called for Elijah.

36 And one ran and filled a sponge with vinegar, and tied it up on a reed to give him a drink; and he said, Hush, let us see if Elijah will come to take him down.

37 But Jesus cried with a loud voice, and the end came.

38 And the door curtains of the temple were rent in two, from the top to the bottom.

39 ¶ And when the centurion, who stood by near him, saw that he cried out in this manner and passed away, he said, Truly this man was the Son of God.

40 There were also women who were looking from afar, Mary of Magdala, and Mary the mother of James the young and of Joses, and Salome;

41 Who had followed him, when he was in Galilee, and ministered to him; and many other women who had come up with him to Jerusalem.

42 ¶ And when it was Friday evening, which is before the sabbath,

43 There came Joseph of Arimathaea, an honorable counsellor, who was also waiting for the kingdom of God; and he dared and went to Pilate, and asked for the body of Jesus.

44 But Pilate marvelled that he was already dead. So he called the centurion and asked him if he had died before the time.

45 And when he learned it, he gave the body to Joseph.

46 And Joseph bought linen, and took him down and wrapped him in it, and laid

9

him in a tomb which was hewn in a rock; and he rolled a stone against the door of the tomb.

47 But Mary of Magdala and Mary the mother of Joses, saw where he was laid.

CHAPTER 16

WHEN the sabbath had passed, Mary of Magdala and Mary the mother of James, and Salome, bought spices, that they might come and anoint him.

2 Early in the morning, on the first day of the week, they came to the tomb, as the sun was just rising.

3 And they said among themselves, Who will roll away the stone from the door of the tomb for us?

4 And they looked and saw that the stone was rolled away, for it was very large.

5 And they entered the tomb, and saw a young man, sitting on the right, covered in a white robe; and they were astonished.

6 But he said to them, Do not be afraid. You seek Jesus the Nazarene, who was crucified; he has risen; he is not here; behold the place where he was laid.

7 But go away and tell his disciples, and Peter, that he will be before you in Galilee; there you will see him, just as he had told you.

8 And when they heard it, they fled and went out of the tomb, for they were seized with amazement and trembling; and they said nothing to any man, for they were frightened.

9 ¶ Now he rose early on the first day of the week, and appeared first to Mary of Magdala, from whom he had cast seven demons.

10 And she went and brought glad tidings to those who were with him, who now were mourning and weeping.

11 And when they heard them saying that he is alive, and had appeared to them, they did not believe them.[1]

12 ¶ After these things he appeared to two of them in another manner, as they were walking and going to a village.

13 And they went and told the rest; but they did not believe them also.

14 ¶ At last he appeared to the eleven while they were reclining, and he upbraided their little faith and the dulness of their hearts, be-

---

[1] All three women returned from the tomb and brought the news, but Mary of Magdala was the chief speaker.

Cf. dif. verses 5–8–10–11–14

cause they had not believed those who saw him risen.

15 ¶ And he said to them, Go to all the world, and preach my gospel to the whole creation.

16 He who believes and is baptized shall be saved; and he who does not believe shall be condemned.

17 And wonders will follow those who believe these things. In my name they will cast out demons; and they will speak with new tongues;

18 And they will pick up snakes; and if they should drink any poison of death, it will not harm them; and they will lay their hands on the sick, and they will be healed.

19 ¶ Then our Lord Jesus, after he had spoken to them, ascended to heaven, and sat on the right hand of God.

20 And they went out, and preached in every place; and our Lord helped them, and he strengthened their words by the miracles which they performed.

THE GOSPEL ACCORDING TO

St. LUKE

CHAPTER 1

SINCE many have desired to have in writing the story of those works, with which we are familiar;

2 According to what was handed down to us by those who from the beginning were eyewitnesses and ministers of that very word;

3 And since these were seen by me also because I was near and considered them all very carefully, I will therefore write to you everything in its order, most honorable Theophilus,

4 So that you may know the truth of the words, by which you were made a convert.

5 ¶ There was in the days of Herod, king of Judaea, a priest whose name was Zacharias, of the order of ministry of the house of Abijah; and his wife was of the daughters of Aaron, and her name was Elizabeth.

6 They were both righteous before God, and walked in all his commandments, and in the righteousness of the Lord without blame.

7 But they had no son, because Elizabeth was barren, and they were both well on in years.

8 And it happened, while he was ministering in the order of his ministry before God,

9 According to the custom of the priesthood, his turn came to burn incense; so he entered the temple of the Lord.

10 And all the congregation of the people prayed outside, at the time of incense.

11 And the angel of the Lord appeared to Zacharias, standing on the right of the altar of incense.

12 And when Zacharias saw him he became dumbfounded, and fear came upon him.

13 And the angel said to him, Fear not, Zacharias; for your prayer has been heard, and your wife Elizabeth will bear you a son, and you will call his name John.

14 And you will have joy and gladness; and a great many will rejoice at his birth.

15 For he will be great before the Lord, and he will not drink wine and strong drink; and he will be filled with the Holy Spirit, while he is still in the womb of his mother.

16 And many Israelites he will cause to turn to the Lord their God.

17 And he will go before them with the spirit and the power of Elijah, to turn the hearts of parents to their children, and those who are disobedient to the wisdom of the righteous; and he will prepare a true people for the Lord.

18 And Zacharias said to the angel, How will I understand this? for I am an old man, and my wife is well on in years.

19 And the angel answered, and said to him, I am Gabriel, who stand in the presence of God; and I am sent to speak to you, and to bring you these glad tidings.

20 From henceforth you will be dumb, and not able to speak, till the day these things happen, because you did not believe these my words which are to be fulfilled in their time.

21 Now the people stood waiting for Zacharias, and wondered because he remained so long in the temple.

22 When Zacharias came out, he could not speak with them; and they understood that he had seen a vision in the temple; and he made signs to them with his eyes, but remained dumb.

23 And when the days of his ministry were finished, he went to his house.

24 And it happened after those days, his wife Elizabeth conceived, and hid herself for five months; and she said,

25 The Lord has done these things to me in the days that he has been mindful of me, to remove my reproach among men.

26 ¶ Now in the sixth month the angel Gabriel was sent from God to Galilee, to a city called Nazareth,

27 To a virgin who was acquired for a price for a man named Joseph, of the house of David; and the name of the virgin was Mary.

28 And the angel went in and said to her, Peace be to you, O full of grace; our Lord is with you, O blessed one among women.

29 When she saw him, she was disturbed at his word,

and wondered what kind of salutation this could be.

30 And the angel said to her, Fear not, Mary; for you have found grace with God.

31 For behold, you will conceive and give birth to a son, and you will call his name Jesus.

32 He will be great, and he will be called the Son of the Highest; and the Lord God will give him the throne of his father David.

33 And he will rule over the house of Jacob for ever; and there will be no limit to his kingdom.

34 Then Mary said to the angel, How can this be, for no man has known me.

35 The angel answered and said to her, The Holy Spirit will come, and the power of the Highest will rest upon you; therefore the one who is to be born of you is holy, and he will be called the Son of God.

36 And behold, Elizabeth your kinswoman has also conceived a son in her old age; and yet this is the sixth month with her, who is called barren.

37 For nothing is impossible for God.

38 Mary said, Here I am, a handmaid of the Lord; let it be to me according to your word. And the angel went away from her.

39 ¶ In those days, Mary rose up, and went hurriedly to a mountain, to a city of Judaea.

40 And she entered the house of Zacharias, and saluted Elizabeth.

41 And when Elizabeth heard the salutation of Mary, the babe leaped in her womb; and Elizabeth was filled with Holy Spirit.

42 And she cried in a loud voice, and said to Mary, Blessed are you among women, and blessed is the fruit of your womb.

43 How does this happen to me, that the mother of my Lord should come to me?

44 For behold, when the voice of your salutation fell on my ears, the babe in my womb leaped with great joy.

45 And blessed is she who believed; for there will be a fulfillment of the things which were spoken to her from the Lord.

46 And Mary said, My soul magnifies the Lord,

47 And my spirit rejoices in God my Saviour.

48 For he has regarded the meekness of his handmaid; for behold, from henceforth, all generations shall envy me.

49 For he who is mighty has done great things to me; holy is his name.

50 And his mercy is for centuries and generations, upon those who fear him.

51 He has brought victory with his arm; he has scattered the proud in the imagination of their heart.

52 He has put down the mighty from their seats, and he has lifted up the meek.

53 He has filled the hungry with good things; and dismissed the rich empty.

54 He has helped his servant Israel, and has remembered his mercy;

55 Just as he spoke with our forefathers, with Abraham, and with his seed for ever.

56 ¶ Mary stayed with Elizabeth about three months, and she returned to her own home.

57 ¶ Now the time came for Elizabeth to be delivered, and she gave birth to a son.

58 And when her neighbors and relatives heard that God had increased his mercy to her, they rejoiced with her.

59 ¶ And it happened on the eighth day, they came to circumcise the boy; and they would have called him Zacharias, after the name of his father.

60 And his mother answered and said to them, Not so; but he should be called John.

61 And they said to her, There is no man in your family, who is called by this name.

62 Then they made signs to his father, what he wanted to call him.

63 And he asked for a tablet and wrote, saying, John is his name. And every one was surprised.

64 And immediately his mouth and his tongue were opened, and he spoke and blessed God.

65 And fear came on all their neighbors; and these things were spoken throughout the mountain of Judaea.

66 And all who heard it reasoned in their hearts, saying, What a boy he will be! And the hand of the Lord was with him.

67 ¶ And his father Zacharias was filled with the Holy Spirit, and prophesied, and said,

68 Blessed is the Lord, the God of Israel; for he has visited his people and wrought a salvation for them.

69 And he has raised up a horn of salvation for us in the house of his servant David;

70 Just as he spoke by the

mouth of his holy prophets, who have been for ages,

71 That he would save us from our enemies, and from the hand of all who hate us.

72 He has shown mercy to our fathers, and he has remembered his holy covenants;

73 And the oaths which he swore to Abraham our father,

74 To grant to us, that we may be saved from the hand of our enemies, and serve before him without fear,

75 In justice and righteousness all our days.

76 And you, boy, will be called the prophet of the Highest; for you will go before the face of the Lord, to prepare his way;

77 To give knowledge of life to his people by the forgiveness of their sins,

78 Through the mercy and kindness of our God; whereby we shall be visited by a ray from above,

79 To give light to those who sit in darkness and in the shadows of death, to guide our feet into the way of peace.

80 The boy grew and became strong in spirit; and he was in the desert until the day of his appearance to Israel.

CHAPTER 2

AND it happened in those days that there went out a decree from Caesar Augustus, to take a census of all the people in his empire.

2 This first census took place during the governorship of Quirinius in Syria.

3 And every man went to be registered in his own city.

4 Joseph also went up from Nazareth, a city of Galilee, to Judaea, to the city of David, which is called Bethlehem; because he was of the house and family of David;

5 With his acquired wife Mary, while she was with child, that they may be registered there.

6 And it came to pass while they were there, that her days of deliverance were to be fulfilled.

7 And she gave birth to her first-born son; and she wrapped him in swaddling clothes, and laid him in a manger; because they had no place where they were lodging.

8 ¶ Now there were shepherds in that region, where they were staying, and they were watching their flocks at night.

9 And behold, the angel of God came to them, and the glory of the Lord shone on

Cf. dif. verses 72–78–1–2–3–5–7

them; and they were seized with a great fear.

10 And the angel said to them, Do not be afraid; for behold, I bring you glad tidings of a great joy, which will be to all the world.

11 For today is born to you in the city of David, a Saviour, who is the Lord Christ.

12 And this is a sign for you; You will find a babe wrapped in swaddling clothes, and laid in a manger.

13 And suddenly there appeared with the angel, many hosts of heaven, praising God, and saying,

14 Glory to God in the highest, and on earth peace and good hope for men.

15 ¶ And it happened, when the angels departed from them and went to heaven, the shepherds spoke to one another, saying, Let us go to Bethlehem, and see this thing that has happened, as the Lord has shown to us.

16 And they came very hurriedly, and found Mary, and Joseph, and the babe laid in the manger.

17 When they saw it, they made known the word which was spoken to them concerning the boy.

18 And all who heard it were amazed at the things which were spoken by the shepherds.

19 But Mary treasured all these things, and dwelt on them in her heart.

20 And the shepherds returned, glorifying and praising God for all that they had seen and heard, as it was spoken to them.

21 ¶ And when eight days were fulfilled to circumcise the child, his name was called Jesus; because he was named by the angel before he was conceived in the womb.

22 ¶ And when the days for their purification were fulfilled, according to the law of Moses, they brought him up to Jerusalem, to present him to the Lord;

23 As it is written in the law of the Lord, Every male that opens the womb shall be called holy to the Lord;

24 And to offer a sacrifice, as it is said in the law of the Lord, A pair of turtledoves, or two young pigeons.

25 Now there was a man in Jerusalem, whose name was Simon; and this man was pious and righteous, waiting for the consolation of Israel; and the Holy Spirit was upon him.

26 And it was said to him by the Holy Spirit, that he would

not see death, until he sees the Anointed of the Lord.

27 This man was led by the Spirit to the temple; and when the parents brought in the boy Jesus, to do for him according to what is commanded in the law,

28 He received him in his arms, and blessed God, and said,

29 Now dismiss thy servant, O my Lord, in peace, according to your word;

30 For behold, mine eyes have already seen your mercies,

31 Which you have prepared before the face of all peoples;

32 A light for a revelation to the Gentiles, and a glory to your people Israel.

33 ¶ And Joseph and his mother marvelled about these things which were spoken concerning him.

34 And Simon blessed them, and he said to Mary, his mother, Behold, this one is appointed for the fall and for the rise of many in Israel, and for a sign of dispute;

35 And a sword will pierce through your own soul; so that the thoughts of the hearts of many may be revealed.

36 And Hannah the prophetess, the daughter of Phanuel, of the tribe of Asher, was of a great age; and she had lived seven years with her husband from the days of her virginity.

37 Then she became a widow for about eighty-four years, and she never left the temple, and with fasting and prayer she worshipped day and night.

38 She also stood up at that hour, and gave thanks to the Lord, and spoke concerning him to every man who was looking forward to the salvation of Jerusalem.

39 ¶ And when they had done everything according to the law of the Lord, they returned to Galilee, to their own city Nazareth.

40 The boy grew and became strong in spirit, filled with wisdom; and the grace of God was upon him.

41 ¶ And his people went every year to Jerusalem during the feast of the passover.

42 And when he was twelve years old, they went up to the feast, as they were accustomed.

43 And when the feast days were over, they returned; but the boy Jesus remained in Jerusalem; and Joseph and his mother did not know it.

44 They thought that he was with the children of their party; and when they went a

Cf. dif. verses 30–32–34–37–38–42–44

day's journey, they sought for him among their own people and those who knew them.

45 But they could not find him; so they returned again to Jerusalem, looking for him.

46 After three days, they found him in the temple, sitting in the midst of the teachers, listening to them, and asking them questions.

47 And all those who heard him were amazed at his wisdom and his answers.

48 And when they saw him, they were astonished; and his mother said to him, My son, why have you done so to us? behold, I and your father have been looking for you with much anxiety.

49 He said to them, Why were you looking for me? did you not know that I would be in the house of my Father?

50 But they could not understand the word which he said to them.

51 So he went down with them and came to Nazareth; and he was subject unto them. And his mother treasured all these words in her heart.

52 And Jesus grew in his stature and in his wisdom, and in favor with God and men.

CHAPTER 3

IN the fifteenth year of the reign of Tiberius Caesar, during the governorship of Pontius Pilate in Judaea, when Herod was tetrarch of Galilee, and his brother Philip tetrarch of Ituraea and of the region of Trachonitis, and Lysanius tetrarch of Abilene,

2 During the high priesthood of Annas and Caiaphas, the word of God came to John, son of Zacharias, in the wilderness.

3 And he came throughout the country around Jordan, preaching the baptism of repentance for the forgiveness of sins;

4 As it is written in the book of the words of Isaiah the prophet, who said, The voice which calls in the wilderness, Prepare the way of the Lord, make the paths of our God straight in the plain.

5 Let all the valleys be filled up, and all the mountains and hills be levelled; let the crooked places be made straight, and the rough places like a plain;

6 And let every flesh see the salvation of God.

7 ¶ And he said to the people, who were coming to him to be baptized, O offspring of scorpions, who has warned

you to escape from the anger which is coming?

8 Therefore bring forth fruits which are worthy of repentance; and do not begin to say within yourselves, We have Abraham as our father; for I say to you that God can raise up children for Abraham from these stones.

9 Behold, the axe is already placed at the root of the trees; therefore every tree which bears not good fruits will be cut down and dropped in the fire.

10 And the people asked him saying, What then shall we do?

11 He answered and said to them, He who has two shirts, let him give to him who has not; and he who has food, let him do likewise.

12 And there came also publicans to be baptized, and they said to him, Teacher, what shall we do?

13 He said to them, Do not exact anything more over what is commanded you to exact.

14 And the soldiers also asked him saying, What shall we do? And he said to them, Do not molest any man, and do not despise any man; your own wages should be enough for you.

15 ¶ While the people were placing their hope on John, and all of them were thinking in their hearts, that perhaps he is the Christ;

16 John answered and said to them, Behold, I baptize you with water; but one is coming after me, who is greater than I, the strings of whose shoes I am not worthy to untie; he will baptize you with the Holy Spirit and with fire;

17 Who holds a shovel in his hand, and purifies his threshing; the wheat he gathers into his barns, and the straw he burns in the unquenchable fire.

18 Many other things also, he taught and preached to the people.

19 ¶ Now Herod the tetrarch, because he was rebuked by John concerning Herodias wife of Philip his brother, and for all the evil things that he was doing,

20 Added this also to them all, that he put John into prison.

21 ¶ It came to pass when all the people were baptized, Jesus also was baptized, and while he prayed the heaven was opened,

22 And the Holy Spirit descended on him, like a dove, and a voice from heaven,

Cf. dif. verses 14–15–16–17–20

saying, You are my beloved Son, with you I am pleased.

23 ¶ Now Jesus was about thirty years old, and he was supposed to be the son of Joseph, the son of Heli,

24 The son of Matthat, the son of Levi, the son of Melchi, the son of Jannai, the son of Joseph,

25 The son of Mattathias, the son of Amos, the son of Nahum, the son of Esli, the son of Naggai,

26 The son of Maath, the son of Mattathias, the son of Semei, the son of Joseph, the son of Juda,

27 The son of John, the son of Rhesa, the son of Zerubbabel, the son of Shealtiel, the son of Neri,

28 The son of Melchi, the son of Addi, the son of Kosam, the son of Elmodad, the son of Er,

29 The son of Jose, the son of Eliezer, the son of Jorim, the son of Mattitha, the son of Levi,

30 The son of Simon, the son of Juda, the son of Joseph, the son of Jonan, the son of Eliakim,

31 The son of Melea, the son of Mani, the son of Matta, the son of Nathan, the son of David,

32 The son of Jesse, the son of Obed, the son of Boaz, the son of Salmon, the son of Nahshon,

33 The son of Aminadab, the son of Aram, the son of Hezron, the son of Perez, the son of Juda,

34 The son of Jacob, the son of Isaac, the son of Abraham, the son of Terah, the son of Nahor,

35 The son of Serug, the son of Arau, the son of Peleg, the son of Eber, the son of Shalah,

36 The son of Cainan, the son of Arphaxad, the son of Shem, the son of Noah, the son of Lamech,

37 The son of Methuselah, the son of Enoch, the son of Jared, the son of Mahalaleel, the son of Cainan,

38 The son of Enosh, the son of Seth, the son of Adam, who was of God.

CHAPTER 4

NOW Jesus, full of the Holy Spirit, returned from the Jordan, and the Spirit carried him away into the wilderness,

2 Forty days, in order that he might be tempted by the adversary. And he did not eat anything in those days; and when they were over, at last he became hungry.

3 ¶ And the adversary said to him, If you are the Son of

God, command this stone to become bread.

4 Jesus answered and said to him, It is written, That it is not by bread alone that man can live, but by every word of God.

5 Then Satan took him up to a high mountain, and showed him all the kingdoms of the earth in a short time.

6 And the adversary said to him, I will give you all this power and its glory, which are entrusted to me, and I give it to whom I please.

7 If therefore you worship me, it will all be yours.

8 Jesus answered and said to him, It is written, You shall worship the Lord your God, and him only you shall serve.

9 And he brought him to Jerusalem, and made him to stand up on the pinnacle of the temple, and said to him, If you are the Son of God, throw yourself down from here;

10 For it is written, That he will command his angels concerning you, to watch you;

11 And they will take you up in their arms, so that even your foot may not strike a stone.

12 Jesus answered and said to him, It is said, You shall not tempt the Lord your God.

13 When the adversary was through with all his temptations, he left him for some time.

14 ¶ So Jesus returned in the power of the Spirit to Galilee; and the fame about him went out through all the country around them.

15 And he taught in their synagogues, and was praised by every man.

16 ¶ And he came to Nazareth, where he had been brought up; and he entered the synagogue on the sabbath day, as was the custom, and he stood up to read.

17 And the book of the prophet Isaiah was given to him. And Jesus opened the book, and found the place where it is written,

18 The Spirit of the Lord is upon me; because of this he has anointed me, to preach good tidings to the poor; and he has sent me to heal the broken-hearted, and to proclaim release to the captives, and sight to the blind; to strengthen with forgiveness those who are bruised,

19 And to preach the acceptable year of the Lord.

20 And he rolled up the scroll and gave it to the attendant, and went and sat

down. And the eyes of all who were in the synagogue were fixed on him.

21 And he began to say to them, To-day this scripture is fulfilled in your ears.

22 And all testified to him, and were amazed by the words of grace which came out of his mouth. And they said, Is not this man the son of Joseph?

23 Jesus said to them, You might probably tell me this proverb, "Physician, heal yourself"; and all that we heard you did in Capernaum, do also here in your own city.

24 Then he said, Truly I say to you, No prophet is acceptable in his own city.

25 For truly I say to you, There were many widows in Israel in the days of the prophet Elijah, when the heaven was closed for three years and six months, and there was a great famine throughout the land;

26 Yet Elijah was not sent to one of them, but to Zarephath of Sidon, to a widow.

27 And there were many lepers in Israel in the days of the prophet Elisha, and yet not one of them was cleansed, except Naaman the Syrian.

28 When those who were in the synagogue heard these things, they were all filled with anger.

29 And they rose up, and took him outside the city, and brought him to the brow of the mountain, on which their city was built, that they might throw him down from a cliff.

30 But he passed through the midst of them and went away.

31 ¶ And he went down to Capernaum, a city of Galilee, and he taught them on the sabbaths.

32 And they were astonished at his teaching; because his word had power.

33 And there was in the synagogue a man who had an unclean, demonic spirit, and he cried in a loud voice,

34 And said, Leave me alone, what have we in common, O Jesus the Nazarene? have you come to destroy us? I know who you are, "Holy One of God!"

35 And Jesus rebuked him, and said, Keep quiet, and come out of him. The demon threw him in the midst, and went out of him, and did him no harm.

36 And every man was seized with amazement, and spoke among themselves, saying, What kind of word is this, that he commands

unclean spirits with authority and power, and they go out!

37 And the fame about him went out through all the country around them.

38 ¶ And when Jesus went out of the synagogue, he entered the house of Simon. And Simon's mother-in-law was suffering with a severe fever; and they besought him for her.

39 And he stood by her, and rebuked the fever, and it left her; and she rose up immediately and ministered to them.

40 ¶ When the sun was setting, all who had sick people suffering from divers diseases brought them to him; and he laid his hand on each one of them, and healed them.

41 Demons also came out of many, who cried out saying, You are the Christ, the Son of God. And he rebuked them, and he would not allow them to speak; that they might not know that he is the Christ.

42 And in the morning, he came out and went to a desert place; and the people were looking for him, and came where he was; and they held him so that he might not leave them.

43 But Jesus said to them, I must preach the kingdom of God in other cities also; because I was sent for this.

44 And he preached in the synagogues of Galilee.

CHAPTER 5

IT came to pass when the people gathered around him to hear the word of God, he stood on the shore of the lake of Gennesaret.

2 And he saw two boats standing by the lake; but the fishermen had got out of them, and were washing their nets.

3 One of them belonged to Simon Peter; so Jesus went up and sat in it, and he asked to row it a little way from the shore to the water. And he sat and taught the people from the boat.

4 When he was through speaking, he said to Simon, Row out to the deep, and cast your net for a catch.

5 Simon answered and said to him, Teacher, we have toiled all night, and have caught nothing; but just because of your word, I will cast the net.

6 And when they had done this, they inclosed a great many fish; and their net was breaking.

7 So they signalled to their

Cf. dif. verses 41–42–3–6

partners in the other boat, to come and help them. And when they came, they filled both the boats, till they were almost sinking.

8 When Simon Peter saw it, he fell at the feet of Jesus, and said to him, I beg you, my Lord, leave me alone, for I am a sinful man.

9 For he was amazed, and all who were with him, because of the catch of fish which they took.

10 So also was it with James and John, sons of Zebedee, who were partners with Simon. But Jesus said to Simon, Do not be afraid; from henceforth you will be catching men for life.

11 And they brought the boats to land, and left everything, and followed him.

12 ¶ When Jesus was in one of the cities, there came a man who was covered with leprosy; and he saw Jesus and fell on his face, and besought him, and said, My Lord, if you will, you can cleanse me.

13 And Jesus stretched out his hand and touched him, and said to him, I will, be clean; and immediately his leprosy left him.

14 And he charged him not to tell any man; but go and show yourself to the priests, and make an offering for your cleansing, as Moses commanded, for a testimony to them.

15 ¶ And the fame concerning him went out the more; and many people gathered to hear him, and to be healed of their diseases.

16 But he departed into the wilderness, and prayed.

17 ¶ It came to pass on one of the days when Jesus was teaching, the Pharisees and the teachers of the law were sitting, who had come from every town of Galilee and Judaea and Jerusalem. And the power of God was present to heal them.

18 And some men brought a paralytic on a quilt-bed; and they wanted to go in and lay him before him.

19 And when they found they were not able to carry him in, because of many people, they went up on the roof, and they lowered him down on his quilt-bed from the ceiling into the midst before Jesus.

20 When Jesus saw their faith, he said to the paralytic, Man, your sins are forgiven.

21 And the scribes and the Pharisees began to reason saying, Who is this man who talks blasphemy? Who can

forgive sins, except God only?

22 But Jesus knew their thoughts, and he answered and said to them, What do you reason in your heart?

23 Which is easier to say, Your sins are forgiven, or just to say, Arise and walk?

24 But that you may know that the Son of man has authority on earth to forgive sins, he said to the paralytic, I tell you, Arise, take up your quilt-bed and go to your home.

25 And immediately he rose up before their eyes, and he took his quilt-bed and went to his house, praising God.

26 And every man was seized with amazement, and they praised God, and were filled with fear, saying, To-day we have seen wonders.

27 ¶ After these things, Jesus went out and saw a publican named Levi, sitting at the custom house; and he said to him, Follow me.

28 So he left everything, and rose up, and went after him.

29 And Levi gave him a great reception in his house; and there was a large gathering of publicans and others, who were guests with them.

30 And the scribes and the Pharisees murmured and said to his disciples, Why do you eat and drink with publicans and sinners?

31 And Jesus answered and said to them, A physician is not needed for those who are well, but for those who are seriously sick.

32 I have not come to call the righteous, but the sinners to repentance.

33 ¶ They said to him, Why do the disciples of John always fast and pray, and also those of the Pharisees; but yours eat and drink?

34 He said to them, You cannot make the sons of the wedding feast fast, so long as the bridegroom is with them.

35 But the days will come, when the bridegroom is taken from them, then they will fast in those days.

36 And he told them a parable, No man cuts a piece of cloth from a new garment and puts it on a worn out garment; so that he may not cut the new, and the new piece will not blend with the old.

37 No man pours new wine into worn out skins; else the new wine will rend the skins, and the wine will run out, and the skins will be ruined.

38 But they pour new wine into new skins, and both are well preserved.

39 And no man drinks old wine, and immediately wants new wine; for he says, The old is delicious.

CHAPTER 6

IT came to pass on the sabbath, as Jesus walked through the wheat fields, his disciples plucked ears of wheat, and rubbed them in their hands and did eat.

2 But some of the men of the Pharisees said to them, Why are you doing what is unlawful to do on the sabbath?

3 Jesus answered and said to them, Have you not read this, what David did when he and those who were with him were hungry?

4 He entered into the house of God, and took the bread that was on the table of the Lord and did eat it, and he gave it to those who were with him; that which was unlawful to eat but only for the priests.

5 And he said to them, The Son of man is Lord of the sabbath.

6 ¶ And it came to pass on another sabbath, he entered into the synagogue and taught; and there was there a man whose right hand was withered.

7 And the scribes and the Pharisees watched him, to see if he would heal on the sabbath, so that they might find an accusation against him.

8 But he knew their thoughts, and said to the man whose hand was withered, Rise up and come to the center of the synagogue. And when he came and stood up,

9 Jesus said to them, I will ask you, What is lawful to do on the sabbath, that which is good or that which is bad? to save a life or to destroy it?

10 And he looked at all of them, and said to him, Stretch out your hand. And he stretched it out; and his hand was restored like the other.

11 But they were filled with bitterness; and discussed with each other what to do with Jesus.

12 ¶ It happened in those days, Jesus went out to a mountain to pray, and he remained all night in prayer to God.

13 And at daybreak, he called his disciples; and he chose twelve from them, whom he called apostles;

14 Simon who is called Peter, and Andrew his brother, and James and John, and Philip and Bartholomew,

15 And Matthew and Thomas, and James the son of Alphaeus and Simon who is called the Zealot,

16 And Judas the son of James, and Judas of Iscariot, who became the traitor.

17 ¶ And Jesus went down with them and stood up in the plain; and a large group of his disciples, and a large crowd of people, from all over Judaea, and from Jerusalem, and from the sea coast of Tyre and Sidon, who had come to hear his word, and to be healed of their diseases;

18 And those who were suffering from unclean spirits, were healed.

19 And all the people wanted to touch him; because power proceeded from him, and he healed them all.

20 ¶ And he lifted up his eyes on his disciples and said, Blessed are you poor, for the kingdom of God is yours.

21 Blessed are you who hunger now, for you shall be filled. Blessed are you who weep now, for you shall laugh.

22 Blessed are you, when men hate you, and discriminate against you, and reproach you, and publish your names as bad, for the sake of the Son of man.

23 Be glad and rejoice in that day, for your reward is increased in heaven; for their fathers did the same to the prophets.

24 But woe to you, rich men! for you have already received your comforts.

25 Woe to you who are full! for you will hunger. Woe to you who laugh now! for you will weep and mourn.

26 Woe to you when men speak well of you! for so did their fathers to the false prophets.

27 But I say to you who hear, Love your enemies, and do good to those who hate you,

28 And bless those who curse you, and pray for those who compel you to carry burdens.

29 And he who strikes you on your cheek, offer him the other; and he who takes away your robe. do not refuse your shirt also.

30 Give to every one who asks you; and from him who takes away what is yours, do not demand it back again.

31 Just as you want men to do to you, do also to them likewise.

32 For if you love those who love you, what is your favor? for even sinners love those who love them.

33 And if you do good only to those who do good to you, what is your favor? for sinners also do the same.

34 And if you lend only to him from whom you expect to be paid back, what is your favor? for sinners also lend to sinners, to be paid back likewise.

35 But love your enemies, and do good to them, and lend, and do not cut off any man's hope; so your reward will increase, and you will become sons of the Highest; for he is gracious to the wicked and the cruel.

36 Be therefore merciful, as your Father also is merciful.

37 Judge not, and you will not be judged; condemn not, and you will not be condemned; forgive, and you will be forgiven.

38 Give, and it will be given to you; good measure shaken up and running over, they will pour into your robe.[1] For with the measure that you measure, it will be measured to you.

39 And he told them a parable, Can a blind man take care of a blind man? will they not both fall in a pit?

40 There is no disciple who is more important than his teacher; for every man who is well developed will be like his teacher.

41 Why do you see the splinter in your brother's eye, and do not see the beam in your own eye?

42 Or how can you say to your brother, My brother, let me take out the splinter from your eye, when behold, you do not see the beam in your own eye? O hypocrites, first take out the beam from your own eye, and then you will see clearly to take out the splinter from your brother's eye.

43 There is no good tree that bears bad fruits, nor a bad tree that bears good fruits.

44 For every tree is known by its own fruits. For they do not gather figs from thistles, nor gather grapes from a bramble bush.

45 A good man brings out good things from the good treasure of his heart; and a bad man from the bad treasure of his heart brings out bad things; for from the abundance of the heart the lips speak.

46 Why do you call me, My Lord, my Lord, and do not do what I say?

47 Every man who comes to me and hears my words and

[1] Easterners carry wheat from house to house in the folds of their robes.

Cf. dif. verses 33–34–35–38–39–40–41–42

does them, I will show you what he is like.

48 He is like a man who built a house, and dug deep, and laid its foundations upon the rock; and when the flood came, the flood beat upon that house, and could not shake it; for its foundation was laid upon a rock.

49 And he who hears and does not, is like a man who built his house on the earth without a foundation; and when the river beat against it, it fell immediately, and the fall of that house was great.

CHAPTER 7

WHEN he had finished all of these words, in the hearing of the people, Jesus entered Capernaum.

2 Now the servant of a centurion was seriously sick, who was very dear to him; and he was near death.

3 And when he heard about Jesus, he sent to him Jewish elders, and besought him to come and heal his servant.

4 When they came to Jesus, they begged him earnestly, saying, He is worthy to have this done for him;

5 For he loves our people, and has even built us a synagogue.

6 Jesus went with them. And when he was not far from the house, the centurion sent some of his friends to him, and said, My Lord, do not trouble yourself; for I am not worthy that you should enter under my roof;

7 That is why I was not worthy to come to you; but just say a word and my boy will be healed.

8 For I am also a man in government service, and there are soldiers under my command; and I say to this one, Go, and he goes; and to another, Come, and he comes; and to my servant, Do this, and he does it.

9 When Jesus heard these things, he was amazed at him, and he turned and said to the people who followed him, I say to you, not even in Israel have I found such faith as this.

10 So those who were sent returned to the house, and found the servant who was sick, healed.

11 ¶ And it came to pass on the next day, he was going to a city called Nain; and his disciples were with him, and many people.

12 And when they came near the gate of the city, he saw a dead man being carried out, who was the only son of his mother, and his mother was a widow; and

Cf. dif. verses 48–4–7–8–11

many people of the city were with her.

13 When Jesus saw her, he had compassion on her, and said to her, Weep not.

14 Then he went and touched the bier, and those who carried it stood still. And he said, Young man, I tell you, Arise.

15 And the dead man sat up, and began to speak. And he gave him to his mother.

16 And all men were seized with fear; and they praised God, saying, A great prophet is risen among us; and, God has visited his people.

17 And this word about him went out through all Judaea, and through the country around them.

18 ¶ And John's disciples told him all these things.

19 So John called two of his disciples, and sent them to Jesus, and said, Are you the one who is to come? or are we to expect another one?

20 And they came to Jesus and said to him, John the Baptist has sent us to you, saying, Are you the one who is to come? or are we to expect another one?

21 In that very hour, he healed a great many of their diseases and plagues, and of evil spirits; and he gave sight to many blind men.

22 So Jesus answered and said to them, Go and tell John everything that you have seen and heard; that the blind see, and the lame walk, and the lepers are cleansed, and the deaf hear, and the dead rise up, and the poor are given hope.

23 And blessed is he, who does not stumble on account of me.

24 ¶ When John's disciples had gone, Jesus began to speak to the people concerning John, What did you go out to the wilderness to see? A reed which is shaken by the wind?

25 If not so, what did you go out to see? A man dressed in fine clothes? Behold, those who wear fine clothes and live delicately, are in kings' houses.

26 And if not so, what did you go out to see? A prophet? Yes, I say to you, and much more than a prophet.

27 This is he of whom it is written, Behold, I send my messenger before your face, to prepare the way before you.

28 I say to you, that there is no prophet among those who are born of women, who is greater than John the Baptist; and yet even the least person in the kingdom of God is greater than he.

Cf. dif. verses 22–23–25–26

29 And all the people who heard it, even the publicans, justified themselves before God, for they were baptized with the baptism of John.

30 But the Pharisees and the scribes suppressed the will of God in themselves, because they were not baptized by him.

31 ¶ To whom, therefore, shall I liken the men of this generation? and to what are they like?

32 They are like boys who sit in the street, and call to their friends and say, We have sung to you but you did not dance; and we have wailed to you and you did not weep.

33 For John the Baptist came, neither eating bread nor drinking wine; and you say, He is insane.

34 The Son of man came, eating and drinking; and you say, Behold, a glutton and a winebibber, and a friend of publicans and sinners!

35 And yet wisdom is justified by all its works.

36 ¶ Then one of the Pharisees came and asked him to eat with him. And he entered the house of that Pharisee and reclined as a guest.

37 Now there was in that city a woman who was a sinner; and when she knew that he was a guest in the Pharisee's house, she took an alabaster cruse of perfume,

38 And she stood behind him at his feet, weeping, and she began to wet his feet with her tears, and to wipe them with the hair of her head, and she kissed his feet, and anointed them with perfume.

39 When the Pharisee who had invited him saw it, he reasoned in himself and said, If this man were a prophet, he would have known who she was and her reputation; for the woman who has touched him is a sinner.

40 Jesus answered and said to him, Simon, I have something to tell you. He said to him, Say it, teacher. Jesus said to him,

41 There were two men who were debtors to a creditor; one of them owed him five hundred pence, and the other one fifty pence.

42 And because they had nothing to pay, he forgave them both. Which one of them will love him more?

43 Simon answered and said, I think the one to whom he forgave more. Jesus said to him, You have judged truly.

44 And he turned to the

Cf. dif. verses 29–30–32–38–39–44

woman, and said to Simon, Do you see this woman? I entered your house, you did not give me even water for my feet; but she has wet my feet with her tears, and wiped them with her hair.

45 You did not kiss me; but she, since she entered, has not ceased to kiss my feet.

46 You did not anoint my head with oil; but she has anointed my feet with perfume.

47 For this reason, I say to you, Her many sins are forgiven, because she loved much; but he to whom little is forgiven, loves little.

48 And he said to the woman, Your sins are forgiven.

49 Then the guests began to say within themselves, Who is this man who forgives even sins?

50 Jesus said to the woman, Your faith has saved you; go in peace.

CHAPTER 8

AND it came to pass after these things, Jesus was traveling in cities and villages, preaching and giving good news of the kingdom of God. And his twelve were with him,

2 And the women who were healed of diseases and un-clean spirits, Mary who is called of Magdala, from whom seven demons went out,

3 And Joanna, the wife of Chuza the steward of Herod, and Susanna, and many others, who ministered to them of their wealth.

4 ¶ And when many people had gathered, and were coming to him from all the cities, he spoke by parables.

5 The sower went out to sow his seed. And when he sowed, some fell on the roadside; and it was trodden under foot, and the birds ate it.

6 Other fell upon the rock; and sprung up earlier, and because it had no moisture, it dried up.

7 And other fell among thistles; and the thistles sprung up with it and choked it.

8 And other fell in good and fertile ground; and sprung up and bore fruit a hundredfold. And when he said this, he cried out, He who has ears to hear, let him hear.

9 ¶ And his disciples asked him, What is this parable?

10 He said to them, To you it is granted to know the mystery of the kingdom of God; but to the rest it has to be said in figures; for while

they see, they do not perceive; and while they hear, they do not understand.

11 ¶ This is the parable. The seed is the word of God.

12 Those on the roadside are those who hear the word; and the enemy comes and takes away the word from their heart, so that they may not believe and be saved.

13 Those on the rock are those who when they have heard, receive the word with joy; and yet they have no root, but their belief is for a while, and in time of trial they stumble.

14 That which fell among the thistles are those who hear the word, and then choke themselves with worries and riches and worldly covetousness, and bear no fruit.

15 But that in good soil, these are those who hear the word with pure and good heart, and keep it, and bear fruit with patience.

16 ¶ No man lights a lamp and covers it with a vessel, or puts it under the bed; but he puts it on the lamp holder, that whoever enters sees its light.

17 For there is nothing covered which will not be uncovered; and nothing hidden which will not be known, and come to light.

18 Take heed how you hear; for he who has, to him shall be given; and he who has not, even that which he thinks he has shall be taken away from him.

19 ¶ And there came to him his mother and his brothers, and they were not able to speak to him because of the crowd.

20 And they said to him, Your mother and your brothers are standing outside, and they want to see you.

21 He answered and said to them, These are my mother and my brothers, those who hear the word of God and do it.

22 ¶ It came to pass on one of the days, Jesus went up and sat in a boat with his disciples; and he said to them, Let us cross to the other side of the lake.

23 And while they were rowing Jesus fell asleep; and there rose a storm of wind on the lake; and the boat was near sinking.

24 And they came up and awoke him and said to him, Our teacher, our teacher, we are perishing. He got up and rebuked the winds and the waves of water, and they quieted down, and there was a calm.

25 And he said to them, Where is your faith? But as

Cf. dif. verses 13–14–17–18–23–25

they were frightened, they wondered, saying one to another, O who is this man, who even commands the winds, and the waves and the sea obey him?

26 And they rowed and came to the country of the Gadarenes, which is on the coast opposite Galilee.

27 And when he landed, he was met by a man from the city, who had the demon in him for a long time, and he did not wear clothes, and did not live in a house, but in the cemetery.

28 When he saw Jesus, he cried out and fell before him, and said in a loud voice, What have we in common, Jesus, Son of the Most High God? I beg you not to torment me.

29 For Jesus commanded the unclean spirit to go out of the man. For it was a long time since he was possessed, and bound with chains, and kept in fetters; but he would often break off his bonds and was driven into the desert by the demon.

30 Jesus asked him, What is your name? He said, Legion, because many demons had entered into him.

31 And they besought him not to command them to go down into the abyss.

32 Now there was there a herd of many swine feeding on the mountain; and they besought him to permit them to attack the swine. And he permitted them.

33 Then the demons went out of the man, and they attacked the swine; and that whole herd went straight to the cliff, and fell down into the lake and were drowned.

34 When the herdsmen saw what had happened, they fled and told it in the cities and in the villages.

35 And some men went out to see what had happened; and they came to Jesus, and found the man from whom the demons had gone out, dressed, and well behaved, and sitting at the feet of Jesus; and they were afraid.

36 And those who had seen it told them, how that lunatic was healed.

37 Then all the people of the Gadarenes besought him to leave them; because they were seized with a great fear; and Jesus went up into the boat, and returned from thence.

38 But the man from whom the demons had gone out, besought him to remain with him; but Jesus dismissed him, and said to him,

39 Return to your own

house, and declare what God has done for you. And he went away, and preached throughout the city what Jesus had done for him.

40 ¶ When Jesus returned, a large multitude welcomed him, for they were all expecting him.

41 And a man named Jairus, a leader of the synagogue, fell at the feet of Jesus, and besought him to enter into his house.

42 For he had an only daughter, about twelve years old, and she was near death. And as Jesus went with him, a large crowd pressed against him.

43 ¶ Now a woman who had the hemorrhage for twelve years, and had spent all her wealth for doctors, could not be healed by anybody.

44 She came near him from behind, and touched the edge of his cloak; and immediately her hemorrhage stopped.

45 And Jesus said, Who touched me? And when all of them denied it, Simon Peter and those who were with him said to him, Teacher, the crowds are troubling you and pressing on you, and yet you say, Who has touched me?

46 But he said, Some one has touched me, for I know that power has gone out of me.

47 When the woman saw that she could not deceive him, she came trembling, and she fell down and worshipped him; and she said in the presence of all the people for what purpose she had touched him, and how she was healed immediately.

48 Jesus said to her, Have courage, my daughter; your faith has healed you; go in peace.

49 ¶ While he was still talking, there came a man from the house of the leader of the synagogue, and said to him, Your daughter has died, do not trouble the teacher.

50 Jesus heard it and he said to the father of the girl, Do not be afraid, but only believe, and she will be restored to life.

51 Jesus came into the house, and he did not allow anyone to enter with him, except Simon and James and John, and the father and mother of the girl.

52 And all of them were weeping and mourning over her; but Jesus said, Do not weep, for she is not dead but asleep.

53 And they laughed at him, for they knew that she was dead.

54 Then he put everybody out, and held her by her hand, and called her, and said, Little girl, arise.

55 And her spirit returned, and she got up immediately; and he commanded to give her something to eat.

56 And her parents were amazed; but he warned them, not to tell any man what had happened.

CHAPTER 9

THEN Jesus called his twelve, and gave them power and authority over all the demons, and to cure diseases.

2 And he sent them out to preach the kingdom of God, and to heal the sick.

3 And he said to them, Do not take anything for the journey, neither a staff, nor a bag, nor bread, nor money; nor have two shirts.

4 And into whatever house you enter, remain there, and depart from thence.

5 And whoever will not welcome you, when you leave that city, shake off even the sand from your feet for a testimony to them.

6 And the apostles went out, and travelled in villages and cities, preaching the gospel, and healing everywhere.

7 ¶ Now Herod the tetrarch heard of all that was done by his hand; and he was amazed, because some men said that John has risen from the dead.

8 But others, that Elijah has appeared; and others, that one of the old prophets has risen.

9 So Herod said, I have beheaded John; but who is this one concerning whom I hear these things? And he wanted to see him.

10 ¶ When the apostles returned, they told Jesus everything which they had done. And he took them all alone to a lonely place in Bethsaida.

11 When the people found it out, they went after him; and he received them, and spoke to them concerning the kingdom of God, and he healed those who were in need of healing.

12 ¶ And when the day began to wane, his disciples came up and said to him, Dismiss the people, that they may go to the villages around us and to the farms, to lodge there, and find food for themselves; because we are in a lonely place.

13 Jesus said to them, You give them to eat. But they said, We do not have more than five loaves of bread and

two fish; unless we go and buy food for all this people.

14 For there were about five thousand men. Jesus said to them, Make them sit down in groups, fifty men in each group.

15 The disciples did so, and made them all sit down.

16 And Jesus took the five loaves of bread and the two fish, and looked up to heaven, and he blessed them, and broke and gave them to his disciples, to set before the people.

17 And they all ate and were filled; and they took up fragments of what was left over, twelve baskets.

18 ¶ While he prayed by himself, and his disciples were with him, he asked them and said, What do the people say concerning me that I am?

19 They answered and said to him, John the Baptist; and others Elijah; and others that one of the old prophets has risen.

20 He said to them, But you, what do you say that I am? Simon answered and said, The Messiah (the anointed one of God).

21 But he cautioned them, and warned them not to say this to anyone.

22 And he said to them, The Son of man must suffer a great many things, and he will be rejected by the elders and the high priests and the scribes, and they will kill him, and on the third day he will rise.

23 ¶ Then he said in the presence of everyone, He who wishes to come after me, let him deny himself, and take up his cross every day and follow me.

24 For he who wishes to save his life, shall lose it; but he who loses his life for my sake, he shall save it.

25 For how can a man be benefited, if he gain the whole world, but lose his own soul, or even weakens it?

26 For whoever is ashamed of me and of my words, the Son of man will be ashamed of him, when he comes with the glory of his Father, accompanied by his holy angels.

27 I tell you the truth, that there are men who stand here, who will not taste death, until they see the kingdom of God.

28 ¶ And it came to pass about eight days after these words, Jesus took Simon, and James and John, and went up into a mountain to pray.

29 And while he prayed, the appearance of his face was

Cf. dif. verses 14–18–20–22–23–26

changed, and his clothes became white and dazzling.

30 And behold, two men were speaking with him, who were Moses and Elijah;

31 Who appeared in glory, and spoke concerning his departure which was to end at Jerusalem.

32 And Simon and those who were with him were heavy with sleep; and when they awoke they saw his glory, and the two men who stood with him.

33 And when they began to leave him, Simon said to Jesus, Teacher, it is better for us to remain here; and let us make three shelters, one for you, one for Moses, and one for Elijah; but he did not know what he was saying.

34 And when he had said these things, there came a cloud and overshadowed them; and they were frightened when they saw Moses and Elijah enter into the cloud.

35 And there came a voice out of the cloud, saying, This is my beloved Son, hear him.

36 And when the voice was heard, they found Jesus alone. And they kept silent, and in those days they did not tell any man what they saw.

37 ¶ And it came to pass the next day, as they came down from the mountain, they were met by many people.

38 And one of the men of that crowd cried out and said, O teacher, I beg you to have mercy on me. I have an only son,

39 And a spirit seizes him, and he suddenly cries out, and gnashes his teeth and foams; and it hardly leaves him when it has tormented him.

40 And I besought your disciples to cast it out; and they could not.

41 Jesus answered and said, O crooked and faithless generation, how long will I be with you, and preach to you? Bring your son here.

42 And as he brought him, the demon attacked him and convulsed him. And Jesus rebuked the unclean spirit, and healed the boy, and gave him to his father.

43 ¶ And they were all amazed at the greatness of God. And while every man wondered at everything which Jesus did, he said to his disciples,

44 Treasure these words in your ears; for the Son of man will be delivered into the hands of men.

45 But they did not understand this word, because it was hidden from them so that they may not know it;

and they were afraid to ask him concerning this word.

46 ¶ Then a reasoning entered into their minds, as to who was the greatest among them.

47 But Jesus knew the reasoning of their heart, and he took a boy and made him stand by him.

48 And he said to them, Everyone who receives a little boy like this one in my name, receives me; and he who receives me receives him who sent me; for whoever is least among you, let him be great.

49 And John answered and said, Teacher, we saw a man casting out demons in your name; and we forbad him, because he did not come with us, as your follower.

50 Jesus said to them, Do not forbid; for he who is not against you is for you.

51 ¶ And it happened, when the days to go up on his journey were fulfilled, he set his face to go to Jerusalem.

52 So he sent messengers ahead of him; and they went away and entered into a Samaritan village, to prepare for him.

53 But they did not receive him, because his face was set to go straight to Jerusalem.

54 When his disciples James and John saw it, they said to him, Our Lord, would you be willing that we command fire to come down from heaven and consume them, just as Elijah did?

55 He turned and rebuked them and said, You do not know of what spirit you are.

56 For the Son of man did not come to destroy lives, but to save. And they went to another village.

57 ¶ And while they were on the journey, a man said to him, My Lord, I will follow you wherever you go.

58 Jesus said to him, The foxes have holes, and the fowl of the sky a shelter; but the Son of man has no place even to lay his head.

59 He said to another, Follow me; but he said to him, My Lord, permit me first to go and bury my father.

60 Jesus said to him, Let the dead bury their own dead; but you go and preach the kingdom of God.

61 Another one said to him, I will follow you, my Lord; but permit me first to entrust my household to some one, and then come.

62 Jesus said to him, No man who puts his hand on the plough handle, and looks back, is fit for the kingdom of God.

CHAPTER 10

AFTER these things, Jesus selected from his disciples seventy others, and he sent them two by two before his face, to every place and city to which he was to go.

2 And he said to them, The harvest is great, and the laborers are few; ask therefore the owner of the harvest, to bring out laborers to his harvest.

3 Go forth; behold I send you as lambs among wolves.

4 Do not carry purses, nor bags, nor shoes; and do not salute any man on the road.

5 And to whatever house you enter, first say, Peace be to this house.

6 And if a man of peace is there, let your peace rest upon him; and if not, your peace will return to you.

7 Remain in that house, eating and drinking of what they have; for a laborer is worthy of his wages. Do not keep moving from house to house.

8 And into whatever city you enter, and they receive you, eat whatever they set before you;

9 And heal those who are sick in it, and say to them, The kingdom of God is come near to you.

10 But into whatever city you enter, and they do not receive you, go out into the street and say,

11 Even the sand of your city which cleaves to our feet, we shake it off to you; but know this that the kingdom of God has come near to you.

12 I say to you, that it will be much easier for Sodom in that day than for that city.

13 Woe to you, Chorazin! woe to you, Bethsaida! If the mighty works which were done in you, had been done in Tyre and Sidon, perhaps they might have repented with sackcloth and in ashes.

14 But, it will be easier for Tyre and Sidon at the judgement day than for you.

15 And you, Capernaum, which have exalted yourself up to heaven, you will be brought down to Sheol.

16 He who hears you hears me; and he who oppresses you oppresses me; and he who oppresses me oppresses him who sent me.

17 ¶ So the seventy whom he had sent returned with great joy, and they said to him, Our Lord, even the demons have submitted to us in your name.

18 He said to them, I saw Satan falling like lightning from heaven.

Cf. dif. verses 1–2–6–7–11–12–13–15–16

11

19 Behold, I give you power, to tread on snakes and scorpions, and over all the power of the enemy; and nothing shall harm you.

20 But do not rejoice in this that the demons submit to you; but rejoice because your names are written in heaven.

21 ¶ At that very hour, Jesus rejoiced in the Holy Spirit and said, I thank you, O my Father, Lord of heaven and earth, because you did hide these things from the wise and men of understanding, and did reveal them to children; yes, my Father, for so it was well pleasing in your presence.

22 And he turned to his disciples and said to them, Everything has been entrusted to me by my Father; and no man knows who is the Son, except the Father; and who is the Father except the Son, and to whomever the Son wishes to reveal him.

23 Then he turned to his disciples alone and said, Blessed are the eyes which see what you see.

24 For I say to you, that many prophets and kings desired to see what you see, and did not see it; and to hear what you hear, and did not hear it.

25 ¶ And behold, a scribe stood up to test him, and he said, Teacher, what shall I do to inherit eternal life?

26 Jesus said to him, What is written in the law? how do you read it?

27 He answered and said to him, You must love the Lord your God with all your heart, and with all your soul, and with all your strength, and with all your mind; and your neighbor as yourself.

28 Jesus said to him, You said the truth; do this and you shall live.

29 But as he wanted to justify himself, he said to him, And who is my neighbor?

30 Jesus said to him, There was a man who went down from Jerusalem to Jericho, and the bandits attacked him, and robbed him, and beat him, and left him with little life remaining in him, and they went away.

31 And it chanced a priest was going down that road; and he saw him and passed on.

32 And likewise a Levite came and arrived at that place, and saw him and passed on.

33 But a Samaritan, as he journeyed, came where he was, and when he saw him, he had compassion on him.

Cf. dif. verses 20–21–22–25–29–30–31–32

34 And he came to him and bound up his wounds, and poured on them wine and oil; and he put him on his own ass, and brought him to the inn, and took care of him.

35 And in the morning, he took out two pennies and gave them to the innkeeper, and said to him, Take care of him; and whatever you spend more, when I return, I will give it to you.

36 Who therefore of these three, appears to you, became neighbor of him who fell into the hands of the bandits?

37 He said, The one who had compassion on him. Jesus said to him, You go also, and do the same.

38 ¶ And it came to pass while they were journeying, he entered into a village; and a woman named Martha received him into her house.

39 And she had a sister whose name was Mary, and she came and sat at the feet of our Lord, and listened to his words.

40 But Martha was busy with many household cares, and she came and said to him, My Lord, you do not seem to care that my sister has left me to serve alone? tell her to help me.

41 Jesus answered and said to her, Martha, Martha, you are worried and excited about many things;

42 But one thing is more necessary; and Mary has chosen the good portion for herself, which shall not be taken away from her.

CHAPTER 11

AND it came to pass, while he was praying in a certain place, when he finished, one of his disciples said to him, Our Lord, teach us to pray, just as John also taught his disciples.

2 Jesus said to them, When you pray, say like this, Our Father in heaven, Hallowed be thy name. Thy kingdom come. Let thy will be done, as in heaven, so on earth.

3 Give us bread for our needs every day.

4 And forgive us our sins; for we have also already forgiven all who are indebted to us. And do not let us enter into temptation; but deliver us from error.

5 And he said to them, Who is among you who has a friend, and he should go to him at midnight, and say to him, My friend, loan me three loaves;

6 For a friend has come to me from a journey, and I have nothing to set before him.

7 And his friend from inside would answer and say to him, Do not trouble me; the door is already locked, and my children are with me in bed; I cannot get up and give you.

8 I say to you, that if because of friendship he would not give him, yet because of his persistence, he will rise and give him as much as he wants.

9 I say to you also, Ask, and it shall be given to you; seek, and you shall find; knock, and it shall be opened to you.

10 For everyone who asks, receives; and he who seeks, finds; and he who knocks, it is opened to him.

11 For who is among you, a father, if his son should ask him bread, why, would he hand him a stone? and if he should ask him a fish, why, would he hand him a snake instead of a fish?

12 And if he should ask him for an egg, why, would he hand him a scorpion?

13 So if you, who err, know how to give good gifts to your children, how much more will your Father give the Holy Spirit from heaven to those who ask him?

14 ¶ And while he was cast-ing out a demon from a dumb man, it came to pass when the demon went out, the dumb man spoke; and the people were amazed.

15 But some of the men among them said, This man casts out devils by Beelzebub, the prince of devils.

16 And others, tempting him, asked him for a sign from heaven.

17 But Jesus knew their thoughts, and said to them, Every kingdom which is divided against itself, shall be destroyed; and a house which is divided against itself shall fall.

18 And if Satan is divided against himself, how can his kingdom survive? and yet you say I am casting out devils through Beelzebub.

19 If I cast out devils through Beelzebub, by what do your sons cast them out? therefore they will be your judges.

20 But if I cast out devils by the finger of God, then the kingdom of God is come near you.

21 When a strong man is armed and keeps watch over his courtyard,[1] his property is safe;

22 But if there should come

---

[1] The courtyard is often used to house cattle and sheep, which is the main property of an Oriental.

one who is stronger than he, he will conquer him, and take away his armor in which he trusted, and divide his spoil.

23 He who is not with me is against me; and he who does not gather with me will scatter.

24 ¶ When an unclean spirit is gone out of a man, it goes away and travels in places where there is no water, to seek rest; and when it finds it not, it says, I will return to my own house from whence I came out.

25 And if it should come and find it warm and well furnished,

26 Then it goes away and brings seven other spirits worse than itself; and they enter and dwell there; and the end of that man will become worse than the beginning.

27 ¶ While he was saying these things, a woman out of the multitude lifted up her voice and said to him, Blessed is the womb which bore you, and the breasts which gave you suck.

28 He said to her, Blessed are they who hear the word of God and keep it.

29 ¶ And when the people were gathering, he began to say, This evil generation wants a sign; and no sign will be given to it, except the sign of the prophet Jonah.

30 For as Jonah was a sign to the Ninevites, so also will the Son of man be to this generation.

31 The queen of the south will rise up in judgement with the men of this generation, and condemn them; for she came from the far ends of the earth to hear the wisdom of Solomon; and behold, a greater than Solomon is here.

32 The men of Nineveh will rise up in judgement with this generation and condemn it; for they repented at the preaching of Jonah; and behold, a greater than Jonah is here.

33 ¶ No man lights a lamp and puts it in a hidden place, or under a basket, but on a lamp holder, so that those who enter may see its light.

34 The lamp of your body is your eye; when therefore your eye is clear, your whole body will also be lighted; but if it is diseased, your whole body will also be dark.

35 Take heed, therefore, lest the light which is in you be darkness.

36 If your whole body is lighted, and there is no part in it dark, the whole of it will give light, just as a lamp gives you light with its shining.

37 ¶ While he spoke, a Pharisee asked him to dine with him; and he entered and reclined.

38 When the Pharisee saw him, he was amazed because he did not first wash before dinner.

39 And Jesus said to him, Now you Pharisees clean the outside of the cup and the dish; but within you are full of extortion and iniquity.

40 O you shortsighted, did not he who made the outside also make the inside?

41 But give alms of what you have; and, behold, everything is clean to you.

42 But woe to you Pharisees! who take tithes on mint and dill and every kind of vegetable, but overlook justice and the love of God. These were necessary for you to have done, and the same by no means to have left undone.

43 Woe to you Pharisees! for you love chief seats in the synagogues, and salutations in the streets.

44 Woe to you, scribes and Pharisees, hypocrites! for you are like graves that cannot be recognised, and men walk over them and know it not.

45 One of the scribes answered and said to him, Teacher, when you say these things, you reproach us also.

46 But he said, Woe also to you, scribes! for you lay heavy burdens on men, and you yourselves do not touch these burdens even with one of your fingers.

47 Woe to you! for you build the tombs of prophets, whom your fathers killed.

48 Therefore you are witnesses, and you approve the works of your fathers; for they killed them, and yet you build their tombs.

49 For this reason, the wisdom of God also said, Behold, I will send them prophets and apostles, some of them they will persecute and kill;

50 That the blood of all the prophets, which was shed since the creation of the world, may be avenged on this generation;

51 From the blood of Abel to the blood of Zacharias, who was killed between the temple and the altar; yes, I say to you, it will be avenged on this generation.

52 Woe to you, scribes! for you have taken away the keys of knowledge; you did not enter, and those who were entering you hindered.

53 When he had said these things to them, the scribes

and the Pharisees were displeased, and they were enraged, and criticised his words.

54 And they plotted against him in many ways, seeking to catch something from his mouth, so that they might be able to accuse him.

CHAPTER 12

WHEN a large number of people had gathered together, so as to tread on one another, Jesus began to say to his disciples, First of all, Beware you of the leaven of the Pharisees, which is hypocrisy.

2 For there is nothing that is covered, that will not be uncovered; and what is hidden that will not be known.

3 For whatever you have said in darkness will be heard in the light; and what you have whispered in the ears in the inner chambers will be preached on the housetops.

4 I say to you, my friends, Do not be afraid of those who kill the body, and after that have nothing more to do.

5 But I will show you of whom to be afraid; of him who after he has killed has the power to throw into hell; yes, I say to you, Fear him.

6 Are not five sparrows sold for two pennies? and yet not one of them is lost before God.

7 But so far as you are concerned, even the hairs of your head are all numbered; therefore fear not; because you are much more important than many sparrows.

8 I say to you, Whoever will acknowledge me before men, the Son of man will also acknowledge him before the angels of God.

9 But he who denies me before men, I will deny him before the angels of God.

10 And whoever says a word against the Son of man, will be forgiven; but he who blasphemes against the Holy Spirit will not be forgiven.

11 When they bring you to the synagogues before the leaders and authorities, do not worry how you will answer, or what you will say;

12 For the Holy Spirit will teach you at that very hour what you ought to say.

13 ¶ And one of the men from the crowd said to him, Teacher, speak to my brother to divide the inheritance with me.

14 Jesus said to him, Man, who appointed me a judge or a property divider over you?

15 And he said to his disciples, Beware of all covetousness, because life does

not depend on abundance of wealth.

16 Then he told them a parable. The land of a rich man brought him a great many crops.

17 And he reasoned within himself and said, What shall I do, for I have no place to gather my crops?

18 So he said, I will do this; I will tear down my barns, and build them and enlarge them; and gather there all my wheat and my good things.

19 And I will say to myself, Myself, you have many good things stored up for many years; rest, eat, drink, and be happy.

20 But God said to him, O you shortsighted, this very night your life will be demanded of you; and these things which you have prepared, to whom will they be left?

21 Such is he who lays up treasures for himself, and is not rich in God.

22 And he said to his disciples, Therefore I say to you, Do not worry for your life, what you will eat; nor for your body, what you will wear.

23 For the life is much more important than food, and the body than clothing.

24 Observe the ravens; for they do not sow nor reap, and they have no storerooms and barns; and yet God feeds them; how much more important are you than the fowls?

25 Who is among you, who by worrying, can add to his stature one cubit?

26 So if you are not able to do the smaller thing, why do you worry about the rest?

27 Observe the flowers, how they grow; for they do not toil nor do they spin; but I say to you, that not even Solomon with all his glory was covered like one of these.

28 And if God clothes in such fashion the grass of the field, which today is and to-morrow falls into the fire-place; how much more is he to you, O you of little faith?

29 So do not be anxious what you will eat, and what you will drink, and let not your mind be disturbed by these things.

30 For worldly people seek after all these things; and your Father knows that these things are also necessary for you.

31 But you, seek the kingdom of God; and all of these things shall be added to you.

32 Do not be afraid, O little

flock; for your Father is pleased to give you the kingdom.

33 Sell your possessions and give them as alms; make for yourselves purses which do not wear out, and a treasure in heaven that does not run short, where the thief does not come near, and moth does not destroy.

34 For where your treasure is, there also will be your heart.

35 ¶ Let your girdle be fastened on your loins, and your lamps lighted.

36 And be like men who expect their master, when he will return from the wedding house; so that when he comes and knocks, they will immediately open the door for him.

37 Blessed are the servants, those whom when their master comes finds awake; truly I say to you, that he will gird himself, and make them sit down, and come in, and serve them.

38 If he should come in the second or the third watch and find them so, blessed are those servants.

39 But know this, that if the master of the house knew at what watch the thief would come, he would have kept awake, and not allowed his house to be plundered.

40 Therefore, you also be ready; for the Son of man will come in that very hour which you do not expect.

41 ¶ Simon Peter said to him, Our Lord, do you speak this parable to us, or also to all men?

42 Jesus said to him, Who is the faithful and wise steward, whom his master will appoint over his household, to give supplies in due time?

43 Blessed is that servant, whom when his master comes will find him so doing.

44 Truly I say to you, that he will appoint him over all his wealth.

45 But if that servant should say in his heart, My master has delayed his coming; and begins to beat the servants and maidservants of his master, and then begins to eat and drink and get drunk;

46 The master of that servant will come in a day and at an hour that he does not expect or know; and he will severely punish him, and place him with those who are not trustworthy.

47 And the servant who knows the wishes of his master, and does not make ready according to his wishes, will receive severe beating.

48 But he who does not know, and does what is

worthy of punishment will receive less beating. For to whomever more is given, of him more will be required; and to whom much is entrusted, more will be required of his hand.

49 ¶ I came to set the earth on fire; and I wish to do it, if it has not already been kindled.

50 I have a baptism to be baptized with; and I am oppressed until it is fulfilled.

51 Do you think that I have come to bring peace on earth? I say to you, No, but divisions;

52 For from henceforth there will be five in a house, who will be divided, three against two, and two against three.

53 For a father will be divided against his son, and a son against his father; a mother against her daughter, and a daughter against her mother; a mother - in - law against her daughter-in-law, and a daughter - in - law against her mother-in-law.

54 ¶ And he said to the people, When you see a cloud rise from the west, you immediately say, It will rain; and it is so.

55 And when the wind blows from the south, you say, It will be hot; and it is so.

56 O you hypocrites, you know how to discern the face of the earth and of the sky; how then is it that you do not discern this time?

57 Why do you not of yourselves judge what is right?

58 ¶ For when you go with your accuser to the district leader, while you are on the way give something and settle with him; otherwise he might take you to the judge, and the judge will deliver you to the prison warden, and the prison warden will throw you into prison.

59 Truly I say to you, you will not come out from thence, until you pay the last penny.

CHAPTER 13

AT that time, there came some men and told him about the Galileans, whose blood Pilate had mingled with their sacrifices.

2 And Jesus answered and said to them, Do you think that those Galileans were greater sinners than all the Galileans, because this happened to them?

3 No; but I say to you, that all of you also, if you do not repent, you will perish in the same way.

4 Or those eighteen, upon whom the tower in Siloam

fell, and killed them; do you think that they were greater sinners than all the men who live in Jerusalem?

5 No, but I say to you, that unless you repent, all of you will perish like them.

6 ¶ And he said this parable; A man had a fig tree planted in his vineyard; and he came and sought fruit on it, and he did not find any.

7 So he said to the laborer, Behold, for three years, I have been coming and seeking fruit on this fig tree, and found none; cut it down; why should it waste the ground?

8 The laborer said to him, My Lord, let it remain this year also, until I work it and fertilize it.

9 It might bear fruit; and if not, then you can cut it down.

10 ¶ While Jesus was teaching in one of the synagogues on the sabbath,

11 There was there a woman who was afflicted with rheumatism for eighteen years; and was bent down and could never straighten herself at all.

12 Jesus saw her, and called her, and said to her, Woman, you are loosened from your sickness.

13 And he laid his hand on her, and immediately she straightened up, and praised God.

14 But the leader of the synagogue answered with anger, because Jesus healed on the sabbath; and he said to the people, There are six days in which men should work; in those days you ought to come and be healed, and not on the sabbath day.

15 Jesus answered and said to him, O hypocrites, does not each one of you loosen his ox or his ass, from the manger, and go with it to give it drink?

16 This one is a daughter of Abraham, and behold, the adversary has bound her for eighteen years; was it not necessary for her to be loosened from this bond on the sabbath day?

17 And when he said these things, all who opposed him were ashamed; and all the people rejoiced over all the wonders which were done by his hand.

18 ¶ Jesus said, To what is the kingdom of God like? and to what shall I liken it?

19 It is like a grain of mustard seed, which a man took and cast in his garden, and it grew and became a large tree, and the fowls of the sky settled on its branches.

20 ¶ Again Jesus said, To

what shall I liken the kingdom of God?

21 It is like the leaven which a woman took and buried in three measures of flour, until it was all leavened.

22 ¶ And he journeyed through the villages and cities, teaching, and going to Jerusalem.

23 A man asked him, Are there only a few who are to be saved? Jesus said to them,

24 Strive to enter in through the narrow door; for I say to you, that many will seek to enter in, and will not be able.

25 From the hour when the master of the house rises up and locks the door, you will be standing outside and knocking at the door, and you will begin to say, Our Lord, our Lord, open for us; and he will answer and say, I say to you, I do not know you where you come from.

26 And you will begin to say, We have eaten and drunk in your presence, and you taught in our streets.

27 And he will say to you, I do not know you where you come from; depart from me, O you workers of iniquity.

28 There will be weeping and gnashing of teeth, when you see Abraham, and Isaac and Jacob, and all the prophets in the kingdom of God, but you thrown outside.

29 And they will come from the east and from the west, and from the south and from the north, and sit down in the kingdom of God.

30 And behold, there are some who are last, who will be first, and there are some who are first who will be last.

31 ¶ In that very day, some of the men of the Pharisees drew near and said to him, Get out and go away from here; because Herod wants to kill you.

32 Jesus said to them, Go and tell that fox, Behold, I cast out demons, and I heal today and tomorrow, and on the third day I will be through.

33 But I must do my work today and tomorrow, and I will leave the next day; because it is impossible that a prophet should perish outside of Jerusalem.

34 O Jerusalem, Jerusalem, murderess of prophets, and stoner of those who are sent to her! how many times I longed to gather your children together, as a hen which gathers her chickens under her wings, but you were not willing!

Cf. dif. verses 32–33–34

35 Behold, your house is left to you desolate; for I say to you, that you will not see me until you say, Blessed is he who comes in the name of the Lord.

CHAPTER 14

AND it came to pass when he entered the house of one of the leaders of the Pharisees to eat bread on a sabbath day, they watched him.

2 And there was a man before him, who had dropsy.

3 And Jesus answered and said to the scribes and Pharisees, Is it lawful to heal on the sabbath?

4 But they kept silent. So he took him, and healed him, and let him go.

5 And he said to them, Which one of you, if his son or his ox should fall into a pit on the sabbath day, would not immediately pull and bring him out?

6 And they could not answer him concerning this.

7 ¶ And he spoke a parable to those who were invited there, because he saw them choosing places among the front seats.

8 When you are invited of a man to a banquet house, do not go and sit in the front seat; it might be that a more honorable man than you is invited there;

9 And then he who has invited you and him will come, and say to you, Give the place to him; and you will be embarrassed when you get up and take a lower seat.

10 But when you are invited, go and sit at the lower end, so that when he who has invited you comes, he will say to you, My friend, go up and sit higher; and you will have glory before all who sit with you.

11 For whoever exalts himself will be humbled; and whoever humbles himself will be exalted.

12 He also said to him who had invited him, When you give a dinner or a supper, do not invite your friends, nor your brothers, nor your relatives, nor your rich neighbors; they might probably invite you, and you will be repaid for this.

13 But when you give a reception, invite the poor, the maimed, the lame and the blind;

14 And you will be blessed; for they have nothing to repay you; for you will be repaid at the resurrection of the righteous.

15 When one of the guests heard these things, he said to

him, Blessed is he who will eat bread in the kingdom of God.

16 Jesus said to him, A man gave a great supper, and invited many.

17 And he sent his servant at supper time to tell those who were invited, Behold, everything is made ready for you, come.

18 One and all, they began to make excuse. The first said to him, I have bought a field, and I am forced to go and see it; I beg you to excuse me for being called away.

19 Another said, I have bought five yoke of oxen, and I am just going to examine them; I beg you, excuse me for being called away.

20 Another said, I have just taken a wife, and therefore I cannot come.

21 And the servant came and told his master these things. Then the master of the house was angry, and said to his servant, Go out quickly to the streets and lanes of the city, and bring in here the poor, the afflicted, the maimed and the blind.

22 And the servant said, My Lord, it has been done as you commanded, and yet there is more room.

23 Then the master said to his servant, Go out to the highways and hedges, and urge them to come in so that my house may be filled.

24 For I say to you, that not one of those men who were invited shall taste of my supper.

25 ¶ And while many people were going with him, he turned and said to them,

26 He who comes to me and does not put aside his father, and his mother, and his brothers, and his sisters, and his wife, and his children, and even his own life, he cannot be a disciple to me.

27 And he who does not take up his cross and follow me, cannot be a disciple to me.

28 For which of you, who wishes to build a tower, does not at first sit down and consider its cost, to see if he has enough to finish it?

29 Lest after he has laid the foundation, he is not able to finish it, and all who see it will mock him,

30 Saying, This man began to build, but he was not able to finish.

31 Or which king, who goes to war to fight against a king equal to him, would not at first reason, whether he is able with ten thousand to meet the one who is coming

against him with twenty thousand?

32 And if not, while he is far away from him, sends envoys and seeks peace.

33 So every man of you, who would not leave all his possessions, cannot be a disciple to me.

34 Salt is good; but if the salt lose its savor, with what can it be salted?

35 It is good neither for the ground nor for fertilising; but it is thrown out. He who has ears to hear let him hear.

CHAPTER 15

THEN the publicans and sinners drew near to him to hear him.

2 And the scribes and Pharisees murmured, saying, He receives even the sinners and eats with them.

3 ¶ So Jesus told them this parable,

4 What man among you has one hundred sheep, and if one of them should get lost, would he not leave the ninety and nine in the open, and go in search of the one which is lost, until he finds it?

5 And when he finds it he rejoices, and he takes it on his shoulders.

6 And he comes to his house, and invites his friends and

neighbors, and says to them, Rejoice with me, for I have found my sheep which was lost.

7 I say to you, that such will be the joy in heaven over one sinner who repents, than over ninety and nine righteous, who need no repentance.

8 ¶ Or what woman who has ten coins, and should lose one of them, would [not light a lamp and sweep the house, and search for it carefully, until she finds it?

9 And when she finds it, she calls her women friends and neighbors, and says to them, Rejoice with me, for I have found my coin which was lost.

10 I say to you, that such will be the joy before the angels of God over one sinner who repents.

11 ¶ And Jesus said to them again, A man had two sons;

12 And his younger son said to him, My father, give me the portion, which is coming to me from your house. And he divided to them his possessions.

13 And after a few days, his younger son gathered everything that was his share, and went to a far-away country, and there he scattered his wealth in extravagant living.

14 And when all he had was

gone, there was a severe famine in that country; and he began to be in need.

15 So he went and got acquainted with one of the men of the city of that country; and he sent him to the field to feed swine.

16 And he craved to fill his stomach with the husks that the swine were eating; and yet no man would give him.

17 And when he came to himself, he said, How many hired workers are now in my father's house, who have plenty of bread, and I am here perishing with hunger!

18 I will rise and go to my father, and say to him, My father, I have sinned before heaven, and before you;

19 And I am no longer worthy to be called your son; just make me like one of your hired workers.

20 And he rose up and came to his father. And while he was yet at a distance, his father saw him, and had compassion on him, and he ran and fell on his neck and kissed him.

21 And his son said to him, My father, I have sinned before heaven and before you, and I am not worthy to be called your son.

22 But his father said to his servants, Bring the best robe and put it on him, and put a ring on his hand, and shoes on his feet;

23 And bring and kill the fat ox, and let us eat and be merry;

24 For this my son was dead, and has come to life; he was lost and is found. And they began to be merry.

25 But his elder son was in the field; and as he came near the house, he heard the voice of the singing of many.

26 And he called one of the boys, and asked him what it was all about.

27 He said to him, Your brother has come; and your father has killed the fat ox, because he received him safe and well.

28 And he became angry and would not go in; so his father came out and besought him.

29 But he said to his father, Behold, how many years I have served you, and I never disobeyed your commandment; and yet you never gave me even a kid, that I might make merry with my friends.

30 But for this son of yours, after he had wasted your wealth with harlots and come back, you have killed the fat ox.

31 His father said to him, My son, you are always with

me, and everything which is mine is yours.

32 It was right for us to make merry and rejoice; for this your brother was dead and has come to life; and was lost and is found.

CHAPTER 16

AND he spoke a parable to his disciples, There was a rich man, who had a steward; and they accused him that he was wasting his wealth.

2 So his master called him and said to him, What is this that I hear concerning you? give me an account of your stewardship; for no longer can you be a steward for me.

3 Then the steward said to himself, What will I do? for my lord will take away from me the stewardship? I cannot dig; and I am ashamed to beg.

4 Now I know what I will do, so that when I leave the stewardship, they will receive me in their houses.

5 And he called his lord's debtors, one by one, and said to the first, How much do you owe my lord?

6 He said to him, A hundred pounds of butter. He said to him, Take your note, sit down quickly, and write fifty pounds.

7 And he said to another, And you, what do you owe to my lord? He said to him, one hundred bushels of wheat. He said to him, Take your note, and sit down and write eighty bushels.

8 And the lord praised the unjust steward because he had done wisely; for the children of this world are wiser in their generation than the children of light.

9 And I also say to you, Make friends for yourselves with this wealth of iniquity; so that when it is gone they will receive you under their shelter for ever.

10 He who is faithful with little, is also faithful with much; and he who is dishonest with little, is also dishonest with much.

11 If therefore, you are not faithful with the wealth of iniquity, who will believe that there is any truth in you?

12 And if you are not found faithful with that which is not your own, who will give you that which is your own?

13 No servant can serve two masters; for either he will hate the one and like the other; or he will honor one and despise the other. You cannot serve God and mammon (wealth).

14 ¶ When the Pharisees

heard all these things, because they loved money, they ridiculed him.

15 But Jesus said to them, You are the ones who make yourselves righteous before men; but God knows your hearts. For what is highly esteemed among men is disgusting in the presence of God.

16 The law and prophets were until John; from that time the kingdom of God is preached, and everyone presses to enter into it.

17 It is easier for heaven and earth to pass away than for one letter of the law to pass away.

18 He who divorces his wife and marries another commits adultery; and he who marries the one who is separated commits adultery.

19 ¶ There was a rich man, who used to wear purple and fine linen, and every day he made merry very lavishly.

20 And there was a poor man named Lazarus, who was laid down at that rich man's door, afflicted with boils;

21 He longed to fill his stomach with the crumbs that fell from the rich man's tray; the dogs also came and licked his boils.

22 Now it happened that the poor man died, and the angels carried him into Abraham's bosom; and the rich man also died and was buried.

23 And while he was tormented in Sheol, he lifted up his eyes from a distance, and saw Abraham, and Lazarus in his bosom.

24 And he called in a loud voice and said, O my father Abraham, have mercy on me, and send Lazarus to dip his finger in water, and wet my tongue; for I am tormented in this flame.

25 Abraham said to him, My son, remember you received your pleasures when you were living, and Lazarus his hardships; and behold now he is comfortable here, and you are suffering.

26 Besides all these things, a great gulf is fixed between us and you; so that those who wish to cross over from here to you cannot, neither from there to cross over to us.

27 He said to him, If that is so, I beseech you, O my father, to send him to my father's house;

28 For I have five brothers; let him go and testify to them, so that they may not also come to this place of torment.

29 Abraham said to him, They have Moses and the

prophets;[1] let them hear them.

30 But he said to him, No, my father Abraham; but if only a man from the dead go to them, they will repent.

31 Abraham said to him, If they will not hear Moses and the prophets, neither will they believe even if a man should rise from the dead.

CHAPTER 17

AND Jesus said to his disciples, It is impossible but that offences should come; but woe to him by whose hand they come!

2 It were better for him that an ass' millstone were hanged on his neck, and he thrown into the sea, than cause one of these little ones to stumble.

3 ¶ Beware among yourselves. If your brother should sin, rebuke him; and if he repents, forgive him.

4 And if he should offend you seven times in a day, and seven times in a day turn to you and say, I repent; forgive him.

5 ¶ And the apostles said to our Lord, Increase our faith.

6 He said to them, If you have faith, even as a grain of mustard seed, you could say to this mulberry tree, Be uprooted and planted in the sea; it would obey you.

7 ¶ Now which of you has a servant who ploughs or feeds sheep, and if he should come from the field, would say to him, Enter in and sit down?

8 But he will rather say to him, Prepare something that I may have my supper, and gird yourself and serve me until I eat and drink; and then you also can eat and drink.

9 Why, will that servant receive praise, because he did what he was commanded to do? I do not think so.

10 Even you also, when you have done all the things which are commanded you, say, We are idle servants; we have only done what was our duty to do.

11 ¶ And it came to pass, while Jesus was going to Jerusalem, he passed through Samaritan territory which is towards Galilee.

12 And when he drew near to enter a village, he was met by ten lepers, and they stood afar off;

13 And they lifted their voices saying, O Jesus, our Master, have mercy on us.

14 And when he saw them he said to them, Go, show yourselves to the priests; and

---

[1] That is, the books of Moses and the prophets.

Cf. dif. verses 9–10–11 153

while they were going, they were cleansed.

15 But one of them, when he saw that he was cleansed, turned back, and with a loud voice praised God.

16 And he fell on his face at the feet of Jesus, thanking him; and this one was a Samaritan.

17 Jesus answered and said, Were there not ten who were cleansed? where are the nine?

18 Why did they separate themselves so as not to come and give praise to God, except this man who is of a strange people?

19 And he said to him, Arise, go, your faith has healed you.

20 ¶ When some of the Pharisees asked Jesus, when the kingdom of God would come, he answered and said to them, The kingdom of God does not come by observation.

21 Neither will they say, Behold, it is here! or, behold, it is there! for behold, the kingdom of God is within you.

22 And he said to his disciples, The days will come when you will covet to see one of the days of the Son of man, and you will not see it.

23 And if they should say to you, Behold, he is here! and behold, he is there! do not go.

24 For just as the lightning flashes from the sky, and all under the sky is lightened, such will be the day of the Son of man.

25 But first he must suffer a great many things, and be rejected by this generation.

26 Just as it happened in the days of Noah, such will it be in the days of the Son of man.

27 For they were eating and drinking, and marrying women, and giving in marriage, until the day when Noah entered the ark, and the flood came, and destroyed every man.

28 And again, just as it happened in the days of Lot; they were eating and drinking, and buying and selling, and planting and building;

29 But in the day when Lot went out of Sodom, the Lord sent down a rain of fire and sulphur from heaven, and destroyed them all.

30 Such will it be in the day when the Son of man appears.

31 In that day, he who is on the roof and his clothes in the house, will not come down to take them; and he

Cf. dif. verses 18—24—30

who is in the field will not return back.

32 Just remember Lot's wife.

33 He who desires to save his life shall lose it; and he who loses his life shall save it.

34 I say to you that in that very night two will be in one bed; one will be taken away, and the other left.

35 And two women will be grinding together; one will be taken away, and the other left.

36 Two will be in the field; one will be taken, and the other left.

37 They answered and said to him, Our Lord, to what place? He said to them, Wherever the corpse is, there will the eagles gather.

CHAPTER 18

HE also spake to them a parable, that they should pray always and not get weary.

2 There was a judge in a city, who did not fear God, and had no regard for men.

3 There was a widow in that city, and she used to come to him, saying, Avenge me of my accuser.

4 And he would not for a long time; but afterwards he said within himself, Though

I am not afraid of God, and have no regard for men;

5 Yet because this widow troubles me, I will avenge her, so that she may not keep coming and annoy me.

6 Then our Lord said, Hear what the unjust judge said.

7 Would not God avenge his chosen ones much more, who call upon him day and night, though he has patience with them?

8 I say to you, he will avenge them promptly. But when the Son of man comes, will he find faith on the earth?

9 ¶ And he said this parable against the men who relied upon themselves that they were righteous, and despised every man.

10 Two men went up to the temple to pray; one a Pharisee, and the other a publican.

11 And the Pharisee stood by himself, and prayed thus, O God, I thank thee, that I am not like the rest of men, extortioners, grafters, and adulterers, and not like this publican.

12 But I fast twice a week, and I give tithes on everything I earn.

13 But the publican stood afar off, and he would not even lift up his eyes to heaven, but smote his breast,

saying, O God, be merciful to me, I am a sinner.

14 I say to you, that this man went down to his house more righteous than the Pharisee. For everyone who exalts himself will be humbled; and everyone who humbles himself will be exalted.

15 ¶ They brought to him also little boys, that he may touch them; and his disciples saw them and rebuked them.

16 But Jesus called them, and said to them, Permit the children to come to me, and do not stop them; for the kingdom of heaven is for those who are like these.

17 Truly I say to you, He who will not receive the kingdom of God like a little boy will never enter into it.

18 And one of the leaders asked him and said to him, O good teacher, what shall I do to inherit life everlasting?

19 Jesus said to him, Why do you call me good? there is no one good, except one, that is God.

20 You know the commandments, You shall not kill; You shall not commit adultery; You shall not steal; You shall not bear false witness; Honor your father and your mother.

21 He said to him, All these I have obeyed from my boyhood.

22 When Jesus heard it, he said to him, You lack one thing; go, sell everything you have, and give it to the poor, and you will have a treasure in heaven; and come and follow me.

23 But when he heard these things, he felt sad, because he was very rich.

24 And when Jesus saw that he felt sad, he said, How difficult it is for those who have wealth to enter into the kingdom of God!

25 It is easier for a rope to go through the eye of a needle, than for a rich man to enter into the kingdom of God.

26 Those who heard it said to him, Who then can be saved?

27 But Jesus said, Those things which are impossible to men are possible to God.

28 Simon Peter said to him, Behold we have left everything and followed you.

29 Jesus said to him, Truly I say to you, that there is no man who leaves houses, or parents, or brothers, or wife, or children for the sake of the kingdom of God,

30 And will not receive many times more at this

time, and in the world to come life everlasting.

31 ¶ Then Jesus took the twelve and said to them, Behold, we are going up to Jerusalem, and all things which are written by the prophets concerning the Son of man will be fulfilled.

32 For he will be delivered to the Gentiles, and they will mock him, and spit on his face.

33 And they will scourge him, and curse him, and kill him; and on the third day he will rise again.

34 But they understood not one of these things; and this saying was hidden from them, and they did not know these things which were spoken to them.

35 ¶ And when he drew near Jericho, a blind man was sitting by the roadside and begging.

36 And he heard the voice of the people passing, and asked, Who is this?

37 They said to him, Jesus the Nazarene is passing.

38 And he cried and said, O Jesus, son of David, have mercy on me.

39 And those who were going before Jesus rebuked him, to keep quiet; but he cried the more, O son of David, have mercy on me.

40 So Jesus stood still, and commanded to call him to him; and as he came near him he asked him,

41 And said to him, What do you wish me to do for you? He answered and said, My Lord, that I may see.

42 And Jesus said to him, See; your faith has healed you.

43 And he saw immediately, and followed him, and praised God; and all the people who saw it, gave praise to God.

CHAPTER 19

AND when Jesus entered and passed through Jericno,

2 There was a man named Zacchaeus, who was rich and chief of the publicans.

3 And he wanted to see who Jesus was; but he could not because of the crowd, for Zacchaeus was small in his stature.

4 So he ran ahead of Jesus, and climbed up into a fig tree without leaves, that he might see him, because he was to pass that way.

5 When Jesus came to that place, he saw him and said to him, Make haste, come down, O Zacchaeus, for to-day I must remain in your house.

6 And he hastened, and came down, and welcomed him with joy.

7 Now when they all saw it, they murmured, saying, He has entered to stay in the house of a sinner.

8 But Zacchaeus rose up and said to Jesus, Behold, my Lord, half of my wealth I will give to the poor; and I will pay fourfold to every man from whom I have extorted.

9 Jesus said to him, Today life has come to this house, because he also is a son of Abraham.

10 For the Son of man came to seek and save that which was lost.

11 ¶ While they were listening to these things, he added and spoke a parable, because he was near Jerusalem, and they were expecting that the kingdom of God was to appear at that very hour.

12 And he said, A great man of a noble family went to a far country to receive for himself a kingdom, and return.

13 And he called his ten servants, and gave them ten pounds, and said to them, Do business until I come back.

14 But the people of his city hated him, and sent messengers after him, saying, We do not want him to rule over us.

15 And when he received the kingdom and returned, he commanded to call his servants, to whom he had given the money, that he might know what each one of them had gained in business.

16 The first one came and said, My lord, your pound has gained ten pounds.

17 He said to him, O good servant, because you are found faithful in a little, you will have charge over ten talents.[1]

18 And the second came and said, My lord, your pound has gained five pounds.

19 He said to this one also, You also will have charge over five talents.

20 And another one came and said, My lord, here is your pound which was with me, which I kept laid up in a purse.

21 For I was afraid of you, because you are a harsh man; you pick up what you have not laid down, and you reap what you have not sown.

22 He said to him, I will judge you from your own

[1]The Aramaic word *Kakra* talent is similar to the word *Karkha* province. The difference between the two words is indicated by a dot. A talent was the largest coin, equal to many pounds.

mouth, O wicked servant. You knew me that I am a harsh man, and pick up what I have not laid down, and reap what I have not sown.

23 Why then did you not give my money to the exchange, so that when I came I could demand it with its interest?

24 And he said to those who stood in his presence, Take away the pound from him, and give it to him who has ten pounds.

25 They said to him, Our lord, he has already with him ten pounds.

26 He said to them, I say to you, to everyone who has shall be given; and from him who has not, even that which he has will be taken away from him.

27 But those my enemies, who were not willing that I should rule over them, bring them here, and kill them before me.

28 ¶ And when Jesus had said these things, he went forward to go to Jerusalem.

29 And when he arrived at Bethphage and Bethany, on the side of the mountain which is called the Home of Olives, he sent two of his disciples,

30 And he said to them, Go to the village which is in front of us; and when you enter it you will find a colt tied up, on which no man has ever ridden; untie it and bring it.

31 And if any man should ask you, Why do you untie it? tell him this, Our lord needs it.

32 And those who were sent went away, and found just as he had told them.

33 And as they were untying the colt, its owners said to them, Why do you untie the colt?

34 And they said to them, Our Lord needs it.

35 And they brought it to Jesus; and they put their garments on the colt, and they set Jesus on it.

36 And as he went on, they spread their garments on the road.

37 And when he came near to the descent of the Mount of the Home of Olives, the whole multitude of the disciples began to rejoice, praising God with a loud voice for all the miracles which they had seen;

38 Saying, Blessed is the king who comes in the name of the Lord; peace in heaven and glory in the highest.

39 But some of the men of the Pharisees who were in

the multitude said to him, Teacher, rebuke your disciples.

40 He said to them, I say to you, that if these should keep silent, the stones would cry out.

41 ¶ And when he drew near and saw the city, he wept over it;

42 And he said, If you had only known those who are concerned in your peace, even in this your day! but now they are hidden from your eyes.

43 But the days will come to you, when your enemies will surround you, and oppress you from every place,

44 And will overthrow you, and your children within you; and they will not leave in you a stone upon a stone; because you did not know the time when you were to be visited.

45 ¶ And when he entered the temple, he began to put out those who were buying and selling in it;

46 And he said to them, It is written, My house is the house of prayer; but you have made it a cave of bandits.

47 And he taught every day in the temple. But the high priests and the scribes and the elders of the people sought to get rid of him;

48 But they were not able to find what to do to him; for all the people hung around him to hear him.

CHAPTER 20

AND it came to pass on one of the days, while he was teaching the people and preaching in the temple, the high priests and the scribes with the elders rose up against him.

2 And they said to him, Tell us by what authority you do these things, and who gave you this authority?

3 Jesus answered and said to them, I will also ask you a word, and you tell me;

4 The baptism of John, was it from heaven or from men?

5 And they reasoned with themselves, saying, If we should say from heaven, he will say to us, Why then did you not believe him?

6 And if we should say from men, all the people will stone us; for they regard John as a prophet.

7 So they said to him, We do not know whence it is.

8 Jesus said to them, Neither will I tell you by what authority I do these things.

9 ¶ And he began to say this parable to the people, A man planted a vineyard, and

Cf. dif. verses 42–43–46–48–1

leased it to laborers, and went on a journey for a long time.

10 And at the season he sent his servant to the laborers to give him of the fruit of the vineyard; but the laborers beat him and sent him back empty.

11 And again he sent another of his servants; but they beat him also, and treated him shamefully, and sent him back empty.

12 And again he sent the third one; but they wounded him also, and threw him outside.

13 Then the owner of the vineyard said, What shall I do? I will send my beloved son; perhaps they will see him and feel ashamed.

14 But when the laborers saw him, they reasoned with themselves, saying, This is the heir; come, let us kill him, and the inheritance will be ours.

15 So they cast him out of the vineyard, and killed him. What therefore will the owner of the vineyard do to them?

16 He will come and destroy those laborers, and give the vineyard to others. And when they heard it, they said, This will never happen.

17 But he looked at them and said, What is it that is written, The stone which the builders rejected, the same became the corner stone?

18 Whoever falls on that stone will be broken; and on whomever it falls it will scatter him.

19 The high priests and the scribes sought to lay hands on him that very hour; but they were afraid of the people; for they knew that he had spoken this parable against them.

20 ¶ So they sent spies disguised as righteous men, to ensnare him by a word, and deliver him to the judge, and then to the authority of the governor.

21 So they asked him, and said to him, Teacher, we know that you speak and teach truthfully, and you do not discriminate between men, but you teach the way of God justly.

22 Is it lawful for us to pay head-tax[1] to Caesar or not?

23 But he understood their craftiness and said, Why do you tempt me?

24 Show me a penny. Whose image and inscription are on it? They said, Caesar's.

25 Jesus said to them, Give therefore to Caesar what is

---

[1] This tax was levied on every male, and it is still resented in the Orient.

Caesar's and to God what is God's.

26 And they were not able to get a word from him before the people; and they were amazed at his answer, and kept silence.

27 ¶ Then came to him some of the men of the Sadducees, those who say there is no resurrection; and they asked him,

28 Teacher, Moses wrote to us, that if a man's brother should die, and has a wife without children, let his brother take his wife and raise up offspring for his brother.

29 Now there were seven brothers; the first married and died without children.

30 The second married his wife, and he died without children.

31 And the third one married her again; and likewise the seven of them; and they died leaving no children.

32 And at last the woman also died.

33 Therefore at the resurrection to which one of them will she be a wife? for seven of them married her.

34 Jesus said to them, The sons of this world marry women, and women are given to men in marriage.

35 But those who are worthy of the other world, and the resurrection from the dead, neither take women in marriage nor are women given in marriage to men.

36 For they cannot die again, because they are like angels; and they are sons of God, because they are sons of the resurrection.

37 Now concerning the resurrection of the dead, even Moses pointed out; for he referred to it at the Bush, when he said, The Lord God of Abraham, and the God of Isaac, and the God of Jacob.

38 God is not the God of the dead but of the living; for all live to him.

39 And some of the men of the scribes answered and said to him, Teacher, you have well said.

40 And they did not dare again to question him concerning anything.

41 ¶ And he said to them, How can the scribes say concerning the Christ, that he is son of David?

42 And yet David said in the book of Psalms, The Lord said to my Lord, Sit at my right hand,

43 Until I put down your enemies under your feet.

44 If therefore David calls him my Lord, how then can he be his son?

Cf. dif. verses 34–35–36–37–41–44

45 ¶ And while all the people were listening, he said to his disciples,

46 Beware of the scribes, who like to walk in long robes, and love to be greeted in the streets, and the chief seats in the synagogues, and the high places at the banquets;

47 Those who embezzle the property of widows with the pretence that they make long prayers; they will receive a greater judgment.

CHAPTER 21

JESUS then looked at the rich men who were casting their offerings into the treasury.

2 And he also saw a poor widow, who cast in two pennies.

3 And he said, Truly I say to you, that this poor widow has cast in more than every man.

4 For all these cast into the house of the offerings of God of their abundance; but she of her poverty cast in everything she had earned.

5 ¶ While some men were talking about the temple, that it was adorned with beautiful stones and gift offerings, Jesus said to them,

6 These things which you see, the days will come when not a stone will be left upon a stone, which will not be torn down.

7 And they asked him, saying, Teacher, when will these things happen? and what is the sign when these things are about to happen?

8 He said to them, Be careful that you may not be deceived; for many will come in my name, and say, I am the Christ; and the time is near; but do not follow them.

9 And when you hear of wars and revolutions, do not be afraid; for all these things must first come to pass; but the end is not yet.

10 For nation will rise against nation, and kingdom against kingdom.

11 And there will be great earthquakes in different places, and famines and plagues; and there will be alarming sights, and great signs will appear from heaven; and the winters will be severe.

12 But before all these things, they will lay hands on you, and persecute you, and deliver you to the synagogues and the prisons; and they will bring you before kings and governors for the sake of my name.

13 It will be to you for a testimony.

14 Treasure it in your heart, and do not try to learn what to answer.

15 For I will give you a mouth and wisdom, which all your enemies will not be able to withstand.

16 You will be delivered up even by your parents and brothers, and your relatives and friends; and they will put some of you to death.

17 And you will be hated by every man because of my name.

18 And yet not a hair of your head will be lost.

19 By your patience you will gain your souls.

20 But when you see Jerusalem surrounded by an army, then know that its destruction is at hand.

21 Then let those who are in Judaea flee to the mountain; and let those who are within it flee; and let those who are in the fields not enter into it.

22 For these are the days of vengeance, so that everything which is written must be fulfilled.

23 But woe to those who are with child, and to those who give suck in those days! for there will be great distress in the land, and wrath to this people.

24 And they will fall by the edge of the sword, and they will be taken captive to every country; and Jerusalem will be trodden under the feet of the Gentiles, until the time of the Gentiles comes to an end.

25 ¶ And there will be signs in sun and moon and stars; and on earth distress of the nations, and confusion because of the roaring of the sea;

26 And upheaval that takes life out of men, because of fear of what is to come on earth; and the powers of the universe will be shaken.

27 Then they will see the Son of man coming in the clouds, with a large army and great glory.

28 But when these things begin to happen, have courage, and lift up your heads; because your salvation is at hand.

29 And he said to them a parable, Look at the fig tree and all the trees;

30 When they put forth leaves, you immediately understand by them that the summer is near.

31 Even so you also, when you see these things happen, know that the kingdom of God is near.

32 Truly I say to you, This generation will not pass

away until all these things happen.

33 Heaven and earth will pass away, but my words shall not pass away.

34 ¶ But take heed to yourselves, that your hearts may not become heavy by extravagance, and drunkenness, and worries of this world, and that day come suddenly upon you.

35 For like a downpour it will entrap all those who dwell on the face of all the earth.

36 Therefore keep watch all the time and pray, so that you may be worthy to escape all these things which are to happen, and that you may stand before the Son of man.

37 ¶ During the day he taught in the temple; and at night he went out, and lodged in the mountain, which is called the Home of Olives.

38 And all the people came ahead of him to the temple, to hear him.

CHAPTER 22

NOW the feast of unleavened bread, which is called the passover, was at hand.

2 And the high priests and the scribes sought how to kill him; but they were afraid of the people.

3 ¶ But Satan had taken possession of Judas who is called of Iscariot, who was of the number of the twelve.

4 So he went away, and spoke with the high priests and the scribes and officers of the temple, about delivering him to them.

5 And they were glad and promised to give him money.

6 And he agreed with them, and sought an opportunity to deliver him to them in the absence of the people.

7 ¶ Then the day of unleavened bread came, on which it was the custom to kill the passover lamb.

8 So Jesus sent Peter and John, and said to them, Go and prepare the passover for us to eat.

9 They said to him, Where do you wish us to prepare?

10 He said to them, Behold, when you enter the city, you will meet a man carrying a skin full of water; follow him. And wherever he enters,

11 Say to the master of the house, Our Teacher says, Where is the guest room, where I may eat the passover with my disciples?

12 And behold, he will show you an upper room, large and furnished; there make ready.

13 And they went and found

just as he had said to them; and they prepared the passover.

14 ¶ And when the time came, Jesus came and sat down, and the twelve apostles with him.

15 And he said to them, I have desired with desire to eat this passover with you before I suffer;

16 For I say to you, that henceforth, I will not eat it, until it is fulfilled in the kingdom of God.

17 And he took the cup and gave thanks and said, Take this, and divide it among yourselves.

18 For I say to you, I will not drink of the fruit of the vine until the kingdom of God comes.

19 ¶ And he took bread and gave thanks and broke it, and gave it to them and said, This is my body, which is given for your sake; this do in remembrance of me.

20 And likewise also the cup, after they had eaten the supper, he said, This is the cup of the new covenant in my blood, which is shed for you.

21 But behold, the hand of him who is to betray me is on the table.

22 And the Son of man will go, just as he has been destined; but woe to the man by whose hand he will be betrayed!

23 And they began to enquire among themselves, which one of them was to do this act.

24 ¶ There was also a dispute among them, as to who is the greatest among them.

25 Jesus said to them, The kings of the Gentiles are also their owners; and those who rule over them are called benefactors.

26 But not so with you; but he who is great among you, let him be the least; and he who is a leader be like a minister.

27 For who is greater, he who sits down or he who serves? Is it not he who sits down? but I am among you as one who serves.

28 You are the ones who have remained with me, throughout my trials.

29 And I promise you, just as my Father has promised me, a kingdom,

30 That you may eat and drink at the table in my kingdom; and you will sit on chairs, and judge the twelve tribes of Israel.

31 ¶ And Jesus said to Simon, Simon, behold Satan wants to sift all of you as wheat;

Cf. dif. verses 21-22-25-26-29-31

32 But I have made supplication for you that your faith may not weaken; and even you in time will repent, and strengthen your brethren.

33 Simon said to him, My Lord, I am ready with you, even for the prison and for death.

34 Jesus said to him, I say to you, Simon, the cock will not crow today, until you have denied three times that you know me.

35 And he said to them, When I sent you out without purses, and without bags, and shoes, why, did you lack anything? They said to him, Not a thing.

36 He said to them, From now on he who has purses, let him take them, and the bag likewise; and he who has no sword, let him sell his robe and buy for himself a sword.

37 For I say to you, that this which is written must be fulfilled in me, He will be numbered among the wicked; for all the things concerning me will be fulfilled.

38 And they said to him, Our Lord, behold here are two swords. He said to them, That is enough.

39 ¶ And he went out and went away, as it was his custom, to the Mount of the Home of Olives; and his disciples also followed him.

40 And when he arrived at a place, he said to them, Pray that you may not enter into temptation.

41 And he separated from them, about the distance of a stone's throw, and he kneeled down, and prayed,

42 Saying, O Father, if you will, let this cup pass from me; but not as I will, but your will be done.

43 And there appeared to him an angel from heaven, to strengthen him.

44 And he was in fear, and prayed earnestly; and his sweat became like drops of blood; and he fell down upon the ground.

45 Then he rose up from his prayer, and came to his disciples, and found them sleeping because of distress.

46 And he said to them, Why do you sleep? rise and pray that you may not enter into temptation.

47 ¶ While he was still speaking, behold, a multitude, and he who is called Judas, one of the twelve, coming before them; and he drew near to Jesus and kissed him. For this was the sign he had given them, He whom I kiss, it is he.

13

48 Jesus said to him, Judas, do you betray the Son of man with a kiss?

49 When those who were with him saw what happened, they said to him, Our Lord, shall we smite them with swords?

50 And one of them struck the servant of the high priest, and cut off his right ear.

51 But Jesus answered and said, It is enough for the present. And he touched the ear of him who was wounded, and healed it.

52 And Jesus said to the high priests and the elders and the officers of the temple, who had come against him, Have you come out against me to arrest me with swords and staves, as if you were against a bandit?

53 I was with you every day in the temple, and you did not even point your hands at me; but this is your turn, and the power of darkness.

54 ¶ And they arrested him, and brought him to the house of the high priest. And Simon followed him afar off.

55 And they kindled a fire in the midst of the courtyard, and they sat around it; and Simon also sat among them.

56 And a young woman saw him sitting by the fire, and she looked at him and said, This man also was with him.

57 But he denied, and said, Woman, I do not know him.

58 And after a little while, another saw him, and said to him, You also are one of them. But Peter said, I am not.

59 And after an hour, another one argued and said, Truly, this man also was with him; for he is also a Galilean.

60 Peter said, Man, I do not know what you are saying. And immediately while he was still speaking, the cock crew.

61 And Jesus turned and looked at Peter. And Simon remembered the word of our Lord, that he said to him, Before the cock crows you will deny me three times.

62 And Simon went outside and wept bitterly.

63 ¶ And the men who held Jesus mocked him,

64 And they covered his head, and they smote him on his face, saying, Prophesy, who has struck you.

65 And many other things they blasphemed and said against him.

66 ¶ As soon as it was daybreak, the elders and the

Cf. dif. verses 49–51–52–53–59

high priests and the scribes gathered together, and brought him up to their council chamber.

67 And they said to him, If you are the Christ, tell us. He said to them, If I tell you, you will not believe me.

68 And if I ask you, you will not answer me nor release me.

69 From henceforth the Son of man will sit at the right hand of the power of God.

70 And they all said, Are you then the Son of God? Jesus said to them, You say that I am.

71 And they said, Why then do we need witnesses? for we have heard it from his own mouth.

CHAPTER 23

THEN the whole company of them rose up, and brought him to Pilate;

2 And began to accuse him, saying, We found this man misleading our people, and forbidding to pay the head-tax to Caesar; and he says concerning himself that he is a king, even the Christ.

3 Pilate asked him and said to him, Are you the king of the Jews? He said to him, You say that.

4 Then Pilate said to the high priests and the people, I cannot find any fault against this man.

5 But they shouted and said, He has stirred up our people, teaching throughout Judaea, and beginning from Galilee even to this place.

6 When Pilate heard the name Galilee, he asked if the man was a Galilean.

7 And when he knew that he was under the jurisdiction of Herod, he sent him to Herod, because he was in Jerusalem in those days.

8 ¶ When Herod saw Jesus he was exceeding glad, for he wanted to see him for a long time, because he had heard many things concerning him; and he hoped to see some miracle by him.

9 And he asked him many words; but Jesus gave him no answer.

10 But the high priests and the scribes stood, and accused him bitterly.

11 And Herod and his soldiers insulted him, and mocked him, and dressed him in a scarlet robe, and sent him to Pilate.

12 And that day Pilate and Herod became friends with each other; for there was a long-standing enmity between them.

13 ¶ Then Pilate called the

Cf. dif. verses 2–5–11

high priests and the leaders of the people,

14 And he said to them, You brought me this man, as if he were misleading your people; and behold, I have examined him before your own eyes, and I have found no fault in this man concerning all that you accuse him.

15 Not even Herod; for I sent him to him; and behold, he has done nothing worthy of death.

16 I will therefore chastise him, and release him.

17 For there was a custom to release to them one at the feast.

18 But all the people cried out saying, Get rid of him, and release to us Bar-Abbas;

19 Who because of sedition and murder which had happened in the city, was cast into prison.

20 Again Pilate spoke to them, desiring to release Jesus.

21 But they cried out, saying, Crucify him, crucify him.

22 And he said to them the third time, What evil has he done? I have found nothing in him, worthy of death; I will therefore chastise him, and release him.

23 But they persisted with loud voices, and asked to crucify him. And their voice and that of the high priests prevailed.

24 Then Pilate commanded to have their request granted.

25 So he released to them the one who because of sedition and murder was cast into prison, whom they asked for; and he delivered Jesus to their will.

26 ¶ And while they took him away, they laid hold of Simon, a Cyrenian, who was coming from the field, and they placed the end of the cross on him, to carry it with Jesus.

27 And many people followed him, and the women who were mourning and wailing over him.

28 But Jesus turned to them and said, O daughters of Jerusalem, do not weep over me; but weep over yourselves, and over your own children.

29 For behold, the days are coming, in which they will say, Blessed are the barren, and the wombs that never gave birth, and the breasts that never gave suck.

30 Then they will begin to say to the mountains, Fall on us; and to the hills, Cover us.

31 For if they do these things with the green wood,

Cf. dif. verses 14–17–18–26–31

what will be done with the dry wood?

32 ¶ And there were coming with him two others, malefactors, to be put to death.

33 And when they came to a place which is called The Skull, they crucified him there, and the malefactors, one on his right and one on his left.

34 And Jesus said, O Father, forgive them, for they know not what they are doing. And they divided his garments and cast lots over them.

35 The people stood looking on. And even the leaders of the synagogue mocked him, and said, He saved others, let him save himself, if he is the Christ, the chosen one of God.

36 And the soldiers ridiculed him, as they came near him and offered him vinegar,

37 Saying to him, If you are the king of the Jews, save yourself.

38 There was also an inscription which was written over him, in Greek and Roman, and Hebrew, THIS IS THE KING OF THE JEWS.

39 ¶ Now one of the malefactors who were crucified with him, blasphemed against him, saying, If you are the Christ, save yourself and save us also.

40 But the other rebuked him, and said to him, Do you not fear even God, for you are also in the same judgement?

41 And ours is just, for we are paid as we deserve and as we have done; but he has done nothing wrong.

42 And he said to Jesus, Remember me, my Lord, when you come in your kingdom.

43 Jesus said to him, Truly I say to you today, You will be with me in Paradise.

44 ¶ Now it was about the sixth hour, and darkness fell upon the whole earth, until the ninth hour.

45 And the sun was darkened, and the door curtains of the temple were torn in the center.

46 Then Jesus cried with a loud voice and said, O my Father, into thy hands I commit my spirit. He said this and passed away.

47 ¶ When the centurion saw what had happened, he praised God and said, Truly this was a righteous man.

48 And all the people who were gathered together to this sight, when they saw what had happened, returned, beating their breasts.

49 And all the acquaintances of Jesus stood afar off, and the women who had come with him from Galilee, and they were beholding these things.

50 ¶ There was a man named Joseph the counsellor of Arimathaea, a city of Judaea, a good and righteous man.

51 He did not agree with their wishes and their actions; and he waited for the kingdom of God.

52 He went to Pilate and asked for the body of Jesus.

53 And he took it down and wrapped it in fine linen, and laid it in a hewn tomb, in which no one was ever laid.

54 This was a Friday, and the sabbath was approaching.

55 ¶ The women who had come with him from Galilee were near, and they saw the tomb, and how his body was laid.

56 And they returned and prepared spices and perfumes. And on the sabbath they rested, as it is commanded.

CHAPTER 24

AND on the first day of the week, early in the morning, while it was yet dark, they came to the tomb, and brought the spices which they had prepared; and there were with them other women.

2 And they found the stone rolled away from the tomb.

3 And they entered in, but they did not find the body of Jesus.

4 And it came to pass as they were confused about this, behold, two men stood above them, and their garments were shining;

5 And they were afraid, and they bowed their faces to the ground; and they said to them, Why do you seek the living among the dead?

6 He is not here, he has risen; remember that he spoke to you while he was in Galilee,

7 Saying, that the Son of man had to be delivered into the hands of sinful men, and be crucified, and rise again on the third day.

8 And they remembered his words.

9 And they returned from the tomb, and told all these things to the eleven and to the rest.

10 They were Mary of Magdala, and Joanna, and Mary the mother of James, and the rest who were with them, who told these things to the apostles.

 Cf. dif. verses 50–51–54

11 And these words appeared in their eyes as delusions; and they did not believe them.

12 But Simon rose up and ran to the tomb; and he looked in and saw the linen laid by itself, and he went away wondering in himself concerning what had happened.

13 ¶ And behold two of them were going on that day to a village called Emmaus, about six miles from Jerusalem.

14 They were talking with one another concerning all these things that had happened.

15 And while they were speaking and asking each other, Jesus came and overtook them, and walked with them.

16 But the sight of their eyes was holden, so that they could not recognize him.

17 And he said to them, What are these words that you are discussing with each other, as you walk, and are sad?

18 One of them, named Cleopas, answered and said to him, Are you a stranger alone from Jerusalem, that you do not know what has happened in it in these days?

19 He said to them, What things? They said to him, About Jesus of Nazareth, a man who was a prophet, mighty in word and deed before God and before all the people.

20 And the high priests and the elders delivered him up to the judgment of death, and they crucified him.

21 But we were hoping that he was the one to save Israel; and behold, it is three days since all these things happened.

22 And some of our women also amazed us, for they went early to the tomb;

23 And when his body was not found, they came, and said to us, We saw angels there, and they said that he is alive.

24 And some of our men also went to the tomb, and they found it so, as the women had said; but they did not see him.

25 Then Jesus said to them, O dull-minded and heavy-hearted, to believe all that the prophets have spoken.

26 Did not Christ have to suffer all these things, and to enter into his glory?

27 And he began from Moses and from all the prophets, and interpreted to them from all the scriptures concerning himself.

28 And they drew near to the village, to which they were going; and he made them think that he was going to a far place.

29 But they urged him and said, Remain with us; because the day is spent and it is near dark. So he entered to stay with them.

30 And it came to pass, as he sat at meat with them, he took bread and blessed it, and broke it, and gave it to them.

31 And immediately their eyes were opened and they recognized him; and he was taken away from them.

32 And they said one to another, Were not our hearts heavy within us, when he spoke with us on the road, and interpreted the scriptures to us?

33 ¶ And they rose up that very hour and returned to Jerusalem; and they found the eleven gathered together, and those who were with them,

34 Saying, Truly our Lord has risen, and he has appeared to Simon.

35 And they also reported those things that happened on the road, and how they knew him as he broke the bread.

36 ¶ And while they were discussing these things, Jesus stood among them, and said to them, Peace be with you; it is I; do not be afraid.

37 And they were confused and frightened, for they thought they saw a spirit.

38 Jesus said to them, Why do you tremble? and why do thoughts arise in your hearts?

39 Look at my hands and my feet, that it is I; feel me and understand; for a spirit has no flesh and bones, as you see I have.

40 When he said these things, he showed them his hands and his feet.

41 And as they still did not believe because of their joy, and they were bewildered, he said to them, Have you anything here to eat?

42 They gave him a portion of a broiled fish, and of a honeycomb.

43 And he took it, and ate before their eyes.

44 And he said to them, These are the words which I spoke to you when I was with you, that everything must be fulfilled which is written in the law of Moses, and in the prophets, and in the psalms, concerning me.

45 Then he opened their mind to understand the scriptures.

Cf. dif. verses 28–31–32–36–37–39–41

46 And he said to them, Thus it is written, and it was right that Christ should suffer, and rise from the dead on the third day;

47 And that repentance should be preached in his name for the forgiveness of sins among all nations; and the beginning will be from Jerusalem.

48 And you are witnesses of these things.

49 And I will send upon you the promise of my Father; but you remain in the city of Jerusalem, until you are clothed with power from on high.

50 ¶ And he took them out as far as Bethany, and he lifted up his hands and blessed them.

51 And it came to pass, while he blessed them, he parted from them, and went up to heaven.

52 And they worshipped him, and returned to Jerusalem with great joy;

53 And they were always in the temple, praising and blessing God. Amen.

THE GOSPEL ACCORDING TO
St. JOHN

CHAPTER 1

THE Word was in the beginning, and that very Word was with God, and God was that Word.

2 The same was in the beginning with God.

3 Everything came to be by his hand; and without him not even one thing came to be of what was created.

4 The life was in him, and the life is the light of men.

5 And the same light shines in the darkness, and the darkness does not overcome it.

6 ¶ There was a man, sent from God, whose name was John.

7 He came as a witness to testify concerning the light, so that every man might believe by means of him.

8 He was not the light, but to testify concerning the light.

9 ¶ He was the true light, which lighteth every man who came into the world.

10 He was in the world, and the world was under his hand, and yet the world knew him not.

11 He came to his own, and his own did not receive him.

12 But those who received him, to them he gave power to become sons of God, especially to those who believe in his name;

13 Those who are not of blood, nor of the will of the flesh, nor of the will of man, but born of God.

14 And the Word became flesh, and dwelt among us, and we saw his glory, a glory like that of the firstborn of the Father, full of grace and truth.

15 John witnessed concerning him and cried and said, This is the one of whom I said, He is coming after me, and yet he is ahead of me, because he was before me.

16 And of his fulness we have all received, grace for grace.

17 For the law was given by Moses; but truth and grace

Cf. dif. verses 1–3–5–7–10–13–15

came into being by Jesus Christ.

18 No man has ever seen God; but the firstborn of God, who is in the bosom of his Father, he has declared him.

19 ¶ This is the testimony of John, when the Jews sent to him priests and Levites from Jerusalem to ask him, Who are you?

20 And he confessed and did not deny it; but he declared, I am not the Christ.

21 Then they asked him again, What then? Are you Elijah? And he said, I am not. Are you a prophet? And he said, No.

22 Then they said to him, Who are you? so that we may give an answer to those who sent us. What do you say concerning yourself?

23 He said, I am the voice of one crying in the wilderness, Straighten the highway of the Lord, as the prophet Isaiah said.

24 Those who were sent were from the Pharisees.

25 And they asked him and said to him, Why then do you baptize, if you are not the Christ, nor Elijah, nor a prophet?

26 John answered and said to them, I baptize with water; but among you stands one whom you do not know;

27 This is the one who comes after me, and is ahead of me; the one even the strings of whose shoes I am not good enough to untie.

28 These things happened in Bethany, at the Jordan crossing, where John was baptizing.

29 ¶ The next day John saw Jesus coming to him, and he said, Behold the lamb of God, who takes away the sin of the world!

30 This is the one of whom I said, The man who comes after me is yet ahead of me, because he was before me.

31 And I did not know him; but that he might be made known to Israel, I came to baptize with water.

32 And John testified and said, I saw the Spirit descending from heaven like a dove, and it rested upon him.

33 And yet I did not know him; but he who sent me to baptize with water, said to me, The one upon whom you see the Spirit descending and resting, he is the one who will baptize with the Holy Spirit.

34 And I saw and testified that this is the Son of God.

35 ¶ The next day John was standing, and two of his disciples;

36 And he looked at Jesus

while he walked, and said, Behold, the lamb of God!

37 And when he said it, two of his disciples heard it; and they went after Jesus.

38 And Jesus turned around and saw them following him, and he said to them, What do you want? They said to him, Rabbi (Teacher), where do you live?

39 He said to them, Come, and you will see. And they came and saw where he stayed, and they remained with him that day; and it was about the tenth hour.

40 One of them who heard John and followed Jesus, was Andrew, the brother of Simon.

41 He saw his brother Simon first, and said to him, We have found the Christ.

42 And he brought him to Jesus. And Jesus looked at him and said, You are Simon the son of Jonah; you are called Kepa (a Stone).

43 ¶ The next day Jesus wanted to leave for Galilee, and he found Philip, and said to him, Follow me.

44 Now Philip was from Bethsaida, the city of Andrew and Simon.

45 Philip found Nathanael, and said to him, We have found that Jesus, the son of Joseph, of Nazareth, is the one concerning whom Moses wrote in the law and the prophets.

46 Nathanael said to him, Can anything good come out of Nazareth? Philip said to him, Come and you will see.

47 Jesus saw Nathanael coming to him and he said of him, Behold truly an Israelite, in whom there is no guile!

48 Nathanael said to him, Whence do you know me? Jesus said to him, Even before Philip called you, while you were under the fig tree, I saw you.

49 Nathanael answered and said to him, Rabbi, you are the Son of God, you are the king of Israel.

50 Jesus said to him, Do you believe because I told you I saw you under the fig tree? you shall see greater things than these.

51 He said to him, Truly, truly, I say to all of you, that from now on you will see the heaven opened, and the angels of God ascending and descending to the Son of man.

CHAPTER 2

ON the third day there was a marriage feast in Cana, a city of Galilee; and the mother of Jesus was there.

Cf. dif. verses 37–42–45–51

2 And Jesus and his disciples were also invited to the marriage feast.

3 And when the wine decreased, his mother said to Jesus, They have no wine.

4 Jesus said to her, What is it to me and to you, woman? my turn has not yet come.

5 His mother said to the helpers, Whatever he tells you, do it.

6 And there were six stone jars placed there for the purification of the Jews, which could hold several gallons each.

7 Jesus said to them, Fill the jars with water; and they filled them up to the brim.

8 Then he said to them, Draw out now, and bring it to the chief guest of the feast. And they brought it.

9 And when the chief guest tasted the water that had become wine, he did not know whence it had come; but the helpers knew, who had drawn the water. Then the chief guest called the bridegroom,

10 And said to him, Every man at first brings the best wine; and when they have drunk, then that which is weak; but you have kept the best wine until now.

11 This is the first miracle which Jesus performed in Cana of Galilee, and he showed his glory; and his disciples believed in him.

12 ¶ After this he went down to Capernaum, he and his mother and his brothers, and his disciples; and they remained there a few days.

13 ¶ And the Jewish passover was nearing; so Jesus went up to Jerusalem.

14 And he found in the temple those who were buying oxen and sheep and doves, and the money changers sitting.

15 And he made a whip of cord, and drove them all out of the temple, even the sheep and the oxen and the money changers; and he threw out their exchange money, and upset their trays;

16 And to those who sold doves he said, Take these away from here; do not make my Father's house a house of trading.

17 And his disciples remembered that it is written, The zeal for your house has given me courage.

18 The Jews answered and said to him, What sign do you show us, that you are doing these things?

19 Jesus answered and said to them, Tear down this temple, and in three days I will raise it up.

20 The Jews said to him, It

took forty-six years to build this temple, and will you raise it up in three days?

21 But he spoke concerning the temple of his body.

22 When he rose from the dead, his disciples remembered that he had said this; and they believed the scriptures, and the word which Jesus had said.

23 ¶ Now when Jesus was in Jerusalem at the passover, during the feast, a great many believed in him, because they saw the miracles which he did.

24 But Jesus did not entrust himself to them, because he understood every man.

25 And he needed no man to testify to him concerning any man; for he knew well what was in man.

CHAPTER 3

THERE was there a man of the Pharisees, named Nicodemus, a leader of the Jews;

2 He came at night to Jesus and said to him, Rabbi, we know that you are a teacher sent from God; for no man can do these miracles that you are doing, except God is with him.

3 Jesus answered and said to him, Truly, truly, I say to you, If a man is not born again[1], he cannot see the kingdom of God.

4 Nicodemus said to him, How can an old man be born again? can he enter again a second time into his mother's womb, and be born?

5 Jesus answered and said to him, Truly, truly, I say to you, If a man is not born of water and the Spirit, he cannot enter into the kingdom of God.

6 What is born of flesh is flesh; and what is born of the Spirit is spirit.

7 Do not be surprised because I have told you that you all must be born again.

8 The wind blows where it pleases, and you hear its sound; but you do not know whence it comes and whither it goes; such is every man who is born of the Spirit.

9 Nicodemus answered and said to him, How can these things be?

10 Jesus answered and said to him, You are a teacher of Israel, and yet you do not understand these things?

11 Truly, truly, I say to you, We speak only what we know, and we testify only to what we have seen; and

---

[1] Born again in Northern Aramaic means to change one's thoughts and habits. Nicodemus spoke Southern Aramaic and hence did not understand Jesus.

Cf. dif. verses 24–25–3–7

yet you do not accept our testimony.

12 If I have told you about earthly things and you do not believe, how then will you believe me, if I tell you about heavenly things?

13 No man has ascended to heaven, except he who came down from heaven, even the Son of man who is in heaven.

14 Just as Moses lifted up the serpent in the wilderness, so the Son of man is ready to be lifted up;

15 So that every man who believes in him should not perish, but have eternal life.

16 For God so loved the world, that he even gave his only begotten Son, so that whoever believes in him should not perish, but have eternal life.

17 For God did not send his Son into the world, to condemn the world; but that the world should be saved by him.

18 He who believes in him will not be condemned; and he who does not believe has already been condemned, for not believing in the name of the only begotten Son of God.

19 And this is the judgement, that light has come into the world, and yet men have loved darkness more than light, because their works were evil.

20 For every one who does detested things hates the light, and he does not come to the light, because his works cannot be covered.

21 But he who does truthful things comes to the light, so that his works may be known, that they are done through God.

22 ¶ After these things, Jesus and his disciples came to the land of Judaea, and he remained there with them, and baptized.

23 John also was baptizing at the spring of Aenon near to Salim, because there was much water there; and they came, and were baptized.

24 For John was not yet cast into prison.

25 ¶ Now it happened that a dispute arose between one of John's disciples and a Jew about the ceremony of purifying.

26 So they came to John and told him, Teacher, he who was with you at the Jordan crossing, concerning whom you testified, behold, he also is baptizing and a great many are coming to him.

27 John answered and said to them, No man can receive anything of his own will, except it is given to him from heaven.

28 You yourselves bear me

Cf. dif. verses 14–20–25–26

witness that I said, I am not the Christ, but only a messenger to go before him.

29 He who has a bride is the bridegroom; and the best man of the bridegroom is he who stands up and listens to him, and rejoices greatly because of the bridegroom's voice; this my joy therefore is fulfilled.

30 He must become greater and I lesser.

31 For he who has come from above is above all; and he who is of the earth is of the earth, and he speaks of earthly things; but he who has come from heaven is above all.

32 And he testifies of what he has seen and heard, and yet no man accepts his testimony.

33 He who accepts his testimony, has set his seal that God is true.

34 For he whom God has sent, speaks the words of God; for God did not give the Spirit by measure.

35 The Father loves the Son, and has placed everything under his hand.

36 He who believes in the Son has eternal life; and he who does not obey the Son, shall not see life, but the wrath of God shall remain on him.

CHAPTER 4

WHEN Jesus knew that the Pharisees had heard he made many disciples, and was baptizing more people than John,

2 Though Jesus himself did not baptize, but his disciples;

3 He left Judaea and came again to Galilee.

4 He had to go through Samaritan territory.

5 Then he came to a Samaritan city, called Sychar, near the field which Jacob had given to his son Joseph.

6 Now Jacob's well was there; and Jesus was tired by the fatigue of the journey, and sat down by the well. It was about the sixth hour.

7 And there came a woman from Samaria to draw water; and Jesus said to her, Give me water to drink.

8 His disciples had entered into the city to buy food for themselves.

9 The Samaritan woman said to him, How is it? You are a Jew, and yet you ask me for a drink, who am a Samaritan woman? For Jews have no social intercourse with Samaritans.

10 Jesus answered and said to her, If you only knew the gift of God, and who is the man who said to you, Give

Cf. dif. verses 30-1-4-5-9

me a drink; you would have asked him, and he would have given you living water.

11 The woman said to him, My lord, you have no leather bucket, and no deep well; where do you get the living water?

12 Why, are you greater than our father Jacob, who gave us this well, and he himself drank from it, and his sons and his sheep?

13 Jesus answered and said to her, Everyone who drinks of this water will thirst again;

14 But whoever drinks of the water which I give him, shall never thirst; but the same water which I give him shall become in him a well of water springing up to life everlasting.

15 The woman said to him, My Lord, give me of this water, so that I may not thirst again, and need not come and draw from here.

16 Jesus said to her, Go and call your husband, and come here.

17 She said to him, I have no husband; Jesus said to her, You said well, I have no husband;

18 For you have had five husbands; and the one you now have is not your husband; what you said is true.

19 Then the woman said to him, My Lord, I see that you are a prophet.

20 Our forefathers worshipped on this mountain; and you say the place where men must worship is in Jerusalem.

21 Jesus said to her, Woman, believe me, the time is coming, when neither on this mountain nor in Jerusalem they will worship the Father.

22 You worship what you do not know; but we worship what we do know; for salvation is from the Jews.

23 But the time is coming, and it is here, when the true worshippers shall worship the Father in spirit and in truth; for the Father also desires worshippers such as these.

24 For God is Spirit; and those who worship him must worship him in spirit and in truth.

25 The woman said to him, I know that the Messiah (Christ) is coming; when he is come, he will teach us everything.

26 Jesus said to her, I am he, who is speaking to you.

27 ¶ While he was talking, his disciples came, and they were surprised that he was talking with a married

woman; but no one said to him, What do you want? or, What are you talking with her?

28 The woman then left her water jar, and went to the city and said to the men,

29 Come and see a man who told me everything which I have done; why, is he the Christ?

30 And the men went out of the city, and came to him.

31 ¶ During the interval his disciples begged him, saying, Teacher, eat.

32 But he said to them, I have food to eat, of which you do not know.

33 The disciples said among themselves, Why, did any man bring him something to eat?

34 Jesus said to them, My food is to do the will of him who sent me, and to finish his work.

35 Do you not say that after four months comes the harvest? behold, I say to you, Lift up your eyes, and look at the fields, which have turned white and have long been ready for the harvest.

36 And he who reaps receives wages, and gathers fruits to life everlasting; so that the sower and the reaper may rejoice together.

37 For in this case the say-ing is true, One sows and another reaps.

38 I sent you to reap that for which you did not labor; for others labored, and you have entered upon their labor.

39 ¶ A great many Samaritans of that city believed in him, because of the word of that woman, who testified, He told me everything which I have done.

40 So when the Samaritans came to him, they begged him to stay with them; and he stayed with them two days.

41 And a great many believed in him because of his word;

42 And they were saying to the woman, Henceforth it is not because of your word that we believe him; for we ourselves have heard and know, that this is indeed the Christ, the Saviour of the world.

43 ¶ Two days later, Jesus departed thence and went to Galilee.

44 For Jesus himself testified, that a prophet is not honored in his own city.

45 When he came to Galilee, the Galileans welcomed him, for they had seen all the wonders he did at Jerusalem during the feast; for they also had come to the feast.

46 Then Jesus came again to Cana of Galilee, where he had made the water wine. And there was at Capernaum a servant of a king, whose son was sick.

47 This man heard that Jesus had come from Judaea to Galilee; so he went to him and asked him to come down and heal his son; for he was near death.

48 Jesus said to him, Unless you see miracles and wonders, you will not believe.

49 The king's servant said to him, My Lord, come down before the boy is dead.

50 Jesus said to him, Go, your son is healed. And the man believed the word that Jesus said to him and went away.

51 And as he was going down, his servants met him and brought him good news, saying, Your son is healed.

52 And he asked them, At what time was he healed? They said to him, Yesterday, at the seventh hour, the fever left him.

53 And his father knew that it was at that very hour when Jesus told him, Your son is healed; so he himself believed and his whole household.

54 This is again the second miracle which Jesus did, after he came from Judaea to Galilee.

CHAPTER 5

AFTER these things there was a feast of the Jews; and Jesus went up to Jerusalem.

2 Now there was at Jerusalem a baptismal pool, which is called in Hebrew Bethesda, having five entrances.

3 And at these entrances a great many sick people were lying, the blind, the lame, and the crippled; and they were waiting for the water to be stirred up.

4 For an angel of God went down at a certain time to the baptismal pool and stirred up the water; and whoever went in first after the stirring of the water was healed of any disease he had.

5 A man was there who had been sick for thirty-eight years.

6 Jesus saw this man lying down, and he knew that he had been waiting for a long time; so he said to him, Do you wish to be healed?

7 The sick man answered and said, Yes, my Lord; but I have no man, when the water is stirred up, to put me into the baptismal pool;

but while I am coming, another one goes in before me.

8 Jesus said to him, Rise, take up your quilt-bed, and walk.

9 And the man was healed immediately, and he got up and took his quilt-bed and walked. And that day was the sabbath day.

10 ¶ So the Jews said to him who was healed, It is the sabbath; it is not lawful for you to carry your quilt-bed.

11 He answered and said to them, He who had healed me, he told me, Take up your quilt-bed, and walk.

12 And they asked him, Who is this man who said to you, Take up your quilt-bed, and walk?

13 But he who was healed did not know who he was; for Jesus was pressed by a large crowd which was at that place.

14 After a while, Jesus found him in the temple and said to him, Behold, you are healed; do not sin again, for something worse might happen to you than the first.

15 And the man went away and told the Jews, that it was Jesus who had healed him.

16 ¶ And for this reason the Jews persecuted Jesus and wanted to kill him, because he was doing these things on the sabbath.

17 But Jesus said to them, My Father works even until now, so I also work.

18 And for this the Jews wanted the more to kill him, not only because he was weakening the sabbath, but also because he said concerning God that he is his Father, and was making himself equal with God.

19 Jesus answered and said to them, Truly, truly, I say to you, that the Son can do nothing of his own accord, except what he sees the Father doing; for the things which the Father does, the same the Son does like him also.

20 For the Father loves his Son, and he shows him everything that he does; and he will show him greater works than these, so that you may marvel.

21 For just as the Father raises the dead and gives them life, even so the Son gives life to those whom he wills.

22 For the Father does not judge any man, but he has entrusted all judgement to the Son;

23 So that every man should honor the Son, just as he honors the Father. He who

does not honor the Son, does not honor the Father who sent him.

24 Truly, truly, I say to you, He who hears my word, and believes him who has sent me, has everlasting life; and he does not come before the judgement, but he passes from death to life.

25 Truly, truly, I say to you, The time is coming, and it is now already here, when the dead will hear the voice of the Son of God; and those who hear it will live.

26 For as the Father has life in himself, even so he has given to the Son also to have life in himself.

27 And he has given him authority to execute judgement also, for he is a son of man.

28 Do not wonder at this; for the time is coming, when all those who are in the graves will hear his voice,

29 And they will come out; those who have done good works to the resurrection of life; and those who have done evil works to the resurrection of judgement.

30 I can do nothing of myself; but as I hear I judge, and my judgement is just; for I do not seek my own will, but the will of him who sent me.

31 If I testify concerning myself, my testimony is not true.

32 It is another one who testifies concerning me; and I know that the testimony which he testifies concerning me is true.

33 You sent to John, and he testified concerning the truth.

34 But I do not receive any testimony from men; but I tell you these things so that you may be saved.

35 He was a lamp which burns and gives light; and you were willing to delight in his light for a while.

36 But I have a greater testimony than that of John; for the works which my Father has given me to finish, the same works which I do, testify concerning me, that the Father has sent me.

37 And the Father who sent me has testified concerning me. But you have never heard his voice, nor seen his appearance.

38 And his word does not abide in you; because you do not believe in him whom he has sent.

39 Examine the scriptures, in which you trust that you have eternal life; and even they testify concerning me.

40 Yet you will not come to

me, that you might have life everlasting.

41 I do not receive any praise from men.

42 But I know you well, that the love of God is not in you.

43 I have come in the name of my Father, and you do not receive me; if another should come in his own name, you will receive him.

44 How can you believe, when you accept praise one from another, but the praise from God only, you do not want?

45 Why, do you think that I will accuse you before the Father; there is one who will accuse you, even Moses, in whom you trust.

46 For if you had believed in Moses, you would also have believed in me; because Moses wrote concerning me.

47 If you do not believe his writings, how then can you believe my words?

CHAPTER 6

AFTER these things, Jesus went to the port of the sea of Galilee, at Tiberias.

2 And a great many people followed him, because they saw the miracles which he performed on sick people.

3 So Jesus went up to the mountain, and he sat there with his disciples.

4 And the feast of the passover of the Jews was at hand.

5 ¶ And Jesus lifted up his eyes, and saw a large crowd coming to him, and he said to Philip, Where can we buy bread that all these may eat?

6 He said this merely to test him; for he knew what he would do.

7 Philip said to him, Two hundred pennies worth of bread would not be sufficient for them, even if each one of them should take a little.

8 One of his disciples, Andrew the brother of Simon Peter, said to him,

9 There is a boy here, who has with him five barley loaves and two fishes; but what are these for all of them?

10 Jesus said to them, Make all the men sit down. There was much grass in that place. So the males[1] sat down, five thousand in number.

11 And Jesus took the bread, and blessed it, and distributed it to those who were sitting down; likewise the fish also, as much as they wanted.

12 When they were filled, he said to his disciples, Gather up the broken pieces

[1] Women and children do not eat with men nor are they counted.

which are left over, so that nothing is lost.

13 And they gathered them up, and filled twelve baskets with broken pieces, which were left over by those who ate from five barley loaves.

14 ¶ Then the men who saw the miracle which Jesus performed said, Truly this is the prophet who is to come into the world.

15 But Jesus knew that they were ready to come and seize him to make him a king, so he departed to the mountain alone.

16 And when evening came, his disciples went down to the sea,

17 And entered into a boat, and were going to the port of Capernaum. And now it was dark, and Jesus had not yet come to them.

18 And the sea became rough, because a strong wind was blowing.

19 And they rowed about twenty-five or thirty furlongs, and they saw Jesus walking on[1] the sea; and as he drew towards their boat; they became afraid.

20 But Jesus said to them, It is I, do not be afraid.

21 So they wanted to receive him into the boat; but soon the boat reached the land to which they were going.

22 ¶ The next day, the multitude which stood waiting at the seaport saw no other boat there, except the boat in which the disciples had entered, and that Jesus had not entered the boat with his disciples.

23 But other boats had come from Tiberias, near the place where they had eaten bread, when Jesus blessed it.

24 And when the people saw that Jesus was not there, nor his disciples, they entered the boats and came to Capernaum, looking for Jesus.

25 And when they found him at the seaport, they said to him, Teacher, when did you come here?

26 Jesus answered and said to them, Truly, truly, I say to you, You seek me, not because you saw the miracles, but just because you ate bread and were filled.

27 Do not work for the food which perishes, but for the food which endures unto life everlasting, which the Son of man will give you; for this one God the Father has sealed.

28 They said to him, What

---

[1] The Aramaic *al* means on or by. The disciples were going from Tiberias to Capernaum, and both cities were on the same side of the Sea of Galilee. See further ver. 21.

shall we do to work the works of God?

29 Jesus answered and said to them, This is the work of God, that you should believe in him whom he has sent.

30 They said to him, What miracle do you perform that we may see and believe in you? What have you performed?

31 Our forefathers ate manna in the wilderness; as it is written, He gave them bread from heaven to eat.

32 Jesus said to them, Truly, truly, I say to you, It was not Moses who gave you bread from heaven; but my Father gives you the true bread from heaven.

33 For the bread of God is he who has come down from heaven, and gives life to the world.

34 They said to him, Our Lord, give us this bread always.

35 Jesus said to them, I am the bread of life; he who comes to me shall never hunger; and he who believes in me shall never thirst.

36 But I have said to you, that you have seen me and yet you do not believe.

37 Everyone whom my Father has given me shall come to me; and he who comes to me, I will not cast him out.

38 For I came down from heaven, not merely to do my own will, but to do the will of him who sent me.

39 This is the will of him who sent me, that I should lose nothing of all that he has given me, but should raise it up at the last day.

40 For this is the will of my Father, that whoever sees the Son and believes in him, shall have life everlasting; and I will raise him up at the last day.

41 ¶ Now the Jews murmured against him, for he said, I am the bread which came down from heaven.

42 And they said, Is this not Jesus, the son of Joseph, whose father and mother we know? how can he say, I have come down from heaven?

43 Jesus answered and said to them, Do not murmur one with another.

44 No man can come to me, except the Father who sent me draw him; and I will raise him up at the last day.

45 For it is written in the prophet, They shall all be taught by God. Everyone therefore who hears from the Father and learns from him, will come to me.

46 No man can see the Father, except he who is from God, he can see the Father.

 Cf. dif. verses 40

47 Truly, truly, I say to you, He who believes in me has eternal life.

48 I am the bread of life.

49 Your forefathers ate manna in the wilderness, and yet they died.

50 This is the bread which came down from heaven, that a man may eat of it and not die.

51 I am the living bread because I came down from heaven; if any man eats of this bread, he shall live forever; and the bread which I will give, is my body, which I am giving for the sake of the life of the world.

52 ¶ The Jews argued one with another, saying, How can this man give us his body to eat?

53 Jesus said to them, Truly, truly I say to you, Unless you eat the body of the Son of man, and drink his blood, you have no life in yourselves.

54 He who eats of my body, and drinks of my blood, has eternal life; and I will raise him at the last day.

55 For my body truly is the food, and my blood truly is the drink.

56 He who eats my body and drinks my blood, will abide with me, and I with him.

57 Just as the living Father sent me, and I am living because of the Father, so whoever eats me will also live because of me.

58 This is the bread which came down from heaven; it is not like that manna which your forefathers ate and died; he who eats of this bread shall live forever.

59 These things he said in the synagogue, while he was teaching at Capernaum.

60 ¶ Many of his disciples who heard it said, This is a hard saying, who can listen to it?

61 Jesus knew in himself that his disciples were murmuring about this; so he said to them, Does this cause you to stumble?

62 What then if you should see the Son of man ascending to the place where he was before?

63 It is the spirit that gives life; the body is of no account; the words which I have spoken to you are spirit and life.

64 But there are some of you who do not believe. For Jesus knew for a long while who were those who did not believe, and who was to betray him.

65 And he said to them, For this reason I have told you

that no man can come to me, unless it is given to him by my Father.

66 ¶ Just because of this saying, a great many of his disciples turned away, and did not walk with him.

67 So Jesus said to his twelve, Why, do you also want to go away?

68 Simon Peter answered and said, My Lord, to whom shall we go? you have the words of eternal life.

69 And we have believed and known that you are the Christ, the Son of the living God.

70 Jesus said to them, Did not I choose you, the twelve, and yet one of you is Satan?[1]

71 He said it concerning Judas, the son of Simon Iscariot; for he was one of the twelve, who was going to betray him.

CHAPTER 7

AFTER these things Jesus travelled in Galilee; for he did not wish to travel in Judaea, because the Jews wanted to kill him.

2 ¶ Now the Jewish feast of the tabernacles was at hand.

3 And his brothers said to Jesus, Depart from here and go to Judaea, so that your disciples may see the works that you do.

4 For there is no man, who does anything in secret, and yet wants it to become known. If you are doing these things, show yourself to the people.

5 For not even his own brothers believed in Jesus.

6 Jesus said to them, My time has not yet come; but your time is always ready.

7 The world cannot hate you; but it hates me, because I testify against it, that its works are evil.

8 You go up to this feast; I am not going just now to this feast, for my time is not yet come.

9 He said these things, and remained in Galilee.

10 But when his brothers had gone up to the feast, then he also went up, not openly, but as it were in secret.

11 ¶ The Jews were looking for him at the feast and said, Where is he?

12 And there was much murmuring among the people concerning him; for some said, He is good; and others said, No, but he just deceives the people.

13 But no man spoke openly about him, because of the fear of the Jews.

[1] The Aramaic *satana* (Satan) is derived from *sta*, which means to slide, to slip, or to miss the mark; and applies to one who causes these results.

14 ¶ Now about the middle period of the feast, Jesus went up to the temple and taught.

15 And the Jews marvelled, saying, How does this man know reading, when he has not been instructed?

16 Jesus answered and said, My teaching is not mine, but his who sent me.

17 He who wills to do his will, he will understand if my teaching is from God, or if I am just speaking of my own accord.

18 He who speaks of his own accord seeks glory for himself; but he who seeks the glory of him who sent him, he is true, and there is no deception in his heart.

19 Did not Moses give you the law? and yet no one of you obeys the law. Why do you want to kill me?

20 The people answered, saying, You are crazy; who wants to kill you?

21 Jesus answered and said to them, I have done one work, and all of you marvel.

22 Moses gave you circumcision, not because it is from Moses, but because it is from the forefathers; and yet you circumcise a man on the sabbath.

23 So if a man is circumcised on the sabbath day, that the law of Moses may not be broken; yet you murmur at me, because I healed a whole man[1] on the sabbath day?

24 Do not judge by partiality, but judge a just judgement.

25 ¶ Then some of the men of Jerusalem were saying, Is not this the man whom they want to kill?

26 And yet he speaks openly, but they say nothing to him. Perhaps our elders have found out that he is the Christ?

27 Howbeit we know whence he comes; but when the Christ comes, no man will know whence he comes.

28 ¶ Jesus then lifted up his voice as he taught in the temple, and said, You know me, and you know whence I come; and yet I have not come of my own accord, but he who sent me is true, whom you do not know.

29 But I know him; because I am from him, and he sent me.

30 So they wanted to seize him; and no man laid hands on him, because his time had not yet come.

---

[1] Circumcision affected only one part of the body. Jesus here healed the whole body; and so his work on the sabbath was more important than circumcision.

Cf. dif. verses 15–18–20–23–24–26

31 But a great many of the people believed in him and said, When the Christ comes, why, will he do greater wonders than this man does?

32 The Pharisees heard the people talking about him; so they and the high priests sent soldiers to arrest him.

33 And Jesus said, I am with you just a short while, and I am going to him who sent me.

34 You will seek me, but you will not find me; and where I am you cannot come.

35 Then the Jews said among themselves, Where is he going, that we cannot find him? why, is he planning to go to the countries of the Gentiles, to teach the pagans?

36 What does this word mean which he said, You will seek me and you will not find me; and where I am you cannot come?

37 ¶ Now on the greatest day, which is the last day of the feast, Jesus stood and cried out and said, If any man is thirsty, let him come to me and drink.

38 Whoever believes in me, just as the scriptures have said, the rivers of living water shall flow from within him.

39 He said this concerning the Spirit, which they who believe in him were to receive; for the Spirit was not yet given, because Jesus was not yet glorified.

40 Many of the people who heard his words were saying, This man truly is a prophet.

41 Others were saying, He is the Christ; but others said, Is it possible that Christ should come from Galilee?

42 Does not the scripture say that Christ will come from the seed of David, and from Bethlehem, the town of David?

43 So the people were divided because of him.

44 And there were some men among them, who wanted to seize him; but no man laid hands on him.

45 And the soldiers returned to the high priests and the Pharisees; and the priests said to them, Why did you not bring him?

46 The soldiers said to them, Never a man has spoken as this man speaks.

47 The Pharisees said to them, Why, have you also been deceived?

48 Why, have any of the leaders or of the Pharisees believed in him,

49 Except this cursed people, who do not know the law?

50 Nicodemus, one of them,

who had come to Jesus at night, said to them,

51 Does our law convict a man, unless it first hears from him, and knows what he has done?

52 They answered and said to him, Why, are you also from Galilee? Search and see that no prophet will rise up from Galilee.[1]

53 So everyone went to his own house.

CHAPTER 8

THEN Jesus went to the Mount of Olives.

2 And in the morning he came again to the temple, and all the people were coming to him; and he sat down and taught them.

3 Then the scribes and the Pharisees brought a woman who was caught in adultery; and they made her to stand in the midst.

4 They said to him, Teacher, this woman was caught openly in the act of adultery.

5 Now in the law of Moses it is commanded that women such as these should be stoned; but what do you say?

6 They said this to tempt him, that they might have a cause to accuse him. While Jesus was bent down, he was writing on the ground.

7 When they were through questioning him, he straightened himself up, and said to them, He who is among you without sin, let him first throw a stone at her.

8 And again as he bent down, he wrote on the ground.

9 And when they heard it, they left one by one, beginning with the elders; and the woman was left alone in the midst.

10 When Jesus straightened himself up, he said to the woman, Where are they? did no man convict you?

11 She said, No man, Lord. Then Jesus said, Neither do I convict you; go away, and from henceforth, do not sin again.

12 ¶ Again Jesus spoke to them and said, I am the light of the world; he who follows me shall not walk in darkness, but he shall find for himself the light of life.

13 The Pharisees said to him, You testify concerning yourself; your testimony is not true.

14 Jesus answered and said to them, Even though I testify concerning myself, my

---

[1] Galilee was the land of the Gentiles and of mixed races, the descendants of those who were transferred from Assyria during the captivity.

testimony is true, because I know whence I came and whither I go; but you do not know whence I came, or whither I go.

15 You judge according to the flesh; but I judge no man.

16 And if I should judge, my judgement is true; because I am not alone, but I and my Father who sent me.

17 And it is written in your own law, that the testimony of two men is true.

18 I testify concerning myself, and my Father who sent me testifies concerning me.

19 They said to him, Where is your Father? Jesus answered and said to them, You know neither me, nor my Father; if you knew me, you would know my Father also.

20 These words he spoke in the treasury, while he taught in the temple; and no man arrested him, for his time had not yet come.

21 ¶ Jesus again said to them, I am going away, and you will seek me, and you will die in your sins; and where I am going you cannot come.

22 The Jews said, Why, will he kill himself? for he says, Where I am going, you cannot come.

23 And he said to them, You are from below, and I am from above; you are of this world, but I am not of this world.

24 I told you that you will die in your sins; for unless you believe that I am he, you will die in your sins.

25 The Jews said, Who are you? Jesus said to them, Even though I should begin to speak to you,

26 I have many things to say and to judge concerning you; but he who sent me is true; and I speak in the world only those things which I have heard from him.

27 They did not understand that he spoke to them concerning the Father.

28 Again Jesus said to them, When you have lifted up the Son of man, then you will understand that I am he, and I do nothing of my own accord; but as my Father has taught me, so I speak just like him.

29 And he who sent me is with me; and my Father has never left me alone; because I always do what pleases him.

30 ¶ While he was speaking these words, a great many believed in him.

31 Then Jesus said to the Jews who believed in him,

If you abide by my word, you are truly my disciples.

32 And you will know the truth, and that very truth will make you free.

33 They said to him, We are the seed of Abraham, and we have never been enslaved to any man; how do you say, You will be free sons?

34 Jesus said to them, Truly, truly, I say to you, Whoever commits sin is a servant of sin.

35 And a servant does not remain in the house forever, but the son remains forever.

36 If therefore, the Son shall make you free, you shall truly become free.

37 I know you are the seed of Abraham; but still you want to kill me, because you have no room in you for my word.

38 I speak what I have seen with my Father; and you do what you have seen with your father.

39 They answered and said to him, Our own father is Abraham. Jesus said to them, If you were the sons of Abraham, you would be doing the works of Abraham.

40 But behold, now you want to kill me, even a man who has told you the truth,

which I heard from God; this Abraham did not do.

41 But you do the works of your father. They said to him, We are not born of fornication; we have one Father, God.

42 Jesus said to them, If God were your Father, you would love me, for I proceeded and came from God; I did not come of my own accord, but he sent me.

43 Why therefore do you not understand my word? Because you cannot obey my word?

44 You are from the father of accusation, and you want to do the lusts of your father; he who is a murderer of men from the very beginning and who never stands by the truth, because there is no truth in him. When he speaks he speaks his own lie, because he is a liar, and the father of it.

45 But because I speak the truth, you do not believe me.

46 Which one of you can rebuke me because of sin? If I speak the truth, why do you not believe me?

47 He who is of God, hears God's words; for this reason you do not hear, because you are not of God.

48 The Jews answered and said to him, Did we not say

well, that you are a Samaritan, and that you are crazy?

49 Jesus said to them, I am not crazy; but I honor my Father, and you curse me.

50 I do not seek my glory; there is one who seeks and judges.

51 Truly, truly, I say to you, Whoever obeys my word, shall never see death.

52 The Jews said to him, Now we are sure that you are insane. Abraham and the prophets have died; and yet you say, Whoever obeys my word, shall never taste death.

53 Why, are you greater than our father Abraham who died, and the prophets who died? Whom do you make yourself?

54 Jesus said to them, If I honor myself, my honor is nothing; but it is my Father who honors me, the one whom you say, He is our God.

55 Yet you have not known him, but I do know him; and if I should say, I do not know him, I would be a liar like yourselves; but I do know him, and I obey his word.

56 Your father Abraham rejoiced to see my day; and he saw it and was glad.

57 The Jews said to him, You are not yet fifty years old, and yet have you seen Abraham?

58 Jesus said to them, Truly, truly, I say to you, Before Abraham was born, I was.

59 So they took up stones, to stone him; and Jesus hid himself, and went out of the temple, and he passed through the midst of them, and went away.

CHAPTER 9

AND as he passed by he saw a man who was blind from his mother's womb.

2 And his disciples asked him, saying, Teacher, who did sin, this man, or his parents, that he was born blind?

3 Jesus said to them, Neither did he sin nor his parents. But that the works of God might be seen in him,

4 I must do the works of him who sent me, while it is day; the night comes when no man can work.

5 As long as I am in the world, I am the light of the world.

6 When he said these words, he spat on the ground, and mixed clay with his saliva, and he placed it on the eyes of the blind man.

7 Then he said to him, Go and wash in the baptismal

pool of Siloam. He went and washed, and he came seeing.

8 His neighbors and those who had seen him before begging, said, Is not this he who used to sit down and beg?

9 Some said, It is he; and some said, No, but he resembles him; but he said, I am he.

10 Then they said to him, How were your eyes opened?

11 He answered and said to them, A man whose name is Jesus made clay and placed it on my eyes, and he said to me, Go and wash in the water of Siloam; and I went and washed, and I see.

12 They said to him, Where is he? He said to them, I do not know.

13 ¶ So they brought to the Pharisees him who had been blind from his birth.

14 Now it was the sabbath when Jesus made the clay, and opened his eyes.

15 Again the Pharisees asked him, How did you receive your sight? He said to them, He placed clay on my eyes, and I washed, and I see.

16 Then some of the Pharisees said, This man is not from God, because he does not observe the sabbath; others said, How can a man who is a sinner do these miracles? And there was a division among them.

17 They said to the blind man again, What do you say concerning him who opened your eyes? He said to them, I say he is a prophet.

18 But the Jews did not believe concerning him, that he had been blind and had received his sight, until they called the parents of him who had received his sight.

19 And they asked them, Is this your son, who you say was born blind? how then does he now see?

20 His parents answered and said, We know that he is our son, and that he was born blind.

21 But how he sees now, or who opened his eyes, we do not know; he is of age, ask him, he will speak for himself.

22 His parents said these things because they were afraid of the Jews; for the Jews had decided already, that if any man should confess that he is the Christ, they would put him out of the synagogue.

23 For this reason his parents said, He is of age, ask him.

24 So they called a second time the man who had been blind, and said to him, Give

praise to God, for we know that this man is a sinner.

25 He answered and said to them, If he is a sinner I do not know; but I do know one thing, that I was blind, and now behold, I see.

26 They said to him again, What did he do to you? how did he open your eyes?

27 He said to them, I have already told you, and you did not listen; why do you want to hear it again? why, do you also want to become his disciples?

28 Then they cursed him, and said to him, You are his disciple, but we are disciples of Moses.

29 And we know that God spoke with Moses; but as for this man, we do not know whence he is.

30 The man answered and said to them, This is surprising, that you do not know whence he is, and yet he opened my eyes.

31 We know that God does not hear the voice of sinners; but he hears the one who fears him and does his will.

32 From ages it has never been heard that a man opened the eyes of one who was born blind.

33 If this man were not from God, he could not have done this.

34 They answered and said to him, You were wholly born in sins, and yet do you teach us? And they cast him out.

35 ¶ And Jesus heard that they had cast him out; and he found him and said to him, Do you believe in the Son of God?

36 He who was healed answered and said, Who is he, my Lord, so that I may believe in him?

37 Jesus said to him, You have seen him, and he is the one who is speaking with you.

38 He said, I do believe, my Lord; and he fell down and worshipped him.

39 Then Jesus said to him, I have come for the judgement of this world, so that those who cannot see may see; and those who see may become blind.

40 ¶ When some of the Pharisees who were with him heard these words, they said to him, Why, are we also blind?

41 Jesus said to them, If you were blind, you would have no sin; but now you say, We see; because of this your sin remains.

CHAPTER 10

TRULY, truly, I say to you, He who does not enter by the door into the sheepfold, but climbs up from another place, he is a thief and a bandit.

2 But he who enters by the door, he is the shepherd of the sheep.

3 To him the door-keeper opens the door; and the sheep hear his voice; and he calls his own sheep by their names and brings them out.

4 And when he has brought out his sheep,[1] he goes before them; and his own sheep follow him, because they know his voice.

5 The sheep do not follow a stranger, but they run away from him; because they do not know the voice of a stranger.

6 Jesus spoke this parable to them; but they did not understand what he was telling them.

7 Jesus said to them again, Truly, truly, I say to you, I am the door of the sheep.

8 All who have come are thieves and bandits, if the sheep did not hear them.

9 I am the door; if any man enter by me, he shall live, and he shall come in and go out and find pasture.

10 A thief does not come, except to steal and kill and destroy; I have come that they might have life, and have it abundantly.

11 I am the good shepherd; a good shepherd risks his life for the sake of his sheep.

12 But the hired person, who is not the shepherd, and who is not the owner of the sheep, when he sees the wolf coming, leaves the sheep and runs away; and the wolf comes and seizes and scatters the sheep.

13 The hired person runs away, because he is hired, and he does not care for the sheep.

14 I am the good shepherd, and I know my own, and my own know me.

15 Just as my Father knows me, I also know my Father; and I lay down my life for the sake of the sheep.

16 I have other sheep also, which are not of this fold; them also I must bring, and they will hear my voice; and all the sheep will become one flock and one shepherd.

17 This is why my Father loves me, because I lay down my life, so that I may take it up again.

18 No man takes it away from me, but I lay it down of my own will. Therefore I have the power to lay it down,

---

[1] "His sheep" refers to the several flocks in the fold, "his own sheep" refers to his own flock.

Cf. dif. verses 3–4–8–11

and I have the power to take it up again. This command I received from my Father.

19 ¶ There was again a division among the Jews because of these sayings.

20 And many of them said, He is insane and rambles; why do you listen to him?

21 Others said, These are not the words of a crazy man. Why, can a crazy man open the eyes of the blind?

22 ¶ Then came the feast of dedication at Jerusalem, and it was winter.

23 And Jesus was walking in the temple in Solomon's porch.

24 Then the Jews surrounded him and said to him, How long do you vex our soul with uncertainty? If you are the Christ, tell us openly.

25 Jesus answered and said to them, I have told you, but you do not believe; yet the works which I do, in the name of my Father, testify of me.

26 But you do not believe, because you are not of my sheep, just as I told you.

27 My own sheep hear my voice, and I know them, and they follow me;

28 And I give to them eternal life; and they will never perish, and no man will snatch them from my hands.

29 For my Father who gave them to me is greater than all; and no man can snatch anything from my Father's hand.

30 I and my Father are one in accord.

31 Then the Jews again took up stones to stone him.

32 Jesus said to them, I have showed you many good works from my Father; for which one of them do you stone me?

33 The Jews said to him, It is not because of the good works we stone you, but because you blaspheme; for while you are only a man, you make yourself God.

34 Jesus said to them, Is it not so written in your law, I said, you are gods?

35 If he called them gods, because the word of God was with them, and the scripture cannot be broken;

36 Yet to the one whom the Father sanctified and sent to the world, you say, You blaspheme, just because I said to you, I am the Son of God.

37 If I am not doing the works of my Father, do not believe me.

38 But if I am doing them, even though you do not believe in me, believe in the works; so that you may know

and believe that my Father is with me and I am with my Father.

39 ¶ And they wanted again to seize him; but he escaped from their hands.

40 And he went away to the Jordan crossing, to the place where John was, where he first baptized; and he remained there.

41 And many men came to him and said, John did not perform a single miracle; but everything which John said concerning this man is true.

42 And many believed in him.

CHAPTER 11

NOW there was a man who was sick, Lazarus of the town of Bethany, the brother of Mary and Martha.

2 This is the Mary who anointed the feet of Jesus with perfume and wiped them with her hair. Lazarus who was sick, was her brother.

3 His two sisters therefore sent to Jesus, saying, Our Lord, behold, the one whom you love is sick.

4 Jesus said, This is not a sickness of death, but for the sake of the glory of God, that the Son of God may be glorified on his account.

5 Now Jesus loved Martha and Mary and Lazarus.

6 When he heard he was sick, he remained two days in the place where he was.

7 After that he said to his disciples, Come, let us go again to Judaea.

8 His disciples said to him, Teacher, not long ago the Jews wanted to stone you, and yet are you going there again?

9 Jesus said to them, Are there not twelve hours in the day? If a man walks by day time, he will not stumble, because he sees the light of this world.

10 But if a man travels at night time, he will stumble, because there is no light in it.

11 Jesus said these things; and after that he said to them, Our friend Lazarus is asleep; but I am going to awake him.

12 His disciples said to him, Our Lord, if he is sleeping, he will get well.

13 But Jesus spoke of his death; and they thought that what he said was sleeping in bed.

14 Then Jesus said to them, plainly, Lazarus is dead.

15 And I am glad I was not there, for your sakes, so that you may believe; but let us walk there.

16 Then Thomas, who is called the Twin, said to his

fellow disciples, Let us also go, and die with him.

17 ¶ So Jesus came to Bethany, and he found that he had been four days in the tomb.

18 Now Bethany was towards Jerusalem, a distance of about two miles.

19 And many Jews kept coming to Martha and Mary, to comfort their hearts concerning their brother.

20 When Martha heard that Jesus had come, she went out to meet him; but Mary sat in the house.

21 Then Martha said to Jesus, My Lord, if you had been here, my brother would not have died.

22 But even now I know that whatever you ask of God, he will give you.

23 Jesus said to her, Your brother will rise up.

24 Martha said to him, I know he will rise up in the resurrection at the last day.

25 Jesus said to her, I am the resurrection and the life; he who believes in me, even though he die, he shall live.

26 And whoever is alive and believes in me shall never die. Do you believe this?

27 She said to him, Yes, my Lord; I do believe that you are the Christ, the Son of God, who is to come to the world.

28 And when she had said these things, she went away and called her sister Mary secretly, and said to her, Our teacher has come, and he is calling you.

29 When Mary heard it, she rose up quickly and came to him.

30 Jesus had not yet come into the town, but he was still at the same place where Martha met him.

31 The Jews also who were with her in the house, comforting her, when they saw Mary rise up quickly and go out, followed her, for they thought she was going to the tomb to weep.

32 When Mary came where Jesus was, and saw him, she threw herself at his feet, and said to him, My Lord, if you had been here, my brother would not have died.

33 When Jesus saw her weeping, and the Jews weeping, who had come with her, he was moved in his spirit, and was greatly disturbed.

34 And he said, Where have you laid him? They said to him, Our Lord, come and see.

35 And Jesus was in tears.

36 The Jews then said, Look, how much he loved him!

37 Some of them said, Could not this man, who

 Cf. dif. verses 31–35–37

opened the eyes of that blind man, have also kept this man from dying?

38 As Jesus was disturbed in himself and because of them, he came to the tomb. That tomb was a cave, and a stone was placed at the entrance.

39 Jesus said, Take away this stone. Martha, the sister of the dead man, said to him, My Lord, he is already disfigured, for he is dead four days.

40 Jesus said to her, Did not I say to you that if you believe, you will see the glory of God?

41 So they took away the stone. And Jesus lifted his eyes upwards, and said, O Father, I thank you for you have heard me,

42 And I know that you always hear me; but I say these things just because of this people who stand around, so that they may believe that you have sent me.

43 And when he had said this, he cried with a loud voice, Lazarus, come outside.

44 And the dead man came out, his hands and feet bound with burial clothes; and his face bound with a burial napkin. Jesus said to them, Loose him and let him go.

45 ¶ Many of the Jews who had come to Mary, when they saw what Jesus had done, believed in him.

46 And some of them went to the Pharisees, and told them everything Jesus had done.

47 ¶ So the high priests and the Pharisees gathered together and said, What shall we do? for this man does many miracles?

48 If we allow him to continue like this, all men will believe in him; and the Romans will come and take over both our country and our people.

49 But one of them, called Caiphas, who was the high priest for that year, said to them, You know nothing;

50 Nor do you reason that it is much better for us that one man should die instead of the people, and not all the people perish.

51 He did not say this of himself; but because he was the high priest for that year, he prophesied that Jesus had to die for the sake of the people;

52 And not only for the sake of the people, but also to gather together the children of God who are scattered abroad.

53 And from that very day, they decided to kill him.

54 ¶ Jesus therefore did not walk openly among the Jews, but went away thence to a place which is close to the wilderness, in the province of Ephraim; and he remained there with his disciples.

55 Now the Jewish passover was at hand; and many went up from the towns to Jerusalem, before the feast, to purify themselves.

56 And they were looking for Jesus, and at the temple they kept saying to one another, What do you think, will he not come to the feast?

57 But the high priests and the Pharisees had already commanded, that if any man should know where he is, to let them know, so that they might seize him.

CHAPTER 12

SIX days before the passover, Jesus came to Bethany, where Lazarus was, whom Jesus had raised from the dead.

2 And they gave him a banquet there; Martha served; but Lazarus was one of the guests who were with him.

3 Then Mary took a cruse containing pure and expensive nard, and anointed the feet of Jesus, and wiped his feet with her hair; and the house was filled with the fragrance of the perfume.

4 And Judas of Iscariot, one of his disciples, who was about to betray him, said,

5 Why was not this oil sold for three hundred pennies, and given to the poor?

6 He said this, not because he cared for the poor; but because he was a thief, and the purse was with him, and he carried whatever was put in it.

7 Jesus then said, Leave her alone; she has kept it for the day of my burial.

8 For you have the poor always with you, but me you have not always.

9 ¶ Many people of the Jews heard that Jesus was there; so they came, not only on account of Jesus, but also to see Lazarus, whom he had raised from the dead.

10 And the high priests were thinking of killing Lazarus also;

11 Because on his account a great many Jews were leaving and believing in Jesus.

12 ¶ On the next day, a large crowd which had come to the feast, when they heard that Jesus was coming to Jerusalem,

13 Took branches of palm trees, and went out to greet

Cf. dif. verses 54

him, and they cried out and said, Hosanna, Blessed is the king of Israel who comes in the name of the Lord.

14 And Jesus found an ass and sat on it; as it is written,

15 Fear not, O daughter of Zion; behold, your king cometh to you, riding on the colt of an ass.

16 His disciples did not understand these things at that time; but when Jesus was glorified, then his disciples remembered that these things were written concerning him, and they had done these things to him.

17 The people who were with him testified that he had called Lazarus from the tomb, and raised him from the dead.

18 It was on this account that large crowds went out to meet him, for they heard that he had performed this miracle.

19 The Pharisees said one to another, Do you see that you have not been able to gain anything? Behold, all the people have gone after him.

20 ¶ Now there were some Gentiles[1] among them who had come up to worship at the feast.

21 They came and approached Philip of Bethsaida of Galilee, and asked him, saying, My lord, we would like to see Jesus.

22 Philip came and told Andrew; then Andrew and Philip told Jesus.

23 Jesus answered and said to them, The hour has come that the Son of man should be glorified.

24 Truly, truly, I say to you, that unless a grain of wheat falls and dies in the ground, it will be left alone; but if it dies, it produces much fruit.

25 He who loves his life will lose it; and he who has no concern for his life in this world will keep it unto life eternal.

26 If any man serve me, let him follow me; and where I am, there also will my servant be; he who serves me, him my Father will honor.

27 Now my soul is disturbed, and what shall I say? O my Father, deliver me from this hour; but for this cause I came to this very hour.

28 O Father, glorify your name. Then a voice was heard from heaven, I am glorified, and I shall again be glorified.

---

[1] The Aramaic *ammey* means Gentiles, that is, Syrians, Idumaeans, and other neighboring peoples. The word for Greeks is *yonaye*.

29 And the people who stood by heard it, and said, It was a thunder; others said, An angel spoke to him.

30 Jesus answered and said to them, This voice was not on my account, but for your sake.

31 Now is the judgment of this world; now the leader of this world will be cast out.

32 And I, when I am lifted up from the earth, will draw every man to me.

33 He said this, to show by what kind of death he was to die.

34 The people said to him, We have heard from the law that the Christ shall remain forever; how do you say that the Son of man must be lifted up? who is this Son of man?

35 Jesus said to them, The light is with you for a little while; walk while you have the light, so that the darkness may not overcome you; and he who walks in the darkness does not know where he goes.

36 While you have the light, believe in the light, so that you may become the sons of the light. Jesus spoke these things, and went away and hid himself from them.

37 ¶ Even though he had performed all of these miracles before them, yet they did not believe in him;

38 So that the word of the prophet Isaiah might be fulfilled, who said, My Lord, who will believe our report, and to whom has the arm of the Lord been revealed?

39 For this reason, they could not believe, because Isaiah said again,

40 Their eyes have become blind and their heart darkened, so that they cannot see with their eyes and understand with their heart; let them return and I will heal them.

41 Isaiah said these things, when he saw his glory and spoke concerning him.

42 Many of the leading men also believed in him; but because of the Pharisees they did not confess it, so that they might not be cast out of the synagogue.

43 For they loved the honor of men more than the glory of God.

44 ¶ Jesus cried out and said, He who believes in me, believes not in me but in him who sent me.

45 And he who sees me, has already seen him who sent me.

46 I have come into the world as the light, so that

whoever believes in me may not remain in the darkness.

47 And he who hears my words, and does not obey them, I will not judge him; for I have not come to judge the world, but to save the world.

48 He who oppresses me and does not receive my words, there is one who will judge him; the word which I have spoken, it will judge him at the last day.

49 For I did not speak of myself; but the Father who sent me, he commanded me what to say and what to speak.

50 And I know that his commandment is life everlasting; these things therefore which I speak, just as my Father told me, so I speak.

CHAPTER 13

NOW before the feast of the passover, Jesus knew the hour had come to depart from this world to his Father. And he loved his own who were in this world, and he loved them unto the end.

2 ¶ During supper, Satan put into the heart of Judas, son of Simon of Iscariot, to deliver him.

3 But Jesus, because he knew that the Father had given everything into his hands, and that he came from God and was going to God,

4 He rose from supper and laid aside his robes; and he took an apron and tied it around his loins.

5 Then he poured water into a basin, and began to wash the feet of his disciples, and to wipe them with the apron which was tied around his loins.

6 When he came to Simon Peter, Simon said to him, You, my Lord, are you going to wash my feet?

7 Jesus answered and said to him, What I am doing, you do not know now, but later you will understand.

8 Then Simon Peter said to him, You will never wash my feet. Jesus said to him, If I do not wash you, you have no part with me.

9 Simon Peter said to him, Then, my Lord, wash not only my feet, but also my hands and my head.

10 Jesus said to him, He who has bathed does not need except to wash his feet only, for he is already all clean; so you are all clean, but not everyone of you.

11 For Jesus knew him who was to betray him; therefore he said, Not everyone of you is clean.

12 When he had washed their feet, he put on his robes and sat down; and he said to them, Do you know what I have done to you?

13 You call me, our Teacher and our Lord; and what you say is well, for I am.

14 If I then, your Lord and Teacher, have washed your feet, how much more should you wash one another's feet?

15 For I have given you this as an example, so that just as I have done to you, you should also do.

16 Truly, truly, I say to you, There is no servant who is greater than his master; and no apostle who is greater than he who sent him.

17 If you know these things, blessed are you if you do them.

18 I do not say this concerning all of you, for I know those whom I have chosen; but that the scripture might be fulfilled, He who eats bread with me has lifted up his heel against me.

19 I tell you now before it happens, that when it happens, you may believe that I am he.

20 Truly, truly, I say to you, He who receives him whom I send, receives me; and he who receives me receives him who sent me.

21 ¶ Jesus said these things, and he was disturbed in spirit, and testified and said, Truly, truly, I say to you, one of you will betray me.

22 The disciples then looked at each other, because they did not know concerning whom he spoke.

23 Now there was one of his disciples who was leaning on his bosom, the one whom Jesus loved.

24 Simon Peter winked at him, to ask him of whom he spoke.

25 So that disciple leaned himself on the breast of Jesus, and said to him, My Lord, who is he?

26 Jesus answered and said, The one for whom I dip bread and give to him. So Jesus dipped the bread, and gave it to Judas, the son of Simon of Iscariot.

27 And after the bread, Satan took possession of him. So Jesus said to him, What you are going to do, do it soon.

28 But no man of those who were sitting at the table understood about what he said this to him.

29 For some of them thought, because the purse was with Judas, that he ordered him to buy what was needed for the feast;

or to give something to the poor.

30 Judas then received the bread and went outside immediately; it was night when he went out.

31 ¶ Jesus then said, Now the Son of man is glorified, and God is glorified by him.

32 If God is glorified by him, God will also glorify him by himself, and he will glorify him at once.

33 My sons, I am with you yet a little while, and you will want me. And just as I said to the Jews, Where I go, you cannot come; so now I tell you also.

34 A new commandment I give you, that you love one another; just as I have loved you, that you also love one another.

35 By this every man shall know that you are my disciples, if you have love one to another.

36 Simon Peter said to him, Our Lord, where are you going? Jesus answered and said to him, Where I go, you cannot follow me now, but you will follow later.

37 Simon Peter said to him, My Lord, why can I not follow you now? I will even lay down my life for you.

38 Jesus said to him, Will you lay down your life for me? Truly, truly, I say to you, The cock shall not crow, until you have denied me three times.

CHAPTER 14

LET not your heart be troubled; believe in God, and believe in me also.

2 In my Father's house there are many rooms; if it were not so, I would have told you. I am going to prepare a place for you.

3 And if I go and prepare a place for you, I will come again, and take you to me; so that where I am, you may also be.

4 And you know where I am going, and you know the way.

5 Thomas said to him, Our Lord, we do not know where you are going, and how can we know the way?

6 Jesus said to him, I am the way, and the truth, and the life; no man comes to my Father except by me.

7 If you had known me, you would have known my Father also; from henceforth you know him and you have seen him.

8 Philip said to him, Our Lord, show us the Father, and that is enough for us.

9 Jesus said to him, All this time I have been with you, and yet you do not know me,

Philip? he who sees me, has seen the Father; and how do you say, Show us the Father?

10 Do you not believe I am with my Father and my Father with me?[1] the words that I speak, I do not speak of myself; but my Father who abides with me, he does these works.

11 Believe that I am with my Father, and my Father with me; and if not, believe because of the works.

12 Truly, truly, I say to you, He who believes in me, the works which I do he shall do also; even greater than these things he shall do, because I am going to my Father.

13 And whatever you ask in my name, I will do it for you, so that the Father may be glorified through his Son.

14 If you ask me in my own name, I will do it.

15 If you love me, then obey my commandments.

16 And I will ask of my Father, and he will give you another Comforter, to be with you for ever;

17 Even the Spirit of the truth; whom the world cannot receive, because it has not seen him, and does not know him; but you know him because he abides with you, and is in you.

18 I will not leave you orphans, for I will come to you after a little while.

19 And the world will not see me, but you will see me; because I live, you also shall live.

20 In that day you will know that I am with my Father, and you are with me, and I am with you.

21 He who has my commandments with him and obeys them, he is the one who loves me; he who loves me will be loved by my Father, and I will love him, and reveal myself to him.

22 Judas, (not of Iscariot) said to him, My Lord, why is it that you will reveal yourself to us, and not to the world?

23 Jesus answered and said to him, He who loves me, keeps my word; and my Father will love him, and we will come to him, and make a place of abode with him.

24 But he who does not love me, does not keep my word; and this word which you hear, is not mine own, but the Father's who sent me.

25 I have spoken these

---

[1] This is an Aramaic expression meaning, "I stand for my Father and my Father stands for me and backs me up."

things to you, while I am with you.

26 But the Comforter, the Holy Spirit, whom my Father will send in my name, he will teach you everything, and remind you of everything which I tell you.

27 Peace I leave with you; my own peace I give you; not as the world gives, I give to you. Let not your heart be troubled, and do not be afraid.

28 You heard that I told you, I am going away, and I will come to you. If you loved me, you would rejoice because I am going to my Father; for my Father is greater than I.

29 And now behold, I have told you before it happens, so that when it does happen, you may believe.

30 Hereafter I will not talk much with you; for the prince of this world comes; and yet he has nothing against me.

31 But that the world may know that I love my Father; and as my Father has commanded me, so I do. Arise, let us go away from here.

CHAPTER 15

I AM the true vine, and my Father is the worker.

2 Every branch in me that does not bear fruit, he cuts out; and the one which bears fruit, he prunes so that it may bring forth more fruit.

3 You have already been pruned because of the word which I have spoken to you.

4 Remain with me and I with you. Just as a branch cannot give fruit by itself, unless it remains in the vine; even so you cannot, unless you remain with me.

5 I am the vine, you are the branches. He who remains with me and I with him, will bear abundant fruit; because without me you can do nothing.

6 Unless a man remains with me, he will be cast outside, like a branch which is withered; which they pick up and throw into the fire to be burned.

7 If you remain with me, and my words remain with you, whatever you ask shall be done for you.

8 In this the Father will be glorified, that you bear abundant fruit, and be my disciples.

9 ¶ Just as my Father has loved me, I also have loved you; remain in my love.

10 If you keep my commandments, you will remain in my love; even as I have kept my Father's com-

mandments, and I remain in his love.

11 I have spoken these things to you, that my joy may be in you, and that your joy may be full.

12 This is my commandment, that you love one another, just as I have loved you.

13 There is no greater love than this, when a man lays down his life for the sake of his friends.

14 You are my friends, if you do everything that I command you.

15 Henceforth I will not call you servants, because a servant does not know what his master does; but I have always called you my friends, because everything that I heard from my Father I made it known to you.

16 You did not choose me, but I chose you, and I have appointed you, that you also should go and produce fruit, and that your fruit might remain; so that whatever you ask my Father in my name, he will give it to you.

17 I command these things to you, that you love one another.

18 If the world hate you, know well that it has hated me before you.

19 If you were of the world, the world would love its own; but you are not of the world, for I have chosen you out of the world; this is why the world hates you.

20 Remember the word which I said to you, that no servant is greater than his master. If they have persecuted me, they will also persecute you; if they kept my word, they will also keep yours.

21 But they will do all these things to you for the sake of my name, because they do not know him who sent me.

22 If I had not come and spoken to them, they would be without sin; but now they have no excuse for their sins.

23 He who hates me, hates my Father also.

24 If I had not done works before their eyes, such as no other man has ever done, they would be without sin; but now they have seen and hated me and also my Father.

25 So that the word which is written in their law may be fulfilled, They hated me for no reason.

26 But when the Comforter comes, whom I will send to you from my Father, the Spirit of truth, which proceeds from my Father, he will testify concerning me.

27 And you also will testify because you have been with me from the beginning.

CHAPTER 16

I HAVE spoken these things to you, so that you may not stumble.

2 For they will put you out of their synagogues; and the hour will come that whoever kills you, will think that he has offered an offering to God.

3 And these things they will do, because they have not known my Father, nor me.

4 I have spoken these things to you, that when their time does come, you may remember them, that I told you. And these things I did not tell you before, because I was with you.

5 ¶ But now I am going to him who sent me, and yet no one of you asks me, Where are you going?

6 But because I told you these things, sorrow has come and filled your hearts.

7 But I tell you the truth, It is better for you that I should go away; for if I do not go away, the Comforter will not come to you; but if I should go, I will send him to you.

8 And when he is come, he will rebuke the world concerning sin, concerning righteousness, and concerning judgement.

9 Concerning sin, because they do not believe in me;

10 Concerning righteousness, because I go to my Father, and you will not see me again;

11 Concerning judgement, because the leader of this world has been judged.

12 Again, I have many other things to tell you, but you cannot grasp them now.

13 But when the Spirit of truth is come, he will guide you into all the truth; for he will not speak from himself, but what he hears that he will speak; and he will make known to you things which are to come in the future.

14 He will glorify me; because he will take of my own and show to you.

15 Everything that my Father has is mine; this is the reason why I told you that he will take of my own and show to you.

16 A little while, and you will not see me; and again a little while, and you will see me, because I am going to the Father.

17 Then his disciples said to one another, What is this that he said to us, A little while and you will not see me; and again a little while

and you will see me; and, because I am going to my Father?

18 And they said, What is this that he said, A little while? We cannot understand what he is talking.

19 Jesus knew that they desired to ask him, and he said to them, Are you inquiring among yourselves concerning this, that I told you, A little while and you will not see me; and again a little while and you will see me?

20 Truly, truly, I say to you, that you will weep and wail, and yet the world will rejoice; and you will be sad, but your sadness will be changed into gladness.

21 When a woman is in travail, she is depressed, because her day has arrived; but when she has given birth to a son, she no longer remembers her troubles, because of the joy that a male[1] child is born into the world.

22 So you also are depressed; but I will see you again, and your heart will rejoice, and your joy no man will take away from you.

23 In that day you will not ask me anything. Truly, truly, I say to you, that whatever you ask my Father in my name, he will give it to you.

24 Hitherto you have asked nothing in my name; ask and you will receive, so that your joy may be full.

25 I have spoken these things in figures; but the time is coming, when I will not speak to you in figures, but will plainly explain to you concerning the Father.

26 In that day you will ask in my name; and I will not say to you, I will ask the Father concerning you.

27 For the Father himself loves you, because you have loved me, and have believed that I came forth from the Father.

28 I came forth from the Father, and I came into the world; again, I am leaving the world and I am going to the Father.

29 His disciples said to him, Behold now you speak plainly, and do not utter a single figure.

30 Now we understand that you know everything; and you need no man to ask you; by this we believe that you have come forth from God.

31 Jesus said to them, Believe it.

---

[1] When a girl is born in the East, the news is kept from the mother for a while if she is in danger. If a boy is born she is at once informed to cheer her up.

32 For behold, the hour is coming, and it has now come, when you will be dispersed, every man to his own country, and you will leave me alone; and yet I am never alone, because the Father is with me.

33 These things I have said to you, that in me you may have peace. In the world you will have tribulation; but have courage; I have conquered the world.

CHAPTER 17

JESUS spoke these things, and then he lifted up his eyes to heaven and said, O my Father, the hour has come; glorify your Son, so that your Son may glorify you.

2 Just as you have given him power over all flesh, so that to all whom you have given him, he may give life eternal.

3 And this is life eternal, that they might know you, that you are the only true God, even the one who sent Jesus Christ.

4 I have already glorified you on the earth; for the work which you had given to me to do, I have finished it.

5 So now, O my Father, glorify me with you, with the same glory which I had with you before the world was made.

6 I have made your name known to the men whom you gave me out of the world; they were yours and you gave them to me; and they have kept your word.

7 Now they know that whatever you have given me is from you.

8 For the words which you gave me I gave them; and they accepted them, and have known truly that I came forth from you, and they have believed that you sent me.

9 What I request is for them; I make no request for the world, but for those whom you have given to me; because they are yours.

10 And everything which is mine, is yours; and what is yours is mine; and I am glorified by them.

11 Hereafter I am not in the world, but these are in the world; and I am coming to you. O holy Father, protect them in your name, which you have given me, that they may be one, even as we are.

12 While I was with them in the world, I protected them in your name; those you gave me I protected, and not one of them is lost, except the son of perdition, that the scripture might be fulfilled.

13 Now I am coming to you; and these things I speak while I am in the world, that my joy may be complete in them.

14 I have given them your word; and the world hated them, because they were not of the world, just as I am not of the world.

15 What I request is not that you should take them out of the world, but that you should protect them from evil.

16 For they are not of the world, just as I am not of the world.

17 O Father, sanctify them in your truth, because your word is truth.

18 Just as you sent me into the world, so I have sent them into the world.

19 And for their sakes, I am sanctifying myself, so that they also may be sanctified in the truth.

20 I am not making request for these alone, but also for the sake of those who believe in me through their word.

21 So that they all may be one; just as you, my Father, art with me, and I am with you, that they also may be one with us; so that the world may believe you sent me.

22 And the glory which you gave me, I gave them; so that they may be one just as we are one.

23 I with them and you with me, that they may become perfected in one; so that the world may know that you sent me, and that you loved them just as you loved me.

24 O Father, I wish that those whom you have given me, may also be with me where I am; so that they may see my glory which you have given me; for you have loved me before the foundation of the world.

25 O my righteous Father, the world did not know you, but I have known you; and these have known that you have sent me.

26 And I have made your name known to them, and I am still making it known; so that the love with which you loved me may be among them, and I be with them.

CHAPTER 18

JESUS said these things and went out with his disciples across the brook Kidron, to a place where there was a garden, where he and his disciples entered.

2 Judas the traitor also knew that place; because Jesus and his disciples frequently gathered there.

Cf. dif. verses 21–23

3 Judas, therefore, took a company of soldiers, and also guards from the high priests and the Pharisees, and he came there with torches and lamps and weapons.

4 Jesus, knowing everything that was to happen, went out and said to them, Whom do you want?

5 They said to him, Jesus the Nazarene. Jesus said to them, I am he. Judas the traitor was also standing with them.

6 When Jesus said to them, I am he, they drew back and fell to the ground.

7 Jesus again asked them, Whom do you want? They said, Jesus the Nazarene.

8 Jesus said to them, I have told you that I am he; if then you want me, let these men go away;

9 That the word which he said might be fulfilled, Of those whom you gave me, I have lost not even one.

10 But Simon Peter had a sword, and he drew it and struck the high priest's servant, and cut off his right ear. The servant's name was Malech.

11 And Jesus said to Peter, Put the sword into its sheath; shall I not drink the cup which my Father has given me?

12 ¶ Then the soldiers and the captains, and the Jewish guards seized Jesus and bound him,

13 And they brought him first to Annas, because he was the father-in-law of Caiaphas, who was the high priest of that year.

14 For Caiaphas was the one who had counselled the Jews, that it was better for one man to die instead of the people.

15 Simon Peter and one of the other disciples followed Jesus. The high priest knew that disciple, so he entered with Jesus into the courtyard.

16 But Simon stood outside near the door. Then the other disciple, whom the high priest knew, went out and told the portress, and brought in Simon.

17 The young portress then said to Simon, Why, are you also one of the disciples of this man? He said to her, No.

18 And the servants and guards were standing and making a fire, to warm themselves because it was cold; Simon also stood with them and warmed himself.

19 The high priest then questioned Jesus concerning his disciples and concerning his teaching.

20 Jesus said to him, I have spoken openly to the people, and I have always taught in the synagogue and in the temple, where all Jews assemble; and I have spoken nothing secretly.

21 Why do you ask me? ask those who heard what I have spoken to them; behold, they know everything which I said.

22 And as he said these things, one of the guards who stood by, struck Jesus on his cheek, and said to him, Is this how you answer the high priest?

23 Jesus answered and said to him, If I have spoken any evil, testify to the evil; but if it is good, why did you strike me?

24 Annas then sent Jesus bound to Caiaphas the high priest.

25 Now Simon Peter was standing and warming himself. They said to him, Why, are you also one of his dis-sciples? He denied and said, I am not.

26 Then one of the servants of the high priest, said to him, a kinsman of him whose ear Simon had cut off, Did I not see you with him in the garden?

27 Simon again denied, and at that very hour the cock crew.

28 ¶ Then they brought Jesus from Caiaphas to the praetorium; and it was morning; and they did not enter into the praetorium, so that they may not be defiled before they ate the passover.

29 Pilate then went outside where they were, and said to them, What accusation do you have against this man?

30 They answered and said to him, If he were not an evil-doer, we would not have delivered him up also to you.

31 Then said Pilate to them, Take him yourselves, and judge him according to your own law. The Jews said to him, We have no power to kill a man;

32 So that the word which Jesus had said might be fulfilled, when he signified by what kind of death he was to die.

33 Pilate then entered into the praetorium, and called Jesus and said to him, Are you the king of the Jews?

34 Jesus said to him, Do you say this of yourself, or have others told it to you concerning me?

35 Pilate said to him, Why, am I a Jew? Your own people and the high priests have delivered you to me; what have you done?

36 Jesus said to him, My

kingdom is not of this world; if my kingdom were of this world, my servants would have fought so that I should not be delivered to the Jews; but now my kingdom is not from here.

37 Pilate said to him, Then are you a king? Jesus said to him, You say that I am a king.[1] For this I was born, and for this very thing I came to the world, that I may bear witness concerning the truth. Whoever is of the truth will hear my voice.

38 Pilate said to him, What is this truth? And as he said this, he went out again to the Jews, and said to them, I am unable to find even one cause against him.

39 You have a custom that I should release to you one at the passover; do you wish, therefore, that I release to you this "king of the Jews"?

40 They all cried out saying, Not him, but Bar-Abbas. Now this Bar-Abbas was a bandit.

CHAPTER 19

THEN Pilate had Jesus scourged.

2 And the soldiers wove a crown of thorns, and placed it on his head, and they covered him with purple robes;

3 And they said, Peace be to you, O king of the Jews! and they struck him on his cheeks.

4 Pilate again went outside and said to them, Behold, I bring him outside to you, so that you may know that I find not even one cause against him.

5 So Jesus went outside, wearing the crown of thorns and the purple robes. And Pilate said to them, Behold the man!

6 When the high priests and the guards saw him, they cried out, saying, Crucify him, crucify him! Pilate said to them, You take him and crucify him; for I find no cause in him.

7 The Jews said to him, We have a law, and according to our law he is guilty of death, because he made himself the Son of God.

8 When Pilate heard this saying, he was the more afraid;

9 So he entered again into the praetorium, and said to Jesus, Where do you come from? But Jesus gave him no answer.

10 Pilate said to him, Will you not speak even to me? Do you not know that I have the authority to release you,

---

[1] "You are making the assertion that I am a political king, but I am not."

Cf. dif. verses 38–1–3–4 221

and I have the authority to crucify you?

11 Jesus said to him, You would have no authority whatever over me, if it had not been given to you from above; for this reason the sin of him who delivered me to you is greater than yours.

12 And because of this, Pilate wanted to release him; but the Jews cried out, If you release this man you are not a friend of Caesar; for whoever makes himself a king, is against Caesar.

13 When Pilate heard this word, he brought Jesus outside; then he sat down on the judgment seat, at a place which is called the Stone Pavement but in Hebrew it is called, Gabbatha.

14 It was Friday of the passover, and it was about six o'clock; and he said to the Jews, Behold your king!

15 But they cried out, Take him away, take him away, crucify him, crucify him. Pilate said to them, Shall I crucify your king? The high priests said to him, We have no king except Caesar.

16 Then he delivered him to them to crucify him. So they took hold of Jesus and took him out,

17 Carrying his cross, to the place which is called The Skull, but in Hebrew it is called Golgotha;

18 Where they crucified him, and with him two others, one on either side, and Jesus between.

19 Pilate also wrote on a stone tablet, and placed it on his cross. And the writing was, THIS IS JESUS THE NAZARENE, THE KING OF THE JEWS.

20 And a great many Jews read this tablet, for the place where Jesus was crucified was near the city; and it was written in Hebrew[1] and in Greek and in Roman.

21 The high priests then said to Pilate, Do not write that he is the king of the Jews; but that he said, I am the king of the Jews.

22 Pilate said, What I have written, I have written it.

23 ¶ Now when the soldiers had crucified Jesus, they took his clothes and divided them into four parts, a part to each of the soldiers; but his robe was without seam, woven from the top throughout.

24 So they said one to another, Let us not tear it, but cast lots for it, whose lot it

---

[1] "Hebrew" here refers to nationality but the language of the inscription was Aramaic.

shall be. And the scripture was fulfilled, which said, They divided my clothes among them, and for my robe they cast lots. These things the soldiers did.

25 ¶ Now there were standing by the cross of Jesus his mother, and his mother's sister, and Mary of Cleopas, and Mary of Magdala.

26 When Jesus saw his mother and the disciple whom he loved standing, he said to his mother, Woman, behold your son!

27 Then he said to the disciple, Behold your mother! And from that very hour the disciple took her with him.

28 After these things Jesus knew that everything was now accomplished; and that the scripture might be fulfilled, he said, I thirst.

29 Now there was a pitcher full of vinegar placed there; so they filled a sponge with vinegar and put it on the point of a reed, and placed it on his mouth.

30 ¶ When Jesus drank the vinegar, he said, It is fulfilled; and he bowed his head and gave up his breath.

31 Now because it was Friday the Jews said, Let not these bodies remain on their crosses because the sabbath is dawning; for that sabbath was a great day. So they besought Pilate to have the legs of those who were crucified broken, and to have them lowered down.

32 So the soldiers came and broke the legs of the first one, and of the other one who was crucified with him.

33 But when they came to Jesus, they saw that he was dead already, so they did not break his legs.

34 But one of the soldiers pierced his side with a spear, and immediately blood and water came out.

35 And he who saw it testified, and his testimony is true; and he knows well that what he said is true, that you also may believe.

36 For these things happened that the scripture might be fulfilled, which said, Not even a bone shall be broken in him.

37 And again another scripture which said, They shall look on him whom they pierced.

38 ¶ After these things Joseph of Arimathea, who was a disciple of Jesus, but secretly because of fear of the Jews, besought Pilate that he might take away the body of Jesus. And Pilate granted him permission.

So he came and took away the body of Jesus.

39 And there came also Nicodemus, who at first had come to Jesus by night; and he brought with him a mixture of myrrh and aloes, about a hundred pints.

40 So they took away the body of Jesus, and bound it in linen cloths with the spices, according to the custom of the Jews in burial.

41 Now there was a garden in the place where Jesus was crucified; and in the garden a new tomb, in which no man was yet laid.

42 So they laid Jesus there, because the sabbath was approaching, and because the tomb was near.

CHAPTER 20

ON the first day of the week, early in the morning, while it was yet dark, Mary of Magdala came to the tomb; and she saw that the stone was removed from the tomb.

2 Then she ran and came to Simon Peter and to the other disciple whom Jesus loved, and she said to them, They have taken our Lord out of that tomb, and I do not know where they have laid him.

3 So Simon and the other disciple went out, and came to the tomb.

4 And they were both running together; but that disciple outran Simon, and came first to the tomb.

5 And he looked in and saw the linen cloths lying; but he did not enter in.

6 Then Simon came after him, and entered into the tomb; and he saw the linen cloths lying,

7 And the burial napkin which was bound around his head, was not with the linen cloths, but was wrapped up and put in a place by itself.

8 Then the other disciple who had come first to the tomb also entered in, and he saw and believed.

9 For they did yet not understand from the scripture, that he had to rise from the dead.

10 So the disciples went away again to their lodging place.

11 ¶ But Mary was standing near the tomb weeping; as she wept, she looked into the tomb;

12 And she saw two angels in white sitting, one at the head, and the other at the feet, where the body of Jesus had lain.

13 And they said to her, Woman, why do you weep?

Cf. dif. verses 39–42

She said to them, Because they have taken away my Lord, and I do not know where they have laid him.

14 She said this and turned around, and saw Jesus standing, but she did not know that it was Jesus.

15 Jesus said to her, Woman, why do you weep? and whom do you want? She thought he was the gardener, so she said to him, My lord, if you are the one who has taken him away, tell me where you have laid him, and I will go and take him away.

16 Jesus said to her, Mary. She turned around and said to him in Hebrew, Rabbuli! which means, My Teacher!

17 Jesus said to her, Do not come near me; for I have not yet ascended to my Father; but go to my brethren and say to them, I am ascending to my Father and your Father, and my God and your God.

18 Then Mary of Magdala came and brought glad tidings to the disciples, that she had seen our Lord and that he had told her these things.

19 ¶ When it was evening on that first day of the week, and the doors were shut where the disciples were staying for fear of the Jews, Jesus came, stood among them, and said to them, Peace be with you.

20 He said this, and then he showed them his hands and his side. The disciples rejoiced when they saw our Lord.

21 Then Jesus said to them again, Peace be with you; just as my Father has sent me, so I send you.

22 And when he had said these things, he gave them courage and said to them, Receive the Holy Spirit.

23 If you forgive a man his sins, they shall be forgiven to him; and if you hold a man's sins, they are held.

24 ¶ But Thomas, one of the twelve, who is called the Twin, was not there with them when Jesus came.

25 And the disciples said to him, We have seen our Lord. He said to them, Unless I see in his hands the places of the nails, and put my fingers in them, and put my hand into his side, I will not believe.

26 Eight days later, the disciples were again inside, and Thomas with them. Jesus came, when the doors were locked, and stood in the midst, and said to them, Peace be with you.

27 Then he said to Thomas, Bring your finger here, and see my hands; and bring your

hand and put it into my side; and do not be an unbeliever, but a believer.

28 Thomas answered and said to him, O my Lord and my God!

29 Jesus said to him, Now you believe, because you have seen me? Blessed are those who have not seen me, and have believed.

30 ¶ Many other miracles Jesus did in the presence of his disciples, which are not written in this book;

31 Even these are written, so that you may believe that Jesus is the Christ, the Son of God; and when you believe you shall have life everlasting in his name.

CHAPTER 21

AFTER these things, Jesus showed himself again to his disciples by the sea of Tiberias; and he appeared in this way.

2 They were all together, Simon Peter, and Thomas who is called the Twin, and Nathanael of Cana of Galilee, and the sons of Zebedee, and two others of the disciples.

3 Simon Peter said to them, I am going to catch fish. They said to him, We also will come with you. So they went out and went up into the boat; and that night they caught nothing.

4 When morning came, Jesus stood by the sea side; and the disciples did not know that it was Jesus.

5 So Jesus said to them, Boys, have you got anything to eat? They said to him, No.

6 He said to them, Throw your net on the right side of the boat, and you will find. So they threw it, and they were not able to draw the net, because of the many fishes which it had caught.

7 Then the disciple whom Jesus loved said to Peter, That is our Lord. When Simon heard that it was our Lord, he took his cloak and girded it around his waist, because he was naked; and he jumped into the sea to come to Jesus.

8 But the other disciples came by boat; for they were not very far from land, but about a hundred yards, and they were dragging the net of fishes.

9 When they landed, they saw burning coals set, and a fish laid on them, and bread.

10 Jesus said to them, Bring some of the fish which you have now caught.

11 So Simon Peter went up, and drew the net to land, full

of large fishes, one hundred and fifty three; and in spite of this weight, the net did not break.

12 Jesus said to them, Come, break your fast. But not one of the disciples dared to ask him who he was, for they knew he was our Lord.

13 Then Jesus drew near, and took bread and fish, and gave to them.

14 This is the third time that Jesus appeared to his disciples, since he rose up from the dead.

15 ¶ When they had broken their fast, Jesus said to Simon Peter, Simon, son of Jonah, do you love me more than these things? He said to him, Yes, my Lord; you know that I love you. Jesus said to him, Feed my male lambs.

16 He said to him again the second time, Simon, son of Jonah, do you love me? He said to him, Yes, my Lord; you know that I love you. Jesus said to him, Feed my sheep.

17 He said to him again the third time, Simon, son of Jonah, do you love me? It grieved Peter because he said to him the third time, Do you love me? So he said to him, My Lord, you understand well everything, you know that I love you. Jesus said to him, Feed my female lambs.

18 Truly, truly, I say to you, when you were young, you used to tie up your girdle yourself, and walk wherever you pleased; but when you become old, you will stretch out your hands, and another will tie up for you your girdle, and take you where you do not wish.

19 He said this, to show by what death he would glorify God. And when he had said these things, he said to him, Follow me.

20 Simon Peter turned around and saw the disciple whom Jesus loved following him, the one who leaned himself on the breast of Jesus at the supper, and said, My Lord, who will betray you?

21 When Peter saw him, he said to Jesus, My Lord, what about him?

22 Jesus said to him, If I wish him to remain until I come, what difference does that make to you? You follow me.

23 This word then went out among the brethren, that that disciple would not die. But what Jesus said was not that he would not die; but, If I wish that he should remain

until I come back, what difference does that make to you?

24 This is the disciple who testified concerning all of these things, and who also wrote them; and we know that his testimony is true.

25 There are also a great many other things which Jesus did, which, if they were written one by one, not even this world, I believe, could contain the books which would be written.

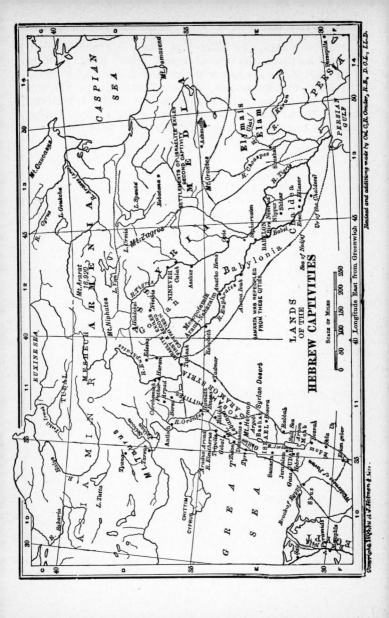

LANDS OF THE HEBREW CAPTIVITIES

Scale of Miles

0   50   100   150   200   250

Longitude East from Greenwich

SAMARIA WAS REPEOPLED FROM THESE CITIES.

Copyright 1895 by A.J. Holman & Co. Revised and additions made by Chas. G.R. Crocker, R.E., D.C.L., LL.D.

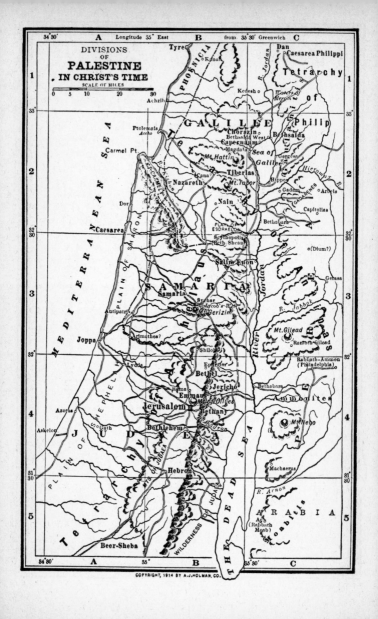

DIVISIONS
OF
PALESTINE
IN CHRIST'S TIME

SCALE OF MILES

0 5 10 20 30